'SAILOR' MALAN
FREEDOM FIGHTER

*This book is dedicated to the inspirational memory of
Group Captain A.G. 'Sailor' Malan: Freedom Fighter.*

'SAILOR' MALAN FREEDOM FIGHTER

The Inspirational Story of a Spitfire Ace

Dilip Sarkar MBE

AIR WORLD

AIR WORLD

'SAILOR' MALAN – FREEDOM FIGHTER
The Inspirational Story of a Spitfire Ace

First published in Great Britain in 2021 by
Air World
An imprint of
Pen & Sword Books Ltd
Yorkshire – Philadelphia

Copyright © Dilip Sarkar, 2021

ISBN 978 1 52679 526 7

The right of Dilip Sarkar to be identified as Author of this work has been asserted by
him in accordance with the Copyright, Designs and Patents Act 1988.

A CIP catalogue record for this book is available from the British Library.

Typeset by SJmagic DESIGN SERVICES, India.

Printed and bound in the UK by CPI Group (UK) Ltd, Croydon, CR0 4YY

Pen & Sword Books Limited incorporates the imprints of Atlas, Archaeology,
Aviation, Discovery, Family History, Fiction, History, Maritime, Military, Military
Classics, Politics, Select, Transport, True Crime, Air World, Frontline Publishing, Leo
Cooper, Remember When, Seaforth Publishing, The Praetorian Press, Wharncliffe
Local History, Wharncliffe Transport, Wharncliffe True Crime and White Owl.

For a complete list of Pen & Sword titles please contact

PEN & SWORD BOOKS LIMITED
47 Church Street, Barnsley, South Yorkshire, S70 2AS, England
E-mail: enquiries@pen-and-sword.co.uk
Website: www.pen-and-sword.co.uk

Or
PEN AND SWORD BOOKS
1950 Lawrence Rd, Havertown, PA 19083, USA
E-mail: Uspen-and-sword@casematepublishers.com
Website: www.penandswordbooks.com

Contents

Author's Note & Glossary

The aviation-minded reader will notice that I have referred to German *Messerschmitt* fighters by the abbreviation 'Me' (not 'Bf', which is more technically correct), or simply by their numeric designation, such as '109' or '110'. This not only reads better but is authentic: during the Battle of Britain, Keith Lawrence, a New Zealander, flew Spitfires and once said to me 'To us they were just "Mes", "109s" or "110s", simple, never "Bf".'

In another attempt to preserve accuracy, I have also used the original German, wherever possible, regarding terms associated with the *Luftwaffe*, such as:

Adlerangriff	'Attack of the Eagles'
Adlertag	'Eagle Day'
Eichenlaub	The Oak Leaves, essentially being a bar to the Ritterkreuz.
Erprobungsgruppe	Experimental group, in the case of *Erprobungsgruppe* 210, a skilled precision bombing unit.
Experte	A fighter 'ace'. Ace status, on both sides, was achieved by destroying five enemy aircraft.
Freie hunt	A fighter sweep.
Gefechstand	Operations headquarters.
Geschwader	The whole group, usually of three *gruppen*.
Geschwaderkommodore	The group leader.
Gruppe	A wing, usually of three squadrons.
Gruppenkeil	A wedge formation of bombers, usually made up of vics of three.
Gruppenkommandeur	The wing commander.
Jagdbomber ('*Jabo*')	Fighter-bomber.

Jagdflieger	Fighter pilot.
Jagdgeschwader	Fighter group, abbreviated JG.
Jagdwaffe	The fighter force.
Jäger	Hunter, in this context a fighter pilot or aircraft.
Kampffleiger	Bomber aircrew.
Kampfgeschwader	Bomber group, abbreviated KG.
Kanal	English Channel.
Katchmarek	Wingman.
Lehrgeschwader	Literally a training group, but actually a precision bombing unit, abbreviated LG.
Luftflotte	Air Fleet.
Oberkanone	Literally the 'Top Gun', or leading fighter ace.
Oberkommando der Wehrmacht (OKW)	The German armed forces high command.
Ritterkreuz	The Knight's Cross of the Iron Cross.
Rotte	A pair of fighters, comprising leader and wingman, into which the *Schwarm* broke once battle was joined.
Rottenführer	Leader of a fighting pair.
Schwarm	A section of four fighters.
Schwarmführer	Section leader.
Seelöwe	Sealion, the codename for Hitler's proposed seaborne invasion of England.
Stab	Staff
Staffel	A squadron.
Staffelkapitän	The squadron leader.
Störflug	Harassing attacks, usually by lone Ju 88s.
Stuka	The Ju 87 dive-bomber.
Sturkampfgeschwader	Dive-bomber group, abbreviated StG.
Vermisst	Missing.
Zerstörer	Literally 'destroyer', the term used for the Me 110.
Zerstörergeschwader	Destroyer group, abbreviated ZG.

Each *geschwader* generally comprised three *gruppen*, each of three *staffeln*. Each *gruppe* is designated by Roman numerals, i.e. III/JG 26 refers to the third *gruppe* of Fighter Group (abbreviated 'JG') 26. *Staffeln* are identified by numbers, so 7/JG 26 is the 7th *staffel* and belongs to III/JG 26.

Rank comparisons may also be useful: -

Gefreiter	Private 1st Class
Unteroffizier	Corporal, no aircrew equivalent in Fighter Command.
Feldwebel	Sergeant
Oberfeldwebel	Flight Sergeant
Leutnant	Pilot Officer
Oberleutnant	Flight Lieutenant
Hauptmann	Squadron Leader
Major	Wing Commander
Oberst	Group Captain

RAF Abbreviations:

AAF	Auxiliary Air Force
AASF	Advance Air Striking Force
A&AEE	Aeroplane & Armament Experimental Establishment
AFC	Air Force Cross
AFDU	Air Fighting Development Unit
AI	Airborne Interception radar
AOC	Air Officer Commanding
AOC-in-C	Air Officer Commanding-in-Chief
ATA	Air Transport Auxiliary
ATS	Armament Training School
BEF	British Expeditionary Force
CAS	Chief of the Air Staff
CFS	Central Flying School
CGS	Central Gunnery School
CO	Commanding Officer
DES	Direct Entry Scheme
DFC	Distinguished Flying Cross
DFM	Distinguished Flying Medal
DSO	Distinguished Service Order
E/A	Enemy Aircraft
EFTS	Elementary Flying Training School
FAA	Fleet Air Arm
FIU	Fighter Interception Unit

AUTHOR'S NOTE & GLOSSARY

FTS	Flying Training School
ITW	Initial Training Wing
LAC	Leading Aircraftman
MRAF	Marshal of the Royal Air Force
MSFU	Merchant Ship Fighter Unit
NCO	Non-Commissioned Officer
ORB	Operations Record Book
OTC	Officer Training Corps
OTU	Operational Training Unit
PDC	Personnel Distribution Centre
RAFVR	Royal Air Force Volunteer Reserve
RFS	Reserve Flying School
RN	Royal Navy
RNAS	Royal Navy Air Service
SASO	Senior Air Staff Officer
SOO	Senior Operations Officer
SSC	Short Service Commission
UAS	University Air Squadron
U/S	Unserviceable

Acknowledgements

I must thank Dr Yvonne Malan for her ongoing enthusiasm for this project, and continually raising awareness, especially on social media, of her august ancestor, the legendary Group Captain Sailor Malan.

I am especially grateful to my long-standing friend and independent film-maker Desmond Naidoo in South Africa for so generously providing transcripts of certain interviews filmed for the documentary about Sailor Malan – Freedom Fighter – that has been in the making for some years now. Hopefully funding issues will one day be overcome and Desmond's documentary broadcast…

Chris Hussey kindly supplied some interesting newspaper cuttings, found preserved in his late mother's wartime scrapbook; also grateful to Maggie Wylam for permission to quote from her late father's unpublished memoir concerning the Fall of France, and likewise Steve Child in respect of his uncle's recollections of Sailor.

Fellow author and researcher Mark Hillier helped me unravel confusion over Sailor's postings in 1944, and Air Marshal Cliff Spink – himself a former commander of 74 'Tiger' Squadron – provided some interesting observations regarding the so-called 'Battle of Barking Creek', and it was helpful to discuss that tragic affair with researcher Nick Black.

Being in the orbit of creative (not to mention obsessed!) people is not always easy, and I am grateful to Sue Bradshaw, brother John and his wife Mary, for taking in their stride me shooting off home several days early from a break on the South coast – because I just *had* to write!

As always, Martin Mace and the Pen & Sword team were a pleasure to work with.

Foreword

'Man's dearest possession is life. It is given to him but once, and he must live it so as to feel no torturing regrets for wasted years, never know the burning shame of a mean and petty past; so live that dying he might say: "all my life, all my strength were given to the finest cause in all the world - the fight for the Liberation of Mankind".'

Nikolai Ostrowski[1]

'It does not matter how many people chose moral duty over the rationality of self-preservation – what does matter is that some did. Evil is not all-powerful. It can be resisted. The testimony of the few who did resist shatters the authority of the logic of self-preservation. It shows it for what it is in the end–a choice.'

Zygmunt Bauman[2]

1 Nikolai Ostrowski, *How The Steel Was Tempered* (London, Central Books, 1973), p. 9.

2 Zygmunt Bauman, *Modernity and the Holocaust* (New York, Cornell University Press, 1992), p. 207.

The broad strokes of Adolph Gysbert 'Sailor' Malan's life is relatively well-known, in the United Kingdom at least. The South African of Afrikaner heritage who became one of the most celebrated of 'The Few'.

Sailor Malan's life is the remarkable story of a life dedicated to fighting oppression, not only during the Second World War but also later in his homeland against apartheid. He was more than a fearless fighter pilot; he was a man with a deep sense of justice, and with the courage and character to fight for it.

I am grateful that this biography has been written. Not only because it corrects some of the misconceptions about the man – he was, for example, far from cold-blooded and calculating, but rather reserved to the point of shyness – but because it also tells the story of his life after the war. That part of his story is largely unknown, for reasons this book will make clear.

To understand Sailor Malan we need to understand a man who defied social expectations to choose what was right over what was easy. The man who so many of the Greatest Generation looked up to as the embodiment of heroism, and who later led thousands in protest against apartheid was an outsider in most contexts. In a time when there was heated animosity, even hatred, between Afrikaners and English-speaking South Africans, he was the son of an Afrikaner of French Huguenot descent and British-born mother. As a cadet aboard the *General Botha* training ship he was younger than the other cadets and one of the few Afrikaans-speaking recruits. In the Royal Air Force he was older than most of his fellow pilots, a South African with Afrikaner heritage fighting in a war the vast majority of Afrikaners did not support. And in opposing apartheid as President of the Torch Commando, he was not only white, but of Afrikaner descent.

Adolph Gysbert Malan – known as John to his family and as Sailor to the world – was born on 3 October 1910 in Wellington in South Africa's Cape Province.[3] The happiest days of his early years were spent on the farm 'Slent', a breathtakingly beautiful farm in the Voor-Paardeberg area near Wellington. He retained a life-long love for 'Slent'. Many years later he would remark to Oliver Walker that '[t]he soul of South Africa lies there'.[4] Sadly, Willie Malan, Sailor's father, plagued by poor health, was unable to make a success of the farm and it was sold at a loss. Today 'Slent' is an award-winning wine farm. Providentially – with the Malans having originated in Italy – the owners are Italian. They are proud of the farm's

---

3 Now part of the Western Cape.

4 Oliver Walker, *Sailor Malan* (London, Cassell and Co Ltd, 1953), p. 16.

connection to one of South Africa's most remarkable sons, and have done much to further his legacy.

With the family farm lost, a growing family and increasing financial problems, it was decided that Sailor would join the *General Botha* training ship in Simon's Town near Cape Town. Young Sailor went from a relative care-free existence to a heavily regimented life, enforced by brutal discipline and hazing. It had a profound influence on him. It is here where he acquired his quiet, stoic indifference to physical and mental distress. And it solidified his acute sense of justice and fairness, and his dislike of bullies of any variety. This, along with his outsider's view, undoubtedly informed his keen sense of where the fault lines of injustice lay.

After several years at sea, both in the merchant marine and for a brief stint in the Royal Naval Reserve, Sailor joined the Royal Air Force. Unlike many of his peers, he did not join the RAF out of boredom or the urge for adventure. He knew war was looming, and he had no illusions about the evilness of Nazi Germany. He signed up to fight for values he held dear: freedom, justice, democracy. His deep commitment to these ideals would later put him at odds with the apartheid government. Sailor and three of his brothers would serve in a war that was widely unpopular among Afrikaners. Many openly supported Nazi Germany, joining paramilitary groups like the 'Ossewabrandwag' (Oxwagon sentinel). Several of them – including future apartheid-era leaders – were interned for their pro-Nazi stance and attempts to overthrow the government.

I will not focus on Sailor's wartime career since it is covered in this book in great detail. He was a fearless pilot and leader of men. Yet he was uncomfortable with being labelled a hero, deflecting attention away from himself by always pointing out that thousands of others – and not just 'The Few' – played a vital role in achieving victory. Douglas Tidy probably summarised it best: 'I find the most endearing thing about him was that, apart from being an exceptional shot, he was just an ordinary chap; quiet, unassuming, and gentle in manner. His great gifts came from within when great gifts were called for. Tremendous courage, relentless determination and that quality of leadership which carried the whole Squadron to do great deeds for him.'[5]

In 1946, Sailor returned to South Africa to work for the Oppenheimer family in Johannesburg. After a period of working as the personal and political secretary to Harry Oppenheimer, Sailor became a farmer near

---

5 Douglas Tidy, *I Fear No Man: The Story of No 74 (Fighter) Squadron Royal Flying Corps and Royal Air Force (The Tigers)*, London, Macdonald, 1972, p. 193.

Kimberley, in the northern part of the then Cape Province. It was a lifestyle he relished. As far as he was concerned he was done with war. Indeed, he never discussed the war, not even with his own children. And yet, he soon found himself facing a battle he could not walk away from: The newly elected National Party's assault on democracy and justice, known as apartheid. Having fought in a war against fascism – a war that cost the lives of two of his brothers, Ralph and Francis – he had no intention of standing by while it took hold in his own country.

Sailor was elected President of the Torch Commando, an organisation whose members were former (white) servicemen and women who strongly opposed the apartheid government's policies. Sailor's popularity and appeal to especially younger Afrikaners terrified the apartheid government. He was a war hero, had Afrikaner heritage, and could not be accused of being a Communist (one of the government's strategies to dismiss opposition to its policies was to stoke fears of the 'Red Peril'). Sailor faced relentless attacks from the South African government and Naspers[6] (now Media24), the newspaper empire that functioned as a propaganda machine for the apartheid government. He was ridiculed as a 'flying poodle', accused of being a stooge of the Oppenheimer family,[7] labelled as a traitor to his people. Less venomous but still troubling, he was looked down upon by some of the English-speaking leaders of the Torch Commando who were contemptuous of his lack of higher education and Afrikaner heritage, and who dismissed him as being merely a figurehead. Yet these same individuals were quite happy to hide behind Sailor and let him take (considerable) flak from the apartheid government and its supporters. Torch Commando rallies – which attracted thousands – were targeted by National Party supporters keen to inflict violence on those they saw as traitors. But Sailor stood firm, leading one of the largest anti-apartheid gatherings in South African history in Cape Town in 1951, and calling the apartheid government fascists to their faces.

The Torch Commando unravelled after the government, realising how effective the organisation was at mobilising white opposition to apartheid, banned civil servants, members of the judiciary and military service members from being members. It might have been a short-lived movement, but it remains a profound – and largely unacknowledged – moment in South African history. At its height it had around 250,000 members, with the ability to appeal to especially younger white South Africans who opposed

---

6   The animosity endures to this day.

7   A favourite target of the anti-Semitic Afrikaner press.

apartheid, but who were wary of the Communist Party (the African National Congress, at that stage, did not allow whites to join).

By 1953, his Torch Commando days were over. He never had any enthusiasm for political life. He was not interested in power; to him it was always about justice. And, given his famous lack of tolerance for balderdash, he was ill-suited to a career in politics. Furthermore, he had serious concerns about the prospect of an armed struggle against the apartheid state. He had seen war, and had no illusions about the consequences. And he had doubts about the true intentions of some of those calling for violent resistance: Their true aim seemed to be absolute power, not justice for all South Africans. His concerns proved to be astute. The armed struggle was largely ineffective (while economic sanctions were devastatingly effective), but it unleashed profoundly destructive forces that continue to haunt South Africa.

Sailor returned to fulltime farming. But heartbreakingly the man who fought so others may live in peace enjoyed precious few years of peace himself. By the later 1950s he developed problems with his balance and speech. After consulting doctors in South Africa and the United Kingdom he was diagnosed with Parkinson's Disease. Although the disease has claimed several members of the Malan family, it is highly likely that his wartime service contributed to the speed and aggression with which the disease claimed him. When his close friend Al Deere visited him in 1961 he was barely able to speak, leaving both men in tears.

On 17 September 1963 Sailor Malan passed away in a Kimberley hospital with his beloved wife Lynda by his side. He was 52. Lynda would outlive him by several years. She never remarried.

The apartheid government would not allow Sailor to rest in peace. He was denied a military funeral and members of the South African military were banned from attending. Those in power swiftly erased both Sailor and the Torch Commando from South African history. As with other white anti-apartheid figures – like Bram Fischer, the lawyer who saved Mandela and his co-accused from the gallows – this was deliberate. Not only because they both loathed and feared those who dared oppose them, but also for a perhaps more telling reason: If people of Afrikaner heritage had the courage to oppose them, what excuse did others have? So they had to be demonised and erased from history.

Sailor Malan died less than a year before Nelson Mandela and his co-accused were sentence to life imprisonment on 12 June 1964. The ANC, Communist Party and allied parties had already been banned. Days before Sailor passed away Looksmart Khulile Ngudle became the first anti-apartheid leader to die in police custody on 5 September 1963. He would not be the last. Thousands would be imprisoned, tortured or, in some cases, assassinated by government hit squads before the apartheid government, crippled by international sanctions, unbanned the ANC, freed Nelson Mandela, and entered into the negotiations that would lead to South Africa's first democratic elections in April 1994.

One had hoped that Sailor would be celebrated in post-apartheid South African. Sadly, this has not happened. This is of course partly due to the efficiency with which the apartheid government erased him from history. But it also has much to do with President Mandela's successors emphasising African nationalism over non-racialism. There currently is a reluctance at best – and recently more of an active resistance – to celebrate any anti-apartheid figure who was not a member of the current ruling party, let alone one who happened to be white. Sailor Malan and the Torch Commando were inconvenient to the apartheid state. And they remain inconvenient today because their existence – of a war hero with Afrikaner heritage and white war veterans taking a stand against apartheid – disrupts the narrative of post-apartheid South Africa.

Sailor Malan was one of 'The Few' who fought in the Battle of Britain, with the future of democracy at stake. But he was also one 'the few' in a different sense: that rare breed of individual who will stand against injustice, no matter the price, regardless of the danger; whose moral compass always points true north. He was, as Roger Rosenblatt notes in one of the most iconic essays on the nature of courage, 'the best that we can do'.[8] The motto of 74 Squadron is 'I Fear No Man.' It was more than words to him. It was part of the fibre of his being. For the truly courageous, people like Sailor Malan, fighting the good fight is nearly instinctive. His courage and sense of justice were not willed; they were the consequence of his character and humanity.

Sailor Malan was part of two 'greatest generations': those fought against fascism in Europe, and those who fought against apartheid and for non-racialism in South Africa. Neither his premature death nor (continued) efforts to erase him from history can defeat his legacy. We know the meaning of courage because of people like Sailor Malan. They stood up for justice and they fought for democracy against tremendous odds and when the consequences could be, and often were, fatal. They did it not for glory or power, fortune or fame, but so that others may live. However dark and dangerous the world becomes, especially in the today's uncertain times, we

---

8   Rosenblatt, Roger 'The Man in the Water', *Time Magazine*, 25 January 1982.

FOREWORD

cannot say there were not those who did have the courage to spark a light, to lead the way.

True courage is not an impulsive act. It is deliberate and sustained. It is a choice made and a course kept despite the odds. Sailor Malan kept that course his entire life. For that he deserves to be remembered and honoured. That is the very least we owe him. This book and Desmond Naidoo's documentary are encouraging steps in honouring this duty.

Yvonne Malan, DPhil (Oxon)
Patron and Vice-President
The Spitfire Society

Introduction

It was as a schoolboy growing up in the 1960s that I first encountered the name of 'Sailor' Malan, the great Spitfire and Battle of Britain ace, probably in one of the warlike boys' comics of the period. The name and photograph of Group Captain A.G. Malan, of course, appears in countless books and articles on the Battle of Britain period, and therefore anyone studying the aerial conflict to any degree will be familiar with this legendary South African.

The wartime story, of aerial derring-do, is inspirational and exciting enough alone, but, I was to discover the further I looked into the Malan story, there was much more to this flying sailor. This was a man as brave as a lion, of the highest professional standards and integrity, the best shot in the RAF, but there is much more. I believe that we do not entirely become aware of the extent of Sailor Malan's dedication and commitment to freedom and democracy until he returned to apartheid-riven and nationalist-controlled South Africa after the war. What happened then is a story every bit as fascinating as his wartime years – if not more so.

And yet, in his native South Africa, for reasons we will explore, the name of Sailor Malan is largely unknown. This book will explain why – and hopefully raise awareness of this champion of freedom and human rights.

For some years, my South African friend Desmond Naidoo has been determined to produce a television documentary about Sailor Malan for broadcasting in South Africa. It has been a struggle to achieve funding, for reasons I never fully appreciated until the last few days of writing this book. Knowing what I do now about the situation in South Africa, I can fully understand, and am unsurprised. Like this book, Desmond's film is vitally important to raising awareness and maintaining the currency of Sailor Malan's story. It *must*, one day, be made.

Of all the books I have written, this is possibly the most important. The reasons why will become evident to the reader.

Dilip Sarkar MBE FRHistS

Chapter One

The *Botha* Boy

The Malans are a proud and ancient family. Originating in Italy and later settling in the Franco-Italian Alps during the thirteenth century, Louis IX of France honoured the Malans for their contribution to his Crusades. Firm Protestants, eleven Malans were martyred between the twelfth and seventeenth centuries, preferring death to Catholicism; the family motto *Deus Arx Mea* translates to 'God is my Citadel'. It is not in Europe, however, that our story begins – but in faraway South Africa.

As the name suggests, South Africa is the southernmost state of the African continent, a country with a turbulent past, for centuries home to a volatile mix of races, cultures – and colours. In 1485 the Portuguese explorer Bartolomeu Dias led the first European expedition to land in southern Africa. This was at the start of what became known as the 'Age of Discovery', as European maritime powers increasingly explored the world, expanding trade and taking the first steps towards globalisation. Numerous lands previously unknown to Europeans were found – which, although already inhabited by indigenous peoples, were claimed by the explorers' countries and colonised. So began the age of empires. By the early seventeenth century, however, Portugal's maritime empire was waning, and by 1652 the Dutch East India Company had established a station at the Cape of Good Hope, which in time became Cape Town, and the Dutch became the dominant European settlers. Between 1688 and 1700, protestant refugees – persecuted Huguenots – also arrived in South Africa from Catholic France, some via the Netherlands, following the Revocation of the Edict of Nantes. The Dutch settlers accommodated the Huguenot refugees, the French knowledge of viticulture over time advancing the prosperity of the Cape of Good Hope. Certainly the French knew how to select perfect locations for farms and vineyards, finding refuge from religious oppression and prejudice.

So it was that French place-names became commonplace as farms, one of the first Huguenot settlers, Pierre Joubert, calling his farm 'La Provence' in 1694. Significantly, amongst the Frenchmen was one Jacques Malan, the family having first sought refuge in Leiden, Netherlands, before arriving in South Africa and settling in Wellington, calling his farm 'Versailles' as a reminder of the old country. The French settlers lived side-by-side with the more numerous Dutch, over time intermarriage blending the two races, and ultimately, while English became the language of education and administration, a simplified form of Dutch, known as 'Afrikaans', became the common tongue of frontier farmers like the Malans – collectively known as 'Boers' (being the Dutch word for farmer) – and all the Dutch, French, and indeed German settlers recognised themselves as the 'Afrikaner' community. For agricultural labour the Afrikaner farmers exploited enslaved people from such countries as Madagascar and Malaysia, and even themselves enslaved certain local tribes such as the Khoikoi and San peoples. Without question the white settlers from more technologically advanced and educated European societies considered themselves naturally superior to the indigenous people of South Africa; one Frenchman, Guy Tachard, wrote:

'They lead a miserable existence. They are dirty to excess and it seems they take pleasure in making themselves hideous. When they want to adorn themselves they rub their heads, faces and hands with the soot from their cauldrons… Barbarism such as theirs, however, has not so completely effaced all traces of civilisation so that no vestige of virtue remains. They are faithful to their masters.'

As Vernon February wrote, 'The French refugees who fled France in order to escape oppression and who found their "terrestrial Elysium" at the Cape, did so on the basis of a society based on slave labour and exploitation.' Robert Ross rightly argued that 'a mild slave regime is impossible, everything touched by slavery is brutalised,' emphasising that the white Boer farming class 'had human beings plucked away from their homes and shipped off from all the ports of the Indian Ocean to the Cape. Then they were worked in the fields until they died.' Clearly there was no parity between the white and non-white populations – and it was abundantly clear which was the undisputed master of the other.

The British occupied the Cape from 1795 onwards, and following victory in the Napoleonic Wars, which concluded in 1815, South Africa was ceded to the burgeoning British Empire. From the early 1800s, many Boers left the British-ruled Cape, angered by the British freeing their slave-workers. The enforced cessation of the practice of enslavement, coupled with increasing skirmishes with native tribes, and need for more fertile farming country, led to 10,000 Afrikaner 'Voortrekkers' beginning the 'Great Trek' from the Cape Colony, between 1836 and 1840, into the north and east interior of South Africa, leading to the creation of what are now the states of Natal, Orange Free State and Transvaal. There, in the new 'Boer Republics', the Afrikaners found lands laden with rich natural resources, discovering substantial gold deposits in the late nineteenth century. If the aim of the 'Great Trek' was to achieve freedom for the Afrikaner people and escape British hegemony, it appeared to have been achieved. The Trek, however, led to conflict with African tribes and division within the Afrikaner community, between those whose ancestors made the arduous journey, and those like the Malans who remained in the Cape, with less of a frontier outlook and fear of the 'Black Peril'.

The British coveted the resource-rich lands claimed by the Boers, and inevitably war broke out. In the First Boer War, 1880-81, the Boers successfully resisted British encroachment, but were eventually defeated in the Second Boer War (1899-1902), during which over 27,000 Boer women and children perished in British 'concentration camps', and both Transvaal and the Orange Free State were annexed by the British. The Afrikaner Boers had not just been defeated by the British – they had also been humiliated, leaving a bitter and lasting legacy. During the wars, opinion within the Malan family was divided: some supported the Boer cause while others sympathised with the British. Amongst the latter was Willem Adolph 'Willie' Malan; as South African historian Professor Bill Nasson wrote, 'With an ample place for their French-Huguenot ancestral bloodline, the decent civilities of the Wellington Malans encompassed instinctive loyalty to the British Crown.'

A Boer unit led by General Smuts adopted guerrilla tactics in their forays against British patrols, exploiting the element of surprise before fading away. During one of these skirmishes at Twenty-four Rivers, near Porterville, Willie Malan – who was not a combatant – was somehow hit by two bullets while on horseback. One went through both thighs, exposing his right femur, the other ripped open his right arm. While recovering in Wellington hospital, the shattered leg became infected, but it was not amputated. With one leg two inches shorter than the other and in constant pain, Willie was on crutches until 1908, which he then discarded and resumed riding and farming at Versailles, the smaller part of which had been bequeathed to him upon his father's death. The following year, Willie married Evelyn Forde Jordan, an Englishwoman from Leicester and kindergarten teacher, at Andrew Murray's Dutch Reformed Church in Bradgate. That year, the British South Africa

Act granted the country nominal independence, the Union of South Africa becoming an entity on 31 May 1910. Consequently the Malans' eldest child, Adolph Gysbert Malan – later known universally as 'Sailor', which is how we will refer to him here – born in Wellington on 3 October 1910, was a South African by birth. In time it would become clear that young Sailor Malan possessed his father's courage and grit. Interestingly, throughout the period of Dutch and British rule, racial segregation between whites and non-whites was informal, an assumed position, although the settlement and movement of native peoples was controlled by the Native Location Act of 1879. The Natives' Land Act of 1913 would severely restrict black land ownership, and it was against this backdrop of white supremacy that the young Malan grew up.

At this time, Willie Malan was managing a Rhodes Fruit Farm in the Drakenstein Valley, Groenfontein Farm, looking towards the impressive Klein Drakenstein mountains. It was there, at the Groenfontein home built by his great-grandfather, that Sailor had been born, and in due course his younger brother, Ralph. After a couple of years the family moved to another 'RFF' at Klipvlei, just north-east of Wellington, beneath the Groenberg. In 1915, Willie bought his own farm, Slent, on the Paardeberg's slopes, sixteen miles south of Wellington, to which the family moved. There, within sight of the iconic Table Mountain, the Malan brothers found a wild and exotic place, with baboons in Slent's rocky upper reaches, and a fearsome old boar which wandered around the farmyard at will. Baiting the poor creature became an active pursuit for the two young boys. One day, Sailor 'exploded a clod of earth right on his snout' – the angry pig chased the brothers a mile before wounding the elder Malan's arm, scarring him for life. It was, however, an idyllic childhood, full of adventure in this unspoilt environment.

When Sailor was about seven or eight years old, apparently a small boy for his age, one Sunday afternoon his father gave him a double-barrelled shotgun and ammunition, to shoot something for the pot: 'I went outside and scored a bull's eye on a watering can, which got me into trouble later. Then I tried creeping up behind a turtle-dove. How I was able to get the gun to my shoulder and fire I don't know, but I did. Unfortunately I fired off both barrels at once and the recoil knocked me flat and bruised my shoulder for days after. Then, when I reloaded the gun I got the rim of one of the cartridges jammed in the breech. I struggled very hard to break the gun open, but hadn't the strength. In the end I took it back under my arm, and ran into the lounge to my mother, still wrestling with the triggers and pointing the barrels towards her. She was terribly angry and snatched the gun from me. I was scolded and so was my father for letting me have the gun. I wasn't allowed to handle a shotgun for a long time after that.' This was, though, the start of a lifelong fascination with firearms and gunnery. Like the RAF's ultimately top-scoring fighter pilot, Air Vice-Marshal Johnnie Johnson, Sailor learned to shoot at a young age, birds on the wing being his target of choice. Consequently, Sailor learned very early on the art of deflection shooting, which is to say, anticipating where a moving target and bullets will converge – a crucial skill in aerial combat.

Children in the area attended farm schools, each educating up to twenty pupils. Sailor attended one such, and had this to say of a particular teacher, a 'Miss M from the Transvaal, who remained very bitter about the British Tommies in the Boer War. What she had to say about them – and the English generally, didn't make sense to me. I knew my mother was English-born, and I knew all her family, and played with her brothers Clifford and Edwin. Miss M wanted us to believe that the "rooibaatjes" not only behaved like devils but looked something like them – all pock-marked, with red necks and purple morals. It left a nasty impression on my mind, all that hatred. Perhaps she had some family reason for being so fanatical. But it didn't work on me the way she obviously wished it to.'

After completing education to Standard IV, Sailor went on to Standard V schooling in Stellenbosch, where he experienced linguistic segregation, English-speaking pupils on one side of the classroom, Afrikaans the other. As he later said, 'A thing like that makes a very bad impact on a child's mind. It did on mine. I had friends both sides of the class. Among ourselves there was no question of language dividing us, we talked English or Afrikaans impartially.' Already, then, the young Sailor was baulking at two things he would later actively campaign against: racial prejudice and oppression.

Unfortunately Slent was not as prosperous as Willie had hoped, and he eventually sold the farm during what were depressed years for farming following the First World War, for a quarter of its value in better years. First, the family returned to Stellenbosch, thence to Malherbe Street, Wellington. Willie had a breakdown over the Slent disappointment, responsibility for bringing up their family of now five children now largely falling on Evelyn's shoulders. Sailor – who was already perceived to be both stubborn and independent – completed Standard VI of his education in late 1923 at Wellington Boys' High School. Then, aged 13 (and below the minimum age for admission), largely for financial reasons Sailor became a cadet aboard the training ship *General Botha*, permanently anchored off Simon's Town.

Sailor later commented, 'I don't know how I got my mind fixed on the *General Botha*. I'd never seen the ship and nobody knew much about it in Wellington. It had been established two or three years as a training ship for South Africans, and I think I was first to go from our district.' Aboard the *General Botha*, Sailor – and hence the nickname – found a harsh culture of violent discipline at the rope's end, and institutionalised bullying by older cadets. Sailor became well-known for his 'impish' sense of humour – often at an instructor's expense – but the experience of the *General Botha* was far from easy. As Yvonne Malan says, 'He developed a stoic indifference, but it had a profound effect on him. Not only because it made him tough, but because it solidified his fierce sense of justice and intense hatred of bullies.' This would prove a significant factor throughout Sailor's life.

Simon's Town was the base of Britain's South Atlantic Fleet, and *General Botha* was initially HMS *Thames*. The new South Africa had neither navy nor merchant fleet, and *General Botha* was the first step towards addressing this deficiency. The ship had been purchased by a Durban millionaire, Mr T.B.F. Davis, and was his gift to his country in memory of his son, killed in the First World War and who had been a cadet aboard HMS *Worcester*. *General Botha* was to be a training ship accommodating up to 150 cadets aged between 14 and 16, modelled on the Royal Navy's traditions and eighteen similar training ships. The two-year curriculum was overseen and delivered by the captain and his officers – all ex-RN. General subjects were included in addition to seamanship, gunnery, signalling and drill, which were all much more to Sailor's liking than the mathematics he struggled with – and mathematics are key to navigation, so vitally important to a seafarer.

Life aboard *General Botha* was far from easy, but undoubtedly shaped Sailor into the man and officer he became. The discipline and bullying by the 'Old Salts', the more senior cadets, was barbaric. The ship's official code permitted eight punishments, the severity dependent upon the offence's gravity, with up to twelve strikes of the cane. Cadets, wearing only shorts, were first passed as fit and able to sustain the punishment, then bound to a table and thrashed. Sailor's first biographer, Oliver Walker, wrote in 1953 that 'In talks with Sailor during which he described incidents infinitely more dramatic and perilous than anything occurring aboard the *Botha*, I never saw him more emotionally stirred than when recalling the ceremony of being tied down and thrashed. The memory of it had stayed with him vividly as a deed of outrage, an invasion of pride and privacy that helped fashion a kind of stoicism that became an armour-plating for more strenuous days to come. Its immediate effect was to check in him any desire, when he in turn became an Old Salt, to take advantage of his seniority, and it had much to do with this reluctance, in later years, to join in the horseplay of RAF initiatory customs.'

Sailor achieved an ordinary pass upon completion of the *General Botha* course, but being younger than his peers and still underage to serve at sea, had to spend another six months aboard: 'I had only one urge by that time, and that was to go to sea... I was trained for the sea, and that was the home I wanted. It wasn't an easy time for my parents... I thought that by going away, being completely independent, I would be saving them some anxiety, financial and otherwise. We were a very big family by then, two sisters and four brothers – the youngest, Peter, only a baby and all of them younger than me. Slent had been sold at a bad loss, as I told you. My father's health was in ribbons. When he was well enough to think of work he was offered the managership of a large fruit farm at Riverside in the Golden Valley Citrus Estates, not far from Cookhouse. That happened before I went to sea, so there was a complete uprooting of the family from all the old scenes. I can imagine what a wrench it was. For myself, by that time, I was concentrated on one thing – getting away to sea.'

At last, eight months after Sailor eventually left *General Botha*, he became an officer cadet with the Union-Castle Company, and first went to sea in the *Sandown Castle*, steaming from Port Elizabeth to New York. For nine years this would be his life, largely voyages to New York and Philadelphia. Of his time on the ocean waves, Sailor commented, 'I'd say it bred in me a kind of fatalism. Long voyages get you into a certain frame of mind. You're signed on. You know your destination weeks ahead. In the meantime you jog along in a routine which seldom varies. You get too a feeling of not belonging anywhere in particular.' This was not, however, the life he envisaged long-term. Eventually Sailor wanted more stability than a life at sea provided, and a family – and in 1930, aged 20, he met Lynda Fraser, then 16, at her parents' home in Ruislip, Middlesex, England. Although they would not meet again for another three years, it would eventually be with Lynda that Sailor would carve out the life his heart desired.

That year, 1930, saw the start of a new decade, one described by the British social historian Charles Loch Mowat as 'gloomy'. This was mainly a consequence of the London Stock Exchange crashing in September 1929, with top investors being jailed for fraud, greatly reducing optimism in American and overseas markets. A month later, share prices on the New York Stock Exchange collapsed. The effect of this, the greatest financial crisis of the twentieth century, reverberated around the world, bringing the halcyon 'Roaring Twenties' to an abrupt end and generating the 'Great Depression'. Naturally this had enormous negative implications for global trade, directly affecting merchant shipping – not least Sailor and the Union-Castle Line, trading between South Africa, Britain and America. While apprentices were suspended, the company retained the services of its officers, so Sailor remained gainfully employed and successfully sat for his Second Mate's Certificate in 1930. With such reduced trading however, over a million tonnes of merchant shipping lay at anchor around Britain, Sailor finding himself not navigating oceans, although there were occasional trips to the Continent, but instead a glorified watchman aboard a ship marooned in Southampton. With unemployment and inflation spiralling out of control on a global basis, Sailor's primary concern, naturally, was the effect of this long-term on his career at sea. Would years of study to gain various maritime qualifications and promotions actually be worthwhile, or even possible?

This was clearly a difficult time, with a seafaring life appearing one with little prospect. As an outlet for his natural positivity and enthusiasm, however, Sailor enlisted in the Royal Naval Reserve and was commissioned as a sub-lieutenant. Although the six-week gunnery course at Devonport also involved certain mundane subjects, Sailor later considered the course to have been a 'first-class, intensive, course… Our final tests were at sea when we were given ten salvoes to play with and had to hit a moving target being towed anything between five and ten miles away at high speed. I managed to straddle it four or five times, which gave me extra high marks.' Yet again, Sailor's exceptional ability at deflection shooting, first learned as a young boy on the farm, was obvious. Mowat also described the 1930s as the 'devil's decade' – and by 1933 the devil was abroad in Germany, something, following trips to Hamburg, Sailor had become acutely aware of. Beyond doubt the prospect of another world war was casting a dark shadow across the world.

Between 1914 and 1918, Europe had experienced its first head-on collision with industrial warfare, which left over twenty million dead and at least as many wounded. German forces had ended the war on foreign soil, only a year before expecting victory, and Germany assumed that the Armistice of November 1918 was the prelude to a negotiated peace settlement. In the event it was not. Understandably, victorious Allied leaders wanted to ensure that such a devastating conflict never occurred again, and laid out the foundations for this new post-war world at the Paris Peace Conference, held at the palace of Versailles and signed on 28 June 1919.

Known as the 'Treaty of Versailles', this laid out strict terms between the Allies and Germany – which was held entirely responsible for starting the war. Considering the destructive performance of German armed forces, the Allies dictated that the German army would number no more than 100,000 volunteers, there would be no air force, and the navy would be restricted to a coastal defence flotilla. Amongst other things, Germany was stripped of her overseas colonies, Alsace-Lorraine was restored to France, the Rhineland demilitarised, German unification with Austria was forbidden, and the 'Danzig Corridor' was created, ceding German land to Poland and providing the Poles access to the Baltic. To ensure that Germany's recovery from the war was slower than that of victorious France, Germany was expected to pay substantial reparations in compensation to the Allied victors. Germany was humiliated, the people regarding the Treaty an Allied 'Diktat', too eagerly accepted by the democratic Weimer Republic imposed upon them by the victors. The German people felt betrayed by the leaders who had signed the Treaty. Politically Germany became a fertile breeding ground for extremist politics. Then came the Great Depression, the resulting economic chaos and reparation payments threatening to reduce Germany to poverty, completely destabilising the Weimer government and paving the way for the rise of the fascist Adolf Hitler and his National Socialist Workers' Party, better known as the 'Nazis'.

Hitler had seen action during the First World War as an infantry soldier and, like countless other servicemen, was embittered regarding Germany's defeat. Hitler loathed the Versailles Treaty and criticised it in many speeches, although the effect of this rhetoric on the German people was arguably negligible. Indeed, his supporters were largely concerned with internal domestic issues. But the territorial problems caused by the Versailles treaty and especially the impositions on the German armed forces would ultimately be key to an expanding and economically rebuilt Germany under Hitler, who eventually came to power in 1933. Hitler believed Germans to be racially superior with a God-given right to expropriate the lands and resources of those states he saw as racially inferior – not least the Jews. He was, of course, rabidly anti-Semitic, blaming Germany's ills on a supposed 'International Jewish Conspiracy', which had stabbed Germany in the back at home while her troops fought bravely at the front. On assuming power, Hitler's immediate priority was to feed the nation, which was in economic turmoil, and create jobs to substantially reduce the figure of six million unemployed. Once this recovery had taken place, Hitler believed that the German people were destined for a cataclysmic confrontation with Communism – which he believed was the ultimate manifestation of the Jewish threat to Germany. Believing that in Russia military power was increasing with this same Armageddon in mind, Hitler embarked on his policy of rearmament, the piecemeal dismantling of Versailles, and violent territorial expansion based upon a racist world view. The countdown to the Second World War had begun. Of his trips to Hamburg after Hitler's takeover, Sailor wrote, 'I spent a lot of time talking to German harbour officials, sailors and civilians, and their attitude made me realise that war was inevitable.' There can be no doubt that this, coupled with mediocre prospects at sea, heavily influenced the next leg of Sailor Malan's life-journey.

Chapter Two

'The RAF liked chaps from the Empire'

While the clouds of war gathered over Mowat's 'Devil's decade', it was obvious that after the First World War warfare in future would be fought very differently, mainly because of one thing: air power.

On Christmas Eve 1914, the first German bomb had been dropped on England – albeit exploding harmlessly in a Dover garden. From that point on, Britain's island nation could no longer rely exclusively upon the Royal Navy for security of base – and from then on, the Home Front was also a front line. These primitive air attacks soon intensified and became more effective: by the Armistice, over 100 raids had killed 1,413 people. For the first time in history, London's underground had provided shelter for terrified civilians, the bombing provoking 'mass panics and near riots'. This developed into a disproportionate fear of air attack – but the air power doctrine emerging between the wars confirmed the bomber as supreme. Britain, close to the continent, although surrounded by a moat, was clearly vulnerable to air attack. Early British military aviation was delivered by the Royal Flying Corps, modelled on the Army, and Royal Naval Air Service. 1 April 1918 saw a significant event: the RFC morphed into the Royal Air Force, the world's first independent air force. Now Major General 'Boom' Trenchard, the first Chief of the Air Staff, was responsible for building an air force with aerodromes and logistics, absorbing both RFC and RNAS squadrons.

In November 1919, Trenchard submitted a White Paper outlining his plan for the peacetime air force. The junior service was to remain independent, and include a substantial proportion of commissioned short-term pilots, a cadet training college for permanent officers, an auxiliary facility, and, among other things, a school for aero-engineering apprentices. In 1922 the Lloyd George government became conscious of the fact that while the French air force included a striking force of 600 machines, the RAF Home Defence capacity was just three squadrons. Consequently it was decided to increase the RAF's establishment to 500 aircraft at a cost of £1.1m annually. The RAF was actually, though, fighting a battle for survival in the corridors of Whitehall and Westminster, owing to the more senior services being resentful of having lost their air arms – and because of the determination of many to disarm completely. Against the odds, in 1923 the Salisbury Committee, appointed to review and decide on the air force's fate, decreed a new and enlarged expansion programme for the RAF. Although this involved increasing establishment to fifty-two Home Defence squadrons, to be complete by 1928, given that war with France was unimaginable, and with no other enemy threatening Britain's shores, this ambitious and early expansion plan soon lost momentum. Indeed, peace, not war, was very much in the air following the Western powers signing the Locarno Treaty in 1925, binding each other to preserve peace and unite against any would-be aggressor.

The first half of the 1930s saw Britain and other nations 'hell-bent', according to Sir Maurice Dean, 'for collective security and prepared to accept incalculable risks in that cause'. In 1932, Britain abandoned what had been a miniscule RAF expansion programme; the following year, Adolf Hitler became Chancellor of Germany, changing everything. The *Führer* immediately set about contravening and reversing what were seen as injustices arising from the Versailles Peace Treaty of 1919, namely restrictions on the German military and territorial concessions. Already, in fact, Weimar Germany had begun secretly rebuilding its prohibited Luftwaffe, far away from prying western eyes, deep in Soviet Russia. The Great Depression, caused by the stock-market crash of 1929, had not helped those supporting rearmament, the British government consequently having serious domestic socio-economic issues to address at home. Hitler, however, saw rearmament as a way out of Germany's economic distress and an essential means of enabling his territorial ambitions – hence Germany prioritised remilitarisation. Conversely, Churchill would later write that for British defence spending, the years 1931-35 were those of the 'locust'. Be that as it may, the complete lack of substantial rearmament and deficiencies on doctrinal thinking were caused by three things: fiscal constraints, political indifference or opposition, and Trenchard's unshakeable belief in the bomber.

Although Trenchard had fought to create and preserve the air force, the so-called 'Father of the Royal Air Force' was a confirmed 'Bomber Baron'. Indeed, many influential civilians and militarists firmly believed in the 'knock-out blow', the single devastating strike destroying an enemy's capacity to fight, delivered from the air, by bombers. Trenchard considered it unnecessary 'for an air force, in order to defeat the enemy nation, to defeat its armed forces first. Air power can dispense with that intermediate step, can pass over the enemy navies and armies, and penetrate air defences and attack directly the centre of production, transportation and communication from which the enemy war effort is maintained. It is on the destruction of enemy industries and above all in the lowering of morale of enemy nationals caused by bombing that the ultimate victory lies.' In 1932 the British Prime Minister Stanley Baldwin told the House of Commons, 'I think it is as well for the man in the street to realise that there is no power on earth that can save him from being bombed. Whatever people may tell him, the bomber will always get through. The only defence is offence, which means you have to kill more women and children more quickly than the enemy if you want to save yourselves.' No surprise then that what little spending there was on defence between the wars was 'bombercentric'. Trenchard's view, expressed in 1921, was that fighter aircraft were 'only necessary to keep up the morale of your own people'.

By 1935, however, the threat posed by Hitler's Germany was increasingly plain – and could no longer be ignored. At last Britain, albeit reluctantly, began to rearm. In 1935 there were thirty-five fighter squadrons, the standards of certain squadrons disbanded after the First World War being proudly raised once more – amongst them, on 3 September 1935, 74 (Fighter) Squadron. The first incarnation of 74 'Tiger' Squadron, in 1917-18, had scored all of its victories (140 enemy aircraft destroyed, 85 probably destroyed, and 15 balloons destroyed) in an eight-month period. Its decorations included four DSOs, sixteen DFCs, an MC, an MM and one Mention in Despatches. 74's pilots included no less a hero than Major E.C. 'Mick' Mannock DSO and two bars, MC and bar, shot down and killed by groundfire on 26 July 1918 – and awarded a posthumous VC. The original squadron had clearly set the bar high in terms of fighting spirit and tradition. The new 74 Squadron would in due course become one with which the name of Sailor Malan would become inextricably connected.

With the reluctant acceptance that expansion of the RAF was as essential as it was necessary, so too had dawned the fact that extra personnel, particularly aircrew, would be required – not just more aircraft. Upon formation, the RAF was modelled on the British Army's organisation and rank structure. Army officers were trained at the Royal Military Academy at Sandhurst, which was, according to J. James in *The Paladins* (see bibliography), 'for gentlemen who could afford to pay the fees'. Those 'gentlemen' had exclusively been educated privately at so-called 'public' schools, as were RAF officers between the wars. Branson and Heinemann describe a society 'still stratified into layers divided by rigid class barriers'. Air force officers were trained at the fee-paying RAF College Cranwell, meaning the commissions – legal authority granted by the sovereign to bear arms and issue orders to subordinates – were effectively bought. Cost, in fact, dominated entry to all of the professions, preserving them, like commissions, exclusively for the upper classes.

From 1905 onwards, all public schools had Officer Training Corps delivering a specific military syllabus and examination. Those who passed were awarded Certificate 'A', armed with which, together with a good school report and an application counter-signed by any colonel, were entitled to a commission as of right. Trenchard modelled the new RAF's system on this long-established tradition, preserving commissions for the upper classes. Before the Second World War, 'the RAF had no definition of leadership.' Such 'skills were absorbed rather than taught, and the services reflected the social attitudes of the time, which were rather more inclined to assume leadership on the basis of social class.' In Trenchard's new service, this also extended to flying: all pilots were to be officers, commissioned into the General Duties (flying) branch. The ability to fly is, of course, over and above the traditional officer function of leading men in battle. Aircrew are a breed apart, as Wells explained: 'From the earliest days of aviation, airmen have been regarded as members of an élite group… it took a special type of man to brave the obvious perils.'

The training of Trenchard's officers was undertaken at the RAF College Cranwell, although Flight Cadets, according to Air Vice-Marshal H.A.V. Hogan, were not at Cranwell 'because we wanted to be leaders of men, but simply because we wanted to fly!' Nonetheless, enthusiasm for aviation and a burning ambition to fly was not enough: the fees payable to attend Cranwell were substantial, the amount involved preserving the pilot's cockpit for the British socio-economic pyramid's top 5.2 per cent. Means, however, may have opened the door to a commission – but it could not automatically assume the ability to fly: the failure rate in flying training was 50 per cent, so a privileged social and educational background was no guarantee towards receiving the coveted flying brevet.

Cranwell, however, was too small to produce the quantity of pilots required by the RAF. In 1921, contrary to his original elitist vision for officer pilots, Trenchard, to both achieve the number of pilots he needed and create a trained reserve, began training a small number of NCOs as pilots. The concept was that these men would fly for five years before resuming their original trades, while eligible for recall to flying duties in the event of an emergency. The initiative was both popular and economic, but numbers remained small: in 1925, 13.9 per cent of pilots were NCOs, rising to 17.1 per cent in 1935. Trenchard's next initiative was revolutionary: Short Service Commissions (SSC). In the senior services, officers usually served for the duration of their working lives (hence the term 'Permanent Commission'). This, however, led to a 'dead man's shoes' scenario, which Trenchard wished to avoid given that flying is obviously a young man's activity. The SSC scheme, therefore, provided for officers to serve a fixed contract of four years active service, followed by six on the reserve list. Such officers were only eligible for promotion so far as flight lieutenant but could transfer to a Permanent Commission on successfully passing the required examination. Together with Direct Entrants from the University Air Squadrons, SSC officers were not trained at Cranwell, which remained exclusively for professional career officers, but at Service Flying Training Schools. Interestingly, the minimum entry requirement for an SSC was the School Certificate, obtainable not just at public but also grammar schools. Nonetheless, it was still assumed that 'all applicants would come from the social class that filled the public schools'.

Another sound initiative was creation of the Auxiliary Air Force in 1924, based on the territorial concept; by 1930 such squadrons comprised 5 per cent of the air force's strength. There was no question, though, that auxiliary officers would be anything but public schoolboys. If Cranwellians were drawn from Britain's socio-economic élite, then auxiliaries were the élite of the élite.

The most significant and forward-thinking feature of 1936's Expansion Scheme 'F' was recognition that a trained reserve was essential, leading to creation of the RAF Volunteer Reserve, intended to 'have wide appeal based upon the Citizen Volunteer principle with a common mode of entry and promotion and commissioning on merit... So far as aircrew training was concerned, the system was based upon local town centres for spare time ground training and upon aerodrome centres associated with the town centres for flying training at the weekend, also for a fortnight's annual camp.' Again, commissions were available to all with a School Certificate. All such volunteer aircrew were automatically made sergeants – much to the chagrin of professional NCOs who had taken years to attain that exalted rank. The RAFVR was a huge step forward to seeing fighter pilots and leaders selected not on the basis of social class but on ability.

It was the expansion of the RAF, and the appeal to men from the Dominions to apply, that Sailor Malan heard loud and clear – seeing this as an opportunity for excitement, advancement, and a means of escaping from his current predicament. In 1935 he made his last trip to America as a merchant seaman, aboard *Sandown Castle* – and wrote a letter of application to the Air Ministry in England, seeking an SSC in the General Duties Branch of the RAF. His application was supported by his old training ship *General Botha*, which marked Sailor as 'a young man trying to better himself'. The Sailor was accepted – and after manoeuvres in HMS *Malaya*, sailed for England and a very different life. Having described his nine years at sea as 'uneventful', he wrote, 'I enjoyed myself in the Navy and wouldn't have missed it. But I found it starch-ridden. I didn't like the caste system, although I can see its attractions and value. Within its limits it produces, more often than not, an efficient class of officer. But it didn't suit me, either by temperament or by comparison with the life I'd known in the merchant service. The attitude of regular Naval types to RNR and RNVR was as if we were the lowest forms of life. The biggest mistake, as I saw from an outsider's viewpoint, was the lack of human relations. The men lived, as it were, below stairs, and the officers only addressed them and knew them as underlings.'

As we have seen, the junior service which Sailor Malan was now entering was already changing, officers having both Permanent and Short Service Commissions (SSC), and the service would soon comprise not just regular airmen but also part-time reservists and auxiliaries. This was a very different scenario to the 'starch-ridden' Navy: 'The difference in relationships when I joined the RAF was remarkable. I daresay that as a man from the Dominions I was to some extent favoured. The RAF liked chaps from the Empire. And especially they liked sailors. When I told the officer at the Flying School that I was a sailor, he grabbed me with both arms and said: "If you can only blow up the mercury column, my friend, you're in".'

In one respect, however, while the dynamics between personnel may have been different to the navy, socially and racially progressive though the RAF would soon prove itself to be, it was distinctly similar to Sailor's South African naval experience: at this time, it was exclusively white. Air Ministry regulations, under the Air Force (Constitution) Act of 1917, explicitly excluded recruits not of 'pure European descent' from serving in the RAF. Similar restrictions were also placed on the Royal Navy and British Army. In August 1923, the Air Ministry's 'Recruiting Regulations for the Royal Air Force' confirmed that the nationality and ethnic origin of recruits was restricted to those of 'pure European descent and the sons of natural born or naturalized British subjects'. This remained the case when Sailor Malan joined the RAF in 1935. The world of the time was very much white dominated, the age of Imperialism remaining alive and well. Sailor Malan had been brought up in what was essentially a black country colonised and run by white people who controlled everything. His contact with non-whites would have been as subservient farm-workers and in other non-professional roles; certainly none served alongside him in the navy. Also worthy of note is that the Recruiting Regulations refer only to 'sons'. Women had served in the RAF, in the Women's Royal Air Force, between 1918 and 1920, as non-combatants and not as aircrew, but females were unable to serve thereafter, until 1939 when the Women's Auxiliary Air Force was created.

By this time, the 25-year-old Sailor Malan was possessed of diverse life experience: an officer well-used to leading men, braving the dangers of the oceans, and opposed to injustice and cruelty. He was also a natural marksman.

But could he fly?

Chapter Three

The Flying Sailor

On 6 January 1936, Sailor Malan reported for elementary training at the Civil Flying School, Filton, Bristol. Upon successful completion of the seven-week course, the new pilots would be commissioned as acting pilot officers (on probation) and progress to the next stage of training. There were ten 'Pupil Pilots' on the course, marked out for commissions on the basis of socio-educational background, and three 'Sergeant Pupils' – the latter taking advantage of Trenchard's far-sighted scheme to train a, albeit comparatively small, number of serving NCOs as pilots. The Pupil and Sergeant Pilots lived separately, segregated by rank, in digs away from the airfield, which was home to the Bristol Aeroplane Company. Having previously established himself at sea, Sailor now found himself, nine years later, starting over again, aged 25, with men much younger and without his professional experience; he would not recall this as a happy time. Nonetheless, the *ab initio* flying course was the gateway to the stars – and therefore key to his newly chosen career and future.

Another SSC officer entering the service in 1936 was Group Captain John Wray, who described the training involved:

'In those days, officers and NCO pilots on limited service engagements spent three months at Elementary Flying Training School, completing fifty hours dual and solo flying, and engaging in associated ground subjects. Flying training at EFTS was mainly on the De Havilland Tiger Moth biplane, although where I was, at Hamble, we also had Avro Cadets, which were similar. After EFTS, we then proceeded to the RAF Depot at Uxbridge for general introduction into the service, including issue of, or in the case of officers, the purchase of uniform. This lasted about a month. Then onwards to Service Flying Training School for one year and ten months' conversion to service aircraft types, and instruction into their use as military weapons. Ground subjects were also studied and the whole training experience was now in a service environment, with we officers learning how to be such, and the NCOs learning how to be NCOs.'

The 'Tiger Moth' – or more formally the DH82 – was a dual biplane with a fixed-pitch propeller, maximum ceiling of 13,600 feet, a range of 302 miles and a maximum speed of 109 mph. The 'Tiggie' provided the first air experience for innumerable pilots the world over, although Sailor, perhaps on account of being those few years older, struggled at first, despairingly watching his peers quickly adapting to flying. 'Suddenly,' he later said, 'I got a few landings right and Deacon, the instructor, an ex-fighter pilot from RFC days, smiled and said "Off you go".' Sailor then successfully soloed – a memorable and proud moment for every pilot.

He passed the course, thereby accessing the next stage of training, the introduction to service life at Uxbridge. There, one Squadron Leader Ira Jones was in charge of Direct Entry Officers' Courses, and was himself an impressive individual. Serving with 74 'Tiger' Squadron during the First World War, flying SE5 fighters, in just three months Jones destroyed thirty-seven enemy aircraft, surviving the war decorated with the DSO, MC, MM and DFC and bar. Of Pilot Officer Malan, who arrived at Uxbridge in June 1936, Jones recalled, 'I was immediately attracted by his sincere manner, quiet disposition, resolute speech, and very strong face, which characterised determination and leadership.' Illuminatingly, Jones asked the new pilot officer why he had chosen to join the RAF: 'Captain Beauchamp-Proctor VC is a South African. He has always been my hero, and I've decided to emulate him.' The diminutive Andrew Beauchamp-Proctor had recorded fifty-four aerial victories during the First World War, becoming the SE5's most successful pilot, with the VC, DSO, MC and bar, and DFC to his credit. Sadly, aged 26 he was killed in a flying accident at Upavon while training for the popular Hendon Air Pageant. A state funeral followed in South Africa.

On 1 March 1936, Sailor relinquished his RNR commission and, as Pilot Officer A.G. Malan, reported to 3 Flying Training School at Grantham on 14 March 1936.

At 3 FTS, Sailor's maturity was clearly recognised as on arrival he was appointed Course Commander – and became known as the 'Admiral'. At Grantham the fledgling pilots flew 100 hours over nine months, in service biplanes including the Hawker Hind and Audax. Ground instruction covered such subjects as meteorology, navigation, aircraft rigging and engine maintenance. There was sport too, although Malan is not remembered as an outstanding games player, his years at sea being inconducive to such participation, but he was a keen member of the 3 FTS rugby team. Socially, he would be recalled as a good companion, albeit with a natural reserve. As the course progressed, the young pilots were instructed on various service types, including fighters, as ability was constantly assessed.

On one training flight, Sailor narrowly escaped death when the engine of his Hawker Fury fighter cut at just 100 feet, minutes after take-off. Coolly the pilot pushed the stick forward, diving steeply, gaining speed, and the engine roared back into life – the little silver biplane pulling up far too close to the ground for comfort. As Sailor later said, 'at high speed, there's no time to be sorry.' He next flew the Gloster Gauntlet, which was the RAF's front-line fighter of the period, earning a 'special distinction'. During the nine-month course's second term, the pupils were streamed into either the Fighter or Bomber Flight. According to Sailor, he opted for fighters as he preferred 'something to throw about'. That, however, is something of a simplification. As previously explained, the focus of pre-war air force expansion was primarily on the bomber force, meaning that fewer fighter pilots were required. Group Captain Wray explained that 'only the very good pilots on the Flying Training School course went to fighter squadrons, which meant, of course, the minority. For example, I was posted to an Army Cooperation squadron because, so I was told by the Chief Ground Instructor, "In Army Cooperation squadrons they need gentlemen, because you may have to take port with the general!"' This is interesting, because at Filton, Sailor's instructor had recorded that 'his pilot is inclined to be heavy and impatient at the controls.' Clearly then, if only the 'very good pilots' were posted to fly fighters, Pilot Officer Malan's flying skills must have improved markedly, because it was not a case of an individual *choosing* to fly either bombers or fighters, but being *selected*, based on performance, and fighters were the pinnacle of achievement.

So it was that on 20 December 1936, nearly a year after reporting to Filton for elementary flying training, Pilot Officer Malan was posted to 74 'Tiger' Squadron at Hornchurch. The posting was not a coincidence. At Uxbridge, Squadron Leader Ira Jones had marked Sailor out as a 'good type'. Jones was passionately proud of 74 Squadron, maintained a keen interest in the reconstituted 'Tigers', and helped cherry-pick officers from his courses at Uxbridge. Talking of Malan and two other young 'Tigers' who had also passed through Uxbridge, he later wrote, 'Indeed, I had asked a friend with authority in Air Ministry personnel postings to have them sent to Tiger Squadron. My judgement was good, for they all turned out to be great air fighters and men of steel.'

For the new South African pilot, the posting to 74 'Tiger' Squadron was another landmark moment, the transition from sea to air complete, and an ambition achieved. Already known universally by his peers as 'Sailor', as opposed to the original 'Admiral' moniker, Adolph Gysbert Malan was now a fighter pilot.

Chapter Four

Tigers and Spitfires

74 'Tiger' Squadron had, unusually, been re-formed in secret, on 3 September 1935, as the RAF at last expanded, aboard a troopship at Southampton. Earlier that year, the Ethiopian King, Haile Selassie, had complained to the peace-keeping League of Nations that Italy's fascist dictator Benito Mussolini was contravening an agreement that the border zone between Ethiopia (Abyssinia) and Italian Somaliland should not be occupied by either power. Mussolini responded by sending two divisions to Italy's African colonies, namely Eritrea and Italian Somaliland. In August 1935, Britain's High Seas Fleet sailed from Malta to Alexandria, on the North African mainland; and Malta, that vitally important base in the Mediterranean, was heavily reinforced – and it was there that the newly re-formed 'Tigers' were bound. In October 1935, Italy invaded Ethiopia without a declaration of war. The League of Nations imposed economic sanctions on Italy, which were never enforced, sending a clear signal to nations bent on aggressive territorial expansion that they could do so with impunity. Indeed by 2 May 1936, King Haile Selassie was in exile, and all sanctions against Italy had been dropped. No military action was taken against Italy either, and as British colonial interests were not threatened, 74 Squadron saw no action flying from Malta. The re-formed unit was equipped with the two-seater Hawker Demon fighter, and at first known only as the 'Demon Flights'. On 14 November 1935 however, the Air Ministry decreed that the new formation was authorised to be 74 (Fighter) Squadron, back-dated to 3 September 1935. Flying from Hal Far on Malta, the 'Tigers' participated in many exercises with the RN, and in the event of hostilities would have provided air cover for the High Seas Fleet. On 21 August 1936, 74 Squadron sailed for England aboard HMT *Somersetshire*, its Mediterranean adventure over. On 27 August 1936, the 'Tigers' were posted to RAF Hornchurch, that famous Sector Station north of the Thames estuary in Essex. A new chapter in 74 Squadron's history was about to begin, one with which Sailor Malan would be inexorably connected.

TIGERS AND SPITFIRES

On 20 December 1936, Pilot Officer A.G. Malan, along with two others recommended by Squadron Leader Ira Jones, namely Pilot Officers W.F. 'Treacle' Tracey and V.G. 'Paddy' Byrne, reported to 74 Squadron at Hornchurch, fresh from 3 FTS. This was still, according to 19 Squadron armourer Fred Roberts, the 'Strawberries and cream and fruitcake for tea' era of the still comparatively small between-the-wars RAF – which retained the air of an exclusive peacetime flying club in which everyone knew each other. Operational training to combat-ready status was provided on the squadrons, and fighter squadrons competed against each other in gunnery, aerobatics and other competitions, and delighted the aviation-minded public at annual air displays. It was, in sum, an idyllic existence. At Hornchurch, Sailor found his new Squadron still equipped with the Demon two-seater fighter, which it operated until 21 April 1937, when it re-equipped with Gloster Gauntlets – a type with which Sailor was already familiar from Grantham days. On 21 May 1937, Squadron Leader D.S. Brookes led seven 74 Squadron Gauntlets, including Pilot Officer Malan, across the Irish Sea to Aldergrove, to participate in an affiliation exercise with 502 (Bomber) Squadron of the AAF. Later, Sailor would recall two incidents from this ten-day deployment:

'The idea was that we would give a display of aerobatics – the usual thing, a few rolls and loops. Paddy [Byrne] and I decided we could improve on this when we took off, so after doing our usual stuff he got on my tail in a mock dogfight and I did a few fancy flick half-rolls which pleased the crowd, but shook the CO rigid. When we came down he put us under close arrest – which meant having a guard stand over us. Later he made it open arrest. Next morning the *Belfast Daily Telegraph* gave Paddy and me top marks for the dog fight and the extra flourishes. This impressed the CO sufficiently to make him change his mind and let us off.'

It would not be long, of course, until Sailor was getting 'top marks' in dogfighting for real. He also recalled a 'hairy' moment while practising for the Aldergrove display:

'For twenty minutes I was staring at death. It happened while we were flying north of the aerodrome and well out to sea. Gillam (Denys Edgar, later a fighter ace decorated with the DFC and bar, and, impressively, the DSO with two bars), who was then a Met Officer, was flying with me at the time we lost our way when fog closed down. I knew the sea was right underneath. My petrol was getting lower every minute. I could see nothing ahead. I didn't know how far off the coast still was. For a while I sat on top of Gillam. Then I lost him. I was flying at 0 feet by this time, not more than twenty feet above the waves, and throttled right back. My bowels turned to water. I was sweating like a pig. In fact I had a rash under my arms from that scare for a long time after. I could literally *feel* the sea coming up to take me. My petrol gauge registered nothing. I'd just about given up hope and was clearing myself ready to jump as I hit the water when a bit of coastline showed through a gap ahead. I managed to clear the rocks and force-land on some nice green turf that turned out to be Lord Antrim's private golf-course!'

The Gloster Gauntlet Sailor was flying at this time was a single-seater biplane fighter, its top speed of 230 mph being 56 mph faster than the Bristol Bulldog, which it replaced as the RAF's primary fighter-type in May 1935. With an impressive service ceiling of 33,500 feet, the aircraft had an open cockpit, a fixed-pitch propeller, fixed undercarriage, and two .303 nose-mounted Vickers machine guns – so in most respects was actually little different to the biplane fighters of the First World War. The problem was, the same month and year in which the Gauntlet entered RAF service, a revolutionary new monoplane fighter made its maiden flight at Augsburg in Germany: the Messerschmitt Me 109. Although the RAF continued living its peacetime 'strawberries and cream' existence, the arrival on the scene of the 'Augsburg Eagle' changed everything, making biplane fighters – including the Gauntlet – obsolete overnight. At this juncture, therefore, it is necessary to explore developments concerning both aircraft design and the increasing threat posed by Hitler's Germany.

The Air Clauses of the Versailles Treaty of 1919 were intended to end military aviation in Germany, thereby preventing a resurrection of the German Flying Corps, which had fought so effectively in the First World War. The Treaty failed to stop Germany possessing or manufacturing civil aircraft however. Consequently commercial and civil aviation in Germany expanded, behind which innocent façade future Luftwaffe aircrews would be secretly trained. As early as 1920, General von Seeckt, Chief of the Army Command at the *Reichswehr Ministerium*, was convinced that German military aviation must be revived. Certain officers, including Sperrle, Kesselring and Stumpff – names synonymous with the Battle of Britain – became responsible for the resurgence of German air power, hidden from view in von Seeckt's Ministry. By 1926, Germany was considered the most air-minded European nation, the German society for aviation enthusiasts, the *Deutscher Luftsportverband*, enjoying a membership of over 50,000 by

1930 – this was because the emphasis on civil aviation had made the activity accessible to more people than in other countries. Again, Von Seeckt was driving this, encouraging an interest in gliding to circumvent the Versailles *Diktat*. Thus, in due course, Germany had no shortage of air-minded youngsters with air experience, all eager to aspire to powered flight. Von Seeckt then created a cadre of aircrew, secretly trained in schools ostensibly for the civilian Deutsche Lufthansa airline, and at a military flying training school at Lipetz in Russia, behind the Urals and well beyond prying western eyes. When Adolf Hitler came to power in 1933, therefore, the basis of the new Luftwaffe already existed.

Significantly, the First World War had demonstrated how dangerous air power could be – and it was sure to be even more destructive in any future conflict. Between 1933 and 1939, neighbouring states considered the new Luftwaffe the greatest threat to their security, and the aeroplane as a much more dangerous offensive weapon than even the tank. Indeed, air power was seen as fundamental to the achievement of Hitler's proposed aggressive expansionist foreign policy. At first Hitler's ambitions for *Lebensraum* – 'Living Space' for the German people – lay eastwards, the *Führer* confident that Britain would either not intervene or ally itself with Germany. It soon became clear, though, that Britain was trying to prevent this eastward expansion, and from that point on Hitler had to consider a major war against Britain. With that in mind, the Luftwaffe was conceived as a comparatively short-range force in anticipation of war with Germany's Polish neighbours to the east, and Britain and France to the west. Having experienced bombing during the First World War, albeit on a limited and primitive scale, it was the British civilian population which feared air attack most; this anxiety only increasing when Germany withdrew from the League of Nations and Disarmament Conference in 1933. By 1935 – the year the League of Nations failed to take positive action against Mussolini over the Abyssinian Crisis – Hitler felt sufficiently confident to reveal his new air force to a disbelieving world.

The new Luftwaffe – incredibly comprising 1,888 aircraft and 20,000 personnel – immediately began openly improving its aircraft designs and testing new aircraft in aero-sport competitions and large-scale domestic air exercises. By 1934, Professor Willy Messerschmitt had designed a civilian touring monoplane, the Me 108 *Taifun* (Typhoon), securing impressive results in Poland's *Challenge International de Tourisme*; it was a short step therefrom to the lethal Me 109 fighter. During 1933 the *Reichsluftministerium* (German Air Ministry) had decided that for future defensive and offensive operations, the Luftwaffe required four types of monoplanes: a multi-seat medium bomber, a tactical bomber, a single-seat fighter and a two-seater fighter. The single-seater fighter, which would replace the existing He 51 and Ar 68 biplane fighters, was to have a top speed of at least 250 mph and an operational ceiling of 30,000 feet.

The new 109 featured a metal-alloy framework, flush-riveted stressed metal covering, leading-edge wing slots in conjunction with slotted trailing-edge flaps (which increased or decreased the wing surface area on demand), retractable main undercarriage and an enclosed cockpit with a jettisonable canopy. When the Me 109B entered service in 1937, while the RAF still operated the Gauntlet, Germany's new fighter's top speed was a shade under 300 mph – and an entirely modern design.

During the 1920s both financial constraints and disarmament had severely curtailed resources available to the RAF for research and development, restrictions applying equally to the British aircraft industry generally. Paradoxically, in spite of this, it was actually an exciting time for aviation – thanks to the Schneider Trophy competition. The Frenchman Jacques Schneider, son of an armament manufacturer, was perplexed by the fact that although seven-tenths of the world's surface was covered by water, marine aviation lagged far behind land-based aviation. Schneider saw the sea providing cheap airports with huge potential for aviation – and so inaugurated an international air race for seaplanes over a water course measured by fixed points. Whichever nation won the coveted silver trophy three consecutive times got to keep it. This was also a period of globally emerging nationalism, meaning that the exciting aerial race became a matter of great national pride. It was this more than anything else that drove forward development – leading directly to the fast monoplane fighters of the Second World War. In 1929, the same year that Wall Street crashed, Supermarine's gifted designer R.J. Mitchell won the trophy for a second consecutive time, with his sleek S.6, a bullet-like monoplane. Unfortunately the economic collapse meant that no government funding was forthcoming for Supermarine's next all-important entry. This incensed a wealthy patriot, Lady Houston, who personally funded the £100,000 necessary for Mitchell to compete. Her ladyship's confidence was well-placed: on 12 September 1931, Flight Lieutenant J.N. Boothman flashed over the delighted crowds at 340.08 mph with the throttle not even wide open – winning the Schneider Trophy for Britain once and for all. That afternoon, Flight Lieutenant G.H. Stainforth took up another S.6B and set a new world air speed record at 379.05 mph. British aviation was supreme, delighting the depressed nation and arousing the interest of the Air Member for Supply & Research,

Air Vice-Marshal Hugh Dowding – whose name would become synonymous with the aerial battle for Britain's survival which lay ahead.

At the time, owing to the development and investment emphasis, bombers were getting faster – able to outpace existing fighter types. When Mitchell won the Schneider Trophy, the Air Defence of Great Britain relied entirely upon biplanes such as the Bristol Bulldog, which was 10 mph slower than Hawker Hart light bomber introduced in 1929. Although advised by experts that biplanes were superior to monoplanes, Dowding, who had himself flown biplanes during the First World War, disagreed. He also recognised that Mitchell's more advanced designs used more metal parts than the wood-and-fabric biplanes – which Dowding saw as a potential advantage in the event of Britain ever being blockaded and timber being in short supply. Dowding believed that the experience of British aircraft designers gained during the Schneider Trophy races could and should be applied to new military, land-based, aircraft. Consequently, starting on 1 October 1931, the Air Ministry issued various specifications for a new fighter, inviting British designers to submit proposals. Eventually, in April 1935, the Air Ministry issued its 'Requirements for Single-Engine Single-Seater Day & Night Fighter (F.10/35)'. This new aircraft, among other things, had to feature eight machine guns, an enclosed cockpit, be capable of at least 310 mph at 15,000 feet, and be at least 40 mph faster than contemporary bombers at that height. Interestingly though, there was no requirement for the new 'real killer fighter' to be a monoplane, indicating that not all at Whitehall were as convinced as Dowding that the biplane was obsolete.

On 6 November 1935, Hawker's Chief Test Pilot, P.W.S. 'George' Bulman, successfully flew Sydney Camm's Hurricane fighter prototype on its maiden flight from Brooklands. The flight was successful, and on 3 June 1936 the Air Ministry ordered 600 of the new type – the largest such order to date and indicative of the growing concern regarding German rearmament by this time. On 6 March 1936, another little British monoplane fighter flew for the first time – Mitchell's 'Type 300' – better known as the Spitfire. On 3 June 1936, the Air Ministry also ordered 310 Spitfires from Supermarine, at £4,500 each. According to popular myth, delivery of those machines was delayed by the Spitfire's advanced design, but more accurately this was because Supermarine, a comparatively small company, lacked the facilities and resources for mass production. Camm's Hurricane, the first of the new British fighters to fly, was also first to reach the RAF when 111 Squadron at Northolt took delivery of the first production machine in November 1937. By then, while RAF pilots made the quantum leap from biplane to modern monoplane, the Me 109 was already available in numbers and being blooded in aerial combat over Spain - as Hitler's Condor Legion supported the fascist General Franco in a bitter civil war. The Spitfire – already supreme in the public's imagination owing to its victorious Schneider Trophy lineage – would not be received by the RAF until 4 August 1938.

When Britain had belatedly begun rearming in 1935, air defence was coordinated by the Air Defence of Great Britain (ADGB). In 1936 it was sensibly decided to separate this unwieldy command into two: Fighter and Bomber Commands. Thus Fighter Command was created on 6 July 1936, with its headquarters at Bentley Priory. On 14 July, Dowding was appointed the first Commander-in-Chief. This reorganisation provided an opportunity to overhaul and revise the nation's air defences – giving Dowding freedom to harness sophisticated science and techniques into the mix. For this task, as previously Air Member for Research & Development involved in the commissioning of both new monoplane fighters and Radio Direction Finding (RDF, better known as 'radar'), there could have been no better choice. Unlike many of his peers, Dowding had always been a champion of air defence – arguing against Trenchard's obsession with offence, steadfastly maintaining his belief that 'security of the base must come first'. Here at last was a man with the experience and vision necessary to prepare Britain to resist determined air attack – and it was against this backdrop of wider events that Sailor Malan flew the Gauntlet biplane at Hornchurch.

By now it was clear that Sailor was a fine aerobatic pilot:

'Someone bet me I couldn't take the Gauntlet up and do a roll off the top at hangar height. It's a law that you don't stunt over the airfield. But the CO was away at the time and I knew this Gauntlet and what it could do. It was a perfect machine in which to do a flick half-turn, and you could fly it on its side with perfect safety, although the movement looked as if you were bound to go into a dangerous spin. I took the Gauntlet up and had a lovely time turning it inside out. Unfortunately the CO returned unexpectedly and saw me. I had to report to his office for an offence that could warrant a court martial. He was storming with rage. He finished up: "I won't have it, Malan. Get out of my office." And then, as I was thankfully preparing to go, he said, in a very different voice: "But, you know, I like people to do it".'

On 2 April 1938, Sailor married Lynda Fraser at St Martin's, Ruislip, the girl he had first met in 1930, and who at first considered him 'serious and inarticulate'. The year was important for another reason too, because on

6 July 1938 Sailor was promoted to Acting Flying Officer and made an acting flight commander – another early indication that his leadership skills and maturity had been recognised.

On 19 September 1938, 74 Squadron moved temporarily to Sutton Bridge for Annual Armament Training – only to be recalled to Hornchurch a week later 'on account of the European crisis'. This requires some explanation.

Having come to power in Germany during 1933, as we have seen, Hitler immediately launched a rearmament programme with a two-fold purpose: to both extract Germany from financial depression and provide the weapons for his expansionist foreign policy, which he also considered to be 'a battle against Versailles'. The Treaty of Versailles had redrawn the map of Europe, as certain areas and associated territories were taken away from Germany, ceded either to existing states or forming parts of new ones. The issue with this was that in these areas German-speaking people were minority groups, many wanting to re-join Germany. In January 1935, for example, the Saar coalfield area, administered by the League of Nations since 1919, overwhelmingly voted to return to Germany. In March 1935, Hitler announced compulsory military service and revealed the new Luftwaffe, soon afterwards reaching an agreement with Britain that the *Kriegsmarine* – the German Navy – could legally rearm, although not beyond 35 per cent of the RN's strength. In March 1936, the League of Nations' failure to act against Mussolini over Abyssinia emboldened Hitler sufficiently to reoccupy the demilitarised Rhineland. In November that year, Germany and Italy aligned with each other through the Rome-Berlin Axis, and Hitler signed the Anti-Comintern Pact with Japan – a treaty opposing Russian influence and an alliance Hitler saw as essential, because in the event of war Russia's forces would be forced to fight on two fronts. In August 1936, Hitler despatched transport aircraft and He 51 fighters to assist General Franco's Nationalist forces in the Spanish Civil War – the most significant military event between the two world wars. In Spain, Germany tested new weapons and tactics, and for the Luftwaffe's 'Condor Legion' Franco's war became a proving ground for its new monoplanes. Arriving in the early summer of 1937, the Me 109 rapidly established and maintained aerial superiority. One Werner Mölders went to Spain with the Condor Legion and succeeded Adolf Galland in command of the third fighter squadron (*Staffel*) in *Jagdgeschwader* (fighter group, JG) 88, which was converting from He 51s to the Me 109. With a full complement of 109s, Mölders was instrumental in working out combat tactics with the modern monoplane fighter – achieving fourteen personal victories over Spain.

Mölders rapidly realised that fighter combat was fast and furious, a cut and thrust affair often lasting but a matter of minutes. Given the high speed and manoeuvrability of the new monoplane fighters it was quickly realised that inflexible formation attacks – such as those being practised and rigidly enforced by Fighter Command – were totally inappropriate. Fluency and fluidity were required. Pilots needed to keep a sharp lookout – because enemy fighters could appear and attack in a very short time – and be able to break and respond to any given tactical situation, be that from a perspective of defence or attack. What was required now, Mölders discovered, was a combat formation based on the fighting pair, not a squadron of twelve aircraft flying cohesively in sections of three and in close formation. The pair, or *Rotte*, comprised leader and wingman. Before battle was joined the *Rotte* operated as part of a *Schwarm* of two *Rotten*. This section of four cruised in line abreast, each aircraft some 200 yards apart, slightly stepped up, permitting pilots the freedom to search for the enemy instead of concentrating on avoiding collision with their neighbour. When battle commenced, the *Schwarm* broke into two *Rotten*. The leader's job was to shoot down the enemy while his tail was protected by his wingman, or *Katschmarek*. Mölders' new tactics allowed the Condor Legion to achieve air superiority in 1937 which it never lost. The balance sheet indicated 72 German combat losses against 327 Republican aircraft destroyed. Upon return from Spain, Mölders wrote a new manual of fighter tactics for the monoplane which became standard operating procedure in the Luftwaffe – earning for himself the nickname *Vati* – father – of the Jagdwaffe.

Spain was also important to the Germans because it was where they developed close-support tactics between the air force and army. The understanding of fighter tactics gained in Spain would also be a huge advantage to the Luftwaffe in the early stages of the Second World War. Nonetheless, the bomber emerged from Spain confirmed as the most feared weapon so far created by man. This was because of one word: Guernica.

Guernica was a Basque village with a population of around 5,000. Standing between Franco's forces and the capture of Bilbao it became crucial to the war in northern Spain. The town had no anti-aircraft guns, and defensive sorties by Republican aircraft were not a consideration due to recent heavy losses. The target was of military importance because of the road network and bridge in the suburb of Renteria. The raid was a combined operation between the Germans and Italians, involving twenty-three aircraft carrying twenty-two tons of bombs. After the bombing, Me 109s and He 51s strafed the roads around the target. The attack failed to confine itself to the intended, legitimate, military target and destroyed most of the defenceless village. At the time civilian casualties were reported as 1,654, although more recent research indicates a death toll nearer to 400. Nonetheless the raid was perceived as a deliberate terror attack aimed entirely at a defenceless civilian population, and confirmed the fear of air power prevalent throughout the 1930s. The world's media became virtually hysterical and Guernica's suffering was immortalised in Picasso's stark and emotive rendition of the tortured souls who suffered and died in the attack. German air doctrine did not, in reality, revolve around terror bombing however. In fact the indiscriminate bombing of cities was regarded as largely wasted effort. Although initially the shocked survivors were demoralised, once they recovered their main emotions were anger and defiance. The Germans realised, therefore, that such bombing could actually increase an enemy's will to resist. Consequently Luftwaffe doctrine concentrated instead on supporting land operations. Nonetheless, in Spain the bomber had, indeed, always got through and the global fear of it appeared completely justified.

Spain emboldened Hitler further still, and he marched troops into and annexed Austria – a union forbidden by Versailles – on 12 March 1938. Next, Hitler turned his attention to the Sudetenland area of Czechoslovakia, where the ethnic German population was in the majority. Hitler demanded a solution of the international community. Britain's Prime Minister, Neville Chamberlain, refused to support France in the event of the French providing military support to the Czechs. This could well have averted war with Germany – at a time when Britain remained ill-prepared to meet Hitler on the battlefield. Chamberlain's only option was to resolve the matter through peaceful negotiation, while Hitler played 'brinkmanship', concentrating troops on the Czech border and demanding self-determination for Sudeten Germans. On 15 September 1938, Chamberlain met with Hitler, finding the Führer determined to fight. On 21 September, while 74 Squadron were exercising on the Sutton Bridge ranges, Chamberlain, supported by France, persuaded the Czechs to return to Germany those areas of the Sudetenland with more than a 50 per cent population of ethnic Germans. The following day, Hitler refused any such deal, stating his intention to occupy the Sudetenland. War appeared imminent, and hence the recall of 74 and other fighter squadrons to their home stations. On 29 September, Britain, France and Italy signed an agreement with Hitler at Munich, transferring the Sudetenland to Germany. The Czechs were neither party to the 'agreement' nor were invited to attend this Four Power Conference. The outcome of the 'Munich Crisis' therefore was that war was averted without a shot fired.

It was a close call. Chamberlain's policy of 'Appeasement' has long been debated by historians, but it is clear that Britain was unprepared for war with Hitler in 1938 – especially in the air, considering that the Me 109 had already indicated how it could sweep defending biplanes aside with ease. Given that immediately upon return to London, Chamberlain ordered the rearmament of Britain, it is clear that he fully understood the inevitability of war with Germany. The Under Secretary of State for Air, Harold Balfour, expressed his view:

'In September 1938, the Luftwaffe could have shot the RAF out of the skies… This, from a purely air defence of Britain view, is why I am a man of Munich… If you accept, as any student of modern warfare must, that mastery in the air is essential to any victory, then the year Munich gave us saved us from probable defeat… So far as the air is concerned there can be no doubt that the "breathing space" saved Britain. In the House of Commons in September 1938, Churchill said, "England has been offered a choice between war and shame. She has chosen shame and will get war." True: we got war but also final victory, whereas war in 1938 could have meant not victory but defeat. What, I ask, is the merit of being the bravest hero of a defeated country?

'Together with other Ministers I met Chamberlain at Heston Airport on his return from Germany. I saw him wave that piece of paper and read the declaration that he and Hitler had that day signed, resolving to settle peacefully all future differences between our two countries. Why he said what he did I shall never know. Did he believe it? Was it emotional fatigue and reaction in a man of advancing years who had flown half across Europe in air travel conditions very different to those of today? Did he believe the words "peace with honour"? Did he regret and distrust almost at once? All this will never be answered with certainty. What I do know is that none of this can be reconciled with the urgent drive over the next twelve months to prepare the RAF for war and to build up quick expansion of our aircraft industry. Never from No 10 did any order come to slow up anything. On the contrary, we were encouraged and supported to double our efforts. We did our best in the year left to us and for the air, I repeat, "Thank God for Munich".'

After Munich, the atmosphere was tense. Sailor: - 'Our first real scare came in September 1938, after the Munich climb-down. We flew to Hornchurch in bad fog, and the Station Commander ordered everybody, pilots and all, to get hold of paint-brushes and camouflage the planes. Patrols in formation were started. My Squadron was at "readiness". From that time until war came, we were more or less continually on a war footing.'

The pilots now worked a four-day cycle: the first on 'stand-by', which is to say ready to fly within the hour; on the second, they would be 'available' – ready to fly in just fifteen minutes; 'readiness' was day three, which meant immediately able to take off; the fourth and final day was 'stand-down', when a pilot could leave the aerodrome with his flight commander's permission, although a flight of operational pilots still had to be on duty that day and engaged in training. This routine would soon become a way of life, as Europe, and ultimately the world, slid inexorably into the cannon's mouth.

A month before the Munich agreement, 19 Squadron had received the first Spitfires, following 111 Squadron becoming Hurricane-equipped in November 1937, and the race was now on to produce more of the modern fighter types. 74 Squadron, however, for the time being, continued flying the Gauntlet and life remained much the same. On 7 November 1938, for example, a team of 'Tigers', comprising Flying Officers Malan and Hayward, Pilot Officers Haywood and Meares, and Sergeant-Pilots Hawken and Flinders, qualified for the final of the Sir Phillip Sassoon Challenge Trophy's 'Flight Attack' competition. The final took place at North Weald on 25 November – 74 Squadron's team, led by Sailor, victors by a country mile. This, however, again brought Sailor into conflict with his superiors. Already he had rejected the tight formations and strictly choreographed Fighter Command attacks, appreciating that with aircraft getting faster and more manoeuvrable all the time, these tactics were impractical. In the final, 74 Squadron flew formations and tactics not in the manual – and was forced to fly the sortie twice to satisfy the judges. This emphasises yet again the lack of foresight of the Air Ministry, which still clung to what was the aerial tactical equivalent of trench warfare. According to Doug Tidy in *I Fear No Man* (see Bibliography), 'As usual from about twenty pilots who all achieved a fairly good standard, there was one who had a natural gift for deflection shooting and who did outstandingly better than the others – in this case was Malan. He was always a wonderful shot and held, rightly, that air firing was the key to all success as an air fighter. His great attributes were a steady aim and good deflection shooting, plus a superbly calm mind and body in action.'

Having entered service with 19 Squadron at Duxford in August 1938, the Spitfire next equipped 66 Squadron, based at the same station, in November. Next was 41 Squadron, at Catterick, in January 1939, and then, on 13 February 1939, 74 Squadron was signalled that it was to re-equip with Spitfires – the first of London's defending squadrons to receive the new fighter. Two days later, 'Tiger' pilots began ferrying their obsolete Gauntlets to 24 Maintenance Unit, and by 4 March 1939, 74 Squadron was completely Spitfire-equipped. The squadron worked up on Spitfires, training hard and becoming increasingly familiar with their new mounts. It is hard to imagine two aircraft so different, the Gauntlet biplane and the sleek modern Spitfire monoplane with its enclosed cockpit, retractable undercarriage, superior performance and eight machine guns. The Spitfire was undoubtedly stunning in appearance, its elliptical wings providing a unique signature. Its sight and sound rapidly inspired and excited the British public – here, off the back of the victorious Supermarine Schneider Trophy racers, was the weapon to sweep German bombers aside. As Sailor said, 'It was like changing over from Noah's Ark to the *Queen Mary*!... She had no vices. She was beautifully positive. You could dive until your eyes were popping out of your head, but the wings would still be there – till your inside melted, and she would answer to a touch. The Spitfire had style and was obviously a killer. We knew that from the moment we first fired our eight guns at a ground target. You fix the range on the ground. 250 yards is the deadliest. The idea behind this armament is that each gun has its own little place in heaven. By a criss-cross of fire, ranged at a selected distance, you achieve the maximum lethal pattern.'

This spread of fire was, essentially, a shotgun effect, scattering rounds over an area, offering a greater likelihood of more finding their mark. While a one-second burst delivered 240lbs of lead, the ammunition involved was only .303 – rifle-calibre. The Me 109 was armed with two nose-mounted 7.92mm machine-guns (only very slightly larger than the .303) and, most importantly, two wing-mounted 20mm Oerlikon FF cannons. This heavy-hitter fired a shell as big as a man's fist, with a 520 rounds per minute rate of fire. There was no comparison between the destructive power of a machine-gun bullet and a 20mm round. While the eight machine guns of Spitfires and Hurricanes were a major forward-step from the Gauntlet's two, the lack of cannon armament was an omission which would vex the RAF until the matter was properly resolved in 1941. The only downside to the cannon was that the slower rate of fire required greater shooting accuracy – so the scatter-gun effect of the Browning had merit in that context, and had clearly impressed Flying Officer Malan. While the propagandists lost no time in promoting the Spitfire as a world-beater, the armament issue is one example of how the Spitfire was actually imperfect – as opposed to popular myth.

There were other deficiencies. The Spitfires and Hurricanes of the period were powered by the Rolls-Royce Merlin engine, over which the Me 109's Daimler-Benz 601A enjoyed a significant advantage: it was fuel-injected and therefore unaffected by gravity. The Merlin's float-carburettor *was* affected by negative-g, meaning that the engine momentarily cut out in the dive – allowing a pursuing German fighter to catch up. Another area of concern was airscrews. The RAF fighters' original propeller was two-bladed, carved from mahogany; originally the 109 had a similar 'fixed-pitch' airscrew. 'Pitch' refers to the angle at which a propeller bites into the air, and changing it has a similar effect to changing gear in a car. The Germans upgraded the 109 to have a three-bladed VDM (Vereinigte Deutsche Metallwerke) 'controllable-pitch' propeller, made of duralumin, the blades of which the pilot could rotate at will and thereby select the optimum pitch for any given situation. The Spitfire Mk Is originally supplied to 74 Squadron had the fixed-pitch wooden airscrew. As it happened, at the time, a former commander of the 'Tigers', Squadron Leader D.S. Brookes, was RAF Overseer to Vickers-Supermarine, the manufacturer of the Spitfire, and had completed a course on de Havilland's new two-pitch propeller, fitted to the Fairey Battle light bomber, which was also Merlin-powered. Appreciating the fixed-pitch propeller's inferiority, 'Brookie' suggested that his old Squadron's Spitfires be fitted with Battle two-pitch airscrews. These were too heavy, but De Havilland responded by producing a lighter-weight example, twelve of which Brookie persuaded the Air Ministry to order. This propeller allowed for two pitch settings, 'coarse' and 'fine', improving performance for take-off and climbing, and increased the Spitfire's maximum speed from 360 to 372 mph. It was still inferior to the VDM example, but a step in the right direction.

On 2 March 1939, Sailor was promoted to Acting Flight Lieutenant, commanding 'A' Flight of 74 Squadron, this rank being consistent with a flight commander's role, which he had already undertaken for some time.

Between 10 and 14 July 1939, 74 Squadron operated from Le Bourget, Paris, celebrated the fall of the Bastille with the French Air Force. With war looming large, this public relations exercise was really the swansong of 74 Squadron's 'strawberries and cream and fruit cake for tea' peacetime existence. On 1 September 1939 the storm broke at last: Hitler invaded Poland. On that day Britain ordered general mobilisation by Royal Proclamation. Two days later, Hitler having ignored an ultimatum to withdraw his forces, on Sunday, 3 September 1939, Britain and France declared war on Nazi Germany.

Chamberlain spoke to the nation at 1115 hrs. Countless people huddled anxiously around their wireless sets, listening to the long-awaited but inevitable news:

'This morning the British Ambassador in Berlin handed the German Government a final Note stating that, unless we heard from them by 11 o'clock that they were prepared at once to withdraw their troops from Poland, a state of war would exist between us. I have to tell you now that no such undertaking has been received, and that consequently this country is at war with Germany.'

So, in spite of every effort to avert it, for the second time during the twentieth century Britain and France were at war with Germany. The 'blast of war' sounded once again – a bitter personal blow to the British Prime Minister.

Sailor wrote in a letter home: 'The Spitfire is a formidable machine and they will get a most unpleasant shock if they come over here. We are quite ready for them.'

Chapter Five

Home Defence

With Britain now at war with Germany, this is an appropriate juncture at which to explore how the aerial defences were organised.

Fighter Command, responsible for the air defence of the British Isles, was formed in 1936, the first commander of which, Air Chief Marshal Sir Hugh Dowding, having flown fighters during the Great War, believed that Home Defence must come first: 'The best defence of the country is fear of the fighter. If we are strong in fighters we should probably never be attacked in force. If we are moderately strong we shall probably be attacked and the attacks will gradually be brought to a standstill… If we are weak in fighter strength, the attacks will not be brought to a standstill and the productive capacity of the country will be virtually destroyed.' It was that scripture that underpinned everything Dowding did to update Britain's air defences.

Fighter Command was divided into group areas, each with its own commander and headquarters but answerable directly to him at his Bentley Priory Fighter Command HQ. London and the South East became 11 Group; 12 Group protected the industrial Midlands and the north; 10 Group (which did not become operational until 8 July 1940) presided over the West Country and South Wales; 13 Group's responsibility was the far north, Scotland and Northern Ireland. Groups were then sub-divided into sectors, the epicentre of which was the sector station aerodrome. 74 Squadron was based at Hornchurch Sector Station, in 11 Group, essential to the defence of London.

Dowding had an innovative technical mind. Before this appointment he had overseen RAF Research & Development. In that capacity he had far-sightedly recognised the advantages that Radio Direction Finding – 'radar' – offered in the early detection of an enemy's approach. Integrating this new science into his modern 'System of Air Defence', Britain's approaches were soon guarded by a chain of RDF stations extending from the Shetland Islands down the east coast, along the south coast and up the west as far as Pembrokeshire's Strumble Head.

The keystones of defence became the network of RDF stations, Observer Corps posts and centres, operations rooms, radio-telephony transmitters, landlines and ancillary devices comprising the system of early warning and control. The 'System' was as perfect as technology and resources permitted. At Fighter Command HQ's underground filter room at Stanmore, RDF information was sifted by filterers and filter officers, displayed on a gridded map and passed by tellers through closed speech circuits to both the adjacent Command Operations Room and to appropriate groups and sectors. It took just four minutes between an RDF operator identifying a plot to this information appearing in the operations rooms. The Sector Controller would then guide his fighters by radio telephone to intercept the enemy. Dowding believed that tactical control, especially during periods of hectic action, should not be exercised by either Fighter Command or group, but by the sector controllers themselves.

After incoming aircraft had crossed the coast, the Observer Corps was responsible for tracking their progress. Observer posts reported to observer centres, which were connected by landline to the Command Operations Room. From the latter, instructions were issued to local authorities as to when sirens should be sounded, warning the local populace of impending attack. The Gun Operations Room tied anti-aircraft guns into the system, making a cohesive whole.

In each group operations room there was always at least one controller on duty. He scrutinised the large, gridded map of his group area. Aircraft approaching or passing over were represented by coloured plaques, manipulated by WAAFs armed with magnetized wands and headphones linked to a teller at an observer centre or filter room. Facing the Controller was a 'totalisator', showing the location and readiness state of squadrons available. The Group Controller's job was to decide how to meet each threat: a heavy responsibility.

Sector operations rooms were linked by landlines and loudspeakers directly to the aircraft dispersal points, where pilots and aircraft waited to fly; they were also linked to one or more radio-telephony transmitters, placed far enough away to ensure that intercepted transmissions did not reveal their whereabouts. The Sector Controller brought his squadrons to 'readiness', or sent them off to intercept in accordance with orders received from Group. Once the squadrons were airborne, he was responsible for giving them orders and information to place them in a favourable position to attack the enemy. Controllers and formation leaders used a special code: 'Scramble' meant take off urgently; 'Pancake' was the order to land; 'Angels' corresponded to height measured in thousands of feet, and while 'Bandits' were definitely hostile aircraft, 'Bogeys' were as yet unidentified plots. Pilots were directed by the provision of a compass heading, or 'Vector', expressed in degrees, or by reference to landmarks given codenames. 'Buster' was the instruction for fighters to travel at top speed, 'Liner' was cruising speed. When the formation leader cried 'Tally Ho', the Controller knew that the formation leader had sighted the enemy and was about to attack. After that, tactical control was passed to the formation leader in the air, while those in control rooms anxiously awaited the combat's outcome.

An operational fighter squadron comprised twelve aircraft and pilots, excluding reserves, divided into two 'flights', 'A' and 'B', each commanded by a flight lieutenant. The flights were then sub-divided into two sections of three aircraft, each trio of fighters having its own leader and being identified by a colour. 'A' Flight usually consisted of Red and Yellow Sections, 'B' comprised Blue and Green. Each section was numbered from one to three, one indicating the leader. 'Blue One' would therefore identify the leader of 'B' Flight's Blue Section. Each squadron was identified by its own two code letters, which were applied to the fighters' fuselages in medium sea grey. Individual aircraft were further identifiable by a single letter, choosing from A to K for 'A' Flight, and L to Z for 'B'. Each squadron also had its own radio call sign: 'Dysoe Red One' therefore identified the leader of 74 Squadron's 'A' Flight. The squadron was under the overall command of a squadron leader, who, in addition to flying duties, was responsible, through his adjutant, for administration, discipline and the general day-to-day smooth running of his unit. In the air, officers and non-commissioned pilots flew together, but on the ground, while off duty, they were segregated in this class-conscious society. It should not be forgotten that a fighter squadron also included those in behind-the-scenes but nonetheless essential roles: intelligence officers, airframe riggers, engine fitters, instrument fitters, and armourers amongst them.

The operational centre of the squadron was 'dispersal', usually a wooden hut on the airfield in which was situated the orderly clerk and all-important telephone. There were twelve beds on which the pilots rested between sorties. Outside, their aircraft were dispersed as a precaution against bombing, facing the centre of the airfield so that pilots could take off with the minimum of delay. During the daytime, pilots learned to leave their parachutes, which they sat on, not in their bucket seats but on top of either the port wing or tailplane with the straps hanging down, meaning that they could seize the two shoulder straps, pull the parachute pack off the wing and move towards the cockpit, all without pausing (on the subject of parachutes, it may interest the reader to know that fighter pilots were only given ground tuition in deploying a parachute, so the first time they actually did so was when abandoning a doomed aircraft!). Pilots wore a flying helmet made of leather, containing radio-telephony earphones, the leads of which were plugged into a socket in the cockpit, in which the helmet and goggles were left, usually on the reflector gunsight or control column top. Stout leather flying boots were usually worn, lined with sheepskin, to insulate against the cold in what were unheated cockpits, leather gauntlets, and a life jacket known as a 'Mae West', after the buxom American actress. Oxygen, required at high altitude, was delivered via an oxygen mask, covering the nose, cheeks and mouth, the pilot's eyes being protected by his goggles. What fighter pilots seldom wore, however, in direct contrast to the movies and due to the tight confines of their tiny cockpits, was the bulky, leather and sheepskin flying jacket; instead they preferred to wear uniform shirts and tunics. The brightly coloured silk neck scarf was not altogether a pose but necessary to prevent chafing as the pilot constantly screwed his neck around searching for the enemy. Moreover, neck ties shrank in seawater, another valid reason why their use was discarded on operations. On the ground, the fighter pilot famously wore his tunic top button undone. With their racy modern fighter aircraft, fighter pilots would soon be centre-stage, the 'glamour boys', the aerial knights who would save Britain from the bombers. As in the First World War, the fighter pilot was poised to become a star, and a crucial tool for the propagandists.

Chapter Six

The 'Battle of Barking Creek'

During the early hours of 4 September 1939, Flying Officer Malan and 'A' Flight made their first operational flight of the Second World War, a nocturnal patrol between 0250 hrs and 0435 hrs aimed at intercepting an unidentified aircraft approaching England from across the North Sea. The Spitfire was designed as a short-range daytime interceptor – not as a night-fighter – and, owing to two banks of glowing exhausts either side and in front of the pilot spoiling his night vision, and narrow-track undercarriage making landings tricky, the Spitfire was not a great night-flying aircraft. At this time and for some time ahead, the RAF had no dedicated night-fighters, so Spitfires and Hurricanes, along with the Boulton-Paul Defiant turreted fighter and twin-engined Bristol Blenheim, would have to plug this gap for the foreseeable future. It was a false alarm: friendly bombers returning from Holland via Felixstowe. Nonetheless, the sortie was a landmark moment for 74 Squadron.

The declaration of war had doubtless prompted many to reflect on life in general, because clearly nothing was ever going to be the same again, the future – if there was one – uncertain. On 4 September 1939, Flying Officer Sailor Malan wrote a rare letter home to his parents:

'I started to write this letter to you over a week ago. But the same day we were ordered to readiness and war stations and I hadn't another chance. I suppose I am in the prime of life and yet have a lot to be thankful for. I have had quite a good fling for one. But the biggest factor is that I have had eighteen months of complete happiness and blissful contentment with one of the sweetest women in the world, and thank God for that. It probably seems a strange thing to say but I am more than ready to enter the conflict having had those glorious eighteen months.'

In Britain, fear of the bomber after Guernica was endemic. This is perfectly understandable. No part of the British Isles was beyond

41

a German bomber's range – and the First World War had already demonstrated that in any future war, civilians would find themselves under aerial attack. Between June and September 1939 some 3,750,000 people were evacuated from heavily populated areas and relocated to the country, such movements that month alone affecting up to a third of Britain's population. It was fully expected that Germany would soon seek to deliver the much discussed and dreaded 'knock-out blow' from the skies; for years politicians had expounded that 'the bomber will always get through'. On that fateful Sunday morning when war was declared, at 1127 hrs Londoners truly believed that Armageddon had arrived when air raid sirens wailed across the capital for the first time. Fortunately it was a false alarm, caused by an unannounced visiting French aircraft. Any unidentified plot approaching the east coast represented a potential threat, leading to fighters being scrambled to investigate what was, in RAF jargon, an 'X-Raid'. What happened next highlights just how taut nerves were stretched – and how eager the 'Tigers' were for action.

Shortly after 0600 hrs on 6 September 1939, a searchlight battery reported high-flying aircraft over the Essex coast at West Mersea to the Sector Operations Room at North Weald. Having passed the information to the Observer Corps, the Sector Controller scrambled 151 Squadron's Hurricanes, and those of 56, both based at North Weald, to patrol between Harwich and Colchester at 11,000 feet in response to the 'X-Raid'. Already, there are important facts to consider.

Firstly, the new monoplane fighters remained comparatively new, and squadrons were still gaining experience of them. 56 Squadron, for example, had only converted from biplanes to the Hawker Hurricane in May 1938, and 151 Squadron in December 1938. How tactics for the new fighters would work in practice remained an unknown quantity. Indeed, owing to the greater speeds of the new monoplane fighters, some at the Air Ministry believed that fighter versus fighter combat would be impossible in any future war, because the human body would not cope with the greater stresses imposed, so, consequently, little thought was given to the matter. Moreover, German bombers being escorted by single-engined fighters was unanticipated, the assumption being that any attack would be launched from bases in Germany, and therefore beyond the Me 109's range. Consequently, tactics had been formulated on the basis that only ponderous German bombers would be engaged, the proposed and practised tactics involved revolving around the squadron or flight, flying in sub-sections of three aircraft. Indeed, on 3 April 1939, Air Vice-Marshal

Gossage, AOC 11 Group, had sent a memorandum to his sectors and squadrons emphasising that 'Some squadrons have not had their monoplane fighters long enough to be able to employ them efficiently in formations greater than sections or flights', and that 'interception exercises shall be carried out by flights or sections'. This is significant. Until the enemy was sighted that fateful morning, the North Weald Controller, Group Captain D.F. Lucking, possessed of all the latest incoming information via the 'System', was solely responsible for deploying and directing defending fighters at sector level (not Fighter Command HQ). At 0630 hrs, Lucking began scrambling whole squadrons, not 'flights or sections', to meet the perceived threat. The wisdom of this, considering how little training had been undertaken by squadrons operating both as a cohesive unit or in conjunction with other squadrons, can only be considered questionable from the outset.

At that time, 0630 hrs, Squadron Leader 'Teddy' Donaldson led the whole of his 151 Squadron up from North Weald. Previous accounts have claimed that the CO of 56 Squadron, Squadron Leader Knowles ignored the order to scramble a single flight, and instead took off with his whole Squadron. This, however, cannot be true, because were that the case, and given the tragic end result of this interception, Squadron Leader Knowles would undoubtedly have found himself the subject of a Court of Inquiry. The fact of the matter is that 56 Squadron's 'A' Flight, led by Flight Lieutenant Soden, scrambled from North Weald at 0640 hrs, a total of eight Hurricanes, significantly including, as things would turn out, Pilot Officer Montague Hulton-Harrop and Pilot Officer Frank Rose. Ten minutes later, Squadron Leader Knowles followed with 'B' Flight, adding a further six fighters to those already airborne. With incoming reports from radar plots and the Observer Corps suggesting that a hostile force of over fifty aircraft was approaching London via Southend, the understandably flustered Sector Controller then scrambled the whole of 74 Squadron at 0645 hrs, along with further Spitfires from 54 and 65 squadrons, both also Hornchurch-based, between 0655 and 0710 hrs.

It was a unique moment in time, highly charged with excitement and tension, everyone involved braced for the 'knockout blow'. The RAF fighters, their pilots' senses acutely alert, were converging on each other and all expecting to see the enemy for the first time – and none of the RAF pilots involved had any previous combat experience. Ahead and just west of Ipswich Flight Lieutenant Malan sighted a formation of twelve aircraft, which were not flying the prescribed Fighter Command close-formation vics of three, but spread out more loosely, with two, what appeared to be, covering fighters following behind and below. Given the information available to him, and in the heat of the moment, Sailor shouted 'Tally Ho! (enemy sighted) and ordered 'A' Flight to execute a Fighter Command No 1 Attack by sections. Tragically, as things turned out, it was not the enemy in sight but 56 Squadron's Hurricanes. According to his subsequent testimony, realising seconds later that the 'bandits' were in fact friendly fighters, Sailor claimed to have immediately issued a follow-up verbal order over the radio, cancelling the previously ordered attack. Yellow Section of 'A' Flight still attacked however, Flying Officer Paddy Byrne and Pilot Officer John Freeborn opening fire, shooting down the two trailing Hurricanes of Pilot Officers Hulton-Harrop and Rose. Tragically, the former was killed while the latter safely force-landed his damaged machine.

Group Captain Lucking was immediately removed from office and both Pilot Officers Byrne and Freeborn arrested, a Court of Inquiry convened. Neither pilot claimed to have heard their Flight Commander's second order cancelling the attack. At the subsequent hearing, held at Hendon on 17 October 1939, Flight Lieutenant Malan appeared as witness for the prosecution, stating under oath that he had cancelled the attack - but that Yellow Section had pressed on. The defence barrister, Sir Patrick Hastings, called Malan 'a bare-faced liar!' seeking only to protect himself, which some have cited as evidence that this was the case. Being called a 'liar' by the defence, however, is absolutely no proof whatsoever, because such an accusation is standard practice, in order to discredit a witness and plant doubt in the court's mind. Sailor Malan, however, is remembered as a consummate and mature professional, and even at that early time was a pilot and leader of some experience. Reserved by nature, a man of impeccable integrity with the heart and courage of a lion, to lie would have been out of character and contrary to everything we know about the man. Moreover, were there any case to answer, Flight Lieutenant Malan would also have been charged and been in the dock alongside his two errant pilots. This, then, suggests that the investigators were satisfied with Malan's conduct and clearly felt that the blame lay with Freeborn and Byrne. Wing Commander John Freeborn, as he became, however, maintained to his dying day that Malan never gave a cancellation order.

So what is the explanation?

This question is impossible to answer definitively, on account of the Court of Inquiry report being closed for 100 years, and 'Barking Creek' remains an emotive issue, still vexing historians and wartime enthusiasts years later. To my mind, the most likely explanation for the tragedy lies in the comparatively primitive, and often unreliable, in-aircraft radio telephony involved – and of course, unlike today, there was no onboard radar or heads-up display. RAF fighters used the TR9D High Frequency radio, enabling communication between pilots of a squadron with each other and the ground controller. What the TR9D did not provide for, however, was for airborne squadrons to communicate directly with each other. Had that been possible, then clearly the whole sorry mess could perhaps have been avoided. Moreover, a small number of aircraft in each unit were also fitted with a navigational aid called 'Pip-squeak', on account of the high-pitched 'pip' it emitted. The problem was that for fourteen seconds of every minute, the TR9D of the 'Pip-squeak' aircraft automatically switched channel to transmit a homing signal to ground direction-finding stations, enabling the exact position of friendly formations to be plotted. During those fourteen seconds when the radio channel switched to 'Pip-squeak', the pilot in the transmitting aircraft could neither hear others nor communicate via the TR9D. As the Flight Commander and formation leader, it is highly likely that Sailor's Spitfire carried a 'Pipsqueak' device, and the fourteen second automatic channel-switch could well explain why his cancellation order was not heard. This is certainly the view of academic researcher Nick Black, who forensically deconstructed the events involved (see bibliography), concluding that:

'After researching this incident thoroughly for almost two years, I wholeheartedly believe that Malan was justified to be furious with Freeborn and Byrne; and wanted to see them punished for failing to follow procedures and identify their targets correctly. I do not believe that Malan lied at the Court Martial, despite what the popular narrative tells us. I also affirm that the whole incident may have been avoided, had not "Pipsqueak" interrupted Malan's communications, causing his countermanding order to go unheard. If there had been suspicion that Malan was in any way to blame for this incident it is likely that he would have found himself on charges at the same time. He was not.'

Clearly, however, Freeborn and Byrne had not deliberately ignored an order, and had not taken to the skies that day to destroy friendly aircraft, and were rightly acquitted in what was simply a tragic accident. John Freeborn, later also a decorated ace and one of the Few, survived the war but never forgave

Malan for what he steadfastly maintained until his dying day was a 'bare-faced lie'. In 2000, I asked Wing Commander Freeborn, in person, what he thought of Malan; with utter contempt in his voice, John said simply, 'He was a *unt'.

Conversely, Group Captain Malan, as he became, maintained a life-long dignified silence on what became known as the 'Battle of Barking Creek'.

Air Marshal Cliff Spink:

'With regard to "Barking Creek", perhaps we will never know the exact story, as by definition air combat and the control involved was good for its time but still rudimentary by any standard. I know from first-hand experience that without the advantage of telemetry (ACMI which we did have later in my career) you could come down from a combat sortie and the view of what happened was as many and various as the pilots taking part! Therefore the participants at Barking Creek may all have been telling the truth as they saw it but which differed significantly in appreciation. I met John Freeborn – who fired the fatal shots – on numerous occasions and being the blunt speaking Yorkshireman he was, in later years, he did not mince his words about Sailor Malan. He thought that Sailor had run for cover on this tragedy and had not been truthful about events... Later the two of them worked very effectively together on a professional level although they were obviously never going to be friends. Talking to John it was obvious he respected Malan for the outstanding fighter leader and pilot he was. Malan never recommended Freeborn for either of his subsequent medals.

'I admired them both, although I never met Malan. Both outstanding pilots and wonderful shots.

'As one who is proud to have his name on the "Malan Memorial Sword" as a 74 'Tiger' Squadron Commander, Sailor Malan remains one of my personal heroes both for what he achieved in the RAF and later in South Africa in his courageous fight against discrimination. Even great men have their skeletons and this episode might be his, although I prefer to think that this was truly a fog of war incident in which the participants "told it as they saw it" – sadly the views were somewhat different. You may indeed be right that Pip-squeak was an important factor – that would certainly explain the variation of opinion on what went on'.

Whatever the truth, the incident certainly highlighted the crucial importance of correctly identifying radar plots and accurately reporting sightings of aircraft. Given the background to this early interception and state of high tension, it was, arguably, an inevitable tragedy. Interestingly, over time, 'Pip-squeak' was found to be problematic on account of monopolising one of the TR9D's two channels, meaning that all transmissions were restricted to a single frequency, and because of the constant interruption for fourteen seconds of every minute. By the Battle of Britain, a new system, 'Identification Friend or Foe' (IFF) had been developed, involving the radar network and which did not interrupt radio communication, although it was impossible to replace 'Pip-squeak' with IFF until after the battle.

It was perhaps an ironic twist of fate that on the afternoon of 'Barking Creek', and the following day, 74 Squadron's 'B' Flight, led by Flight Lieutenant 'Treacle' Treacy, provided Spitfires to fly for the making of *The Lion Has Wings*, a feature film intended to reassure the public 'of the power of the Royal Air Force' and its ability to defend Britain from aerial bombardment. Given the fear of German air attack, this was a vitally important propaganda film, which again emphasises the fearful atmosphere of the time. Starring Ralph Richardson, Merle Oberon, June Duprez, Anthony Bushell, and, interestingly, Ronald Adam – an RFC First World War veteran who in 1939 was commissioned in the RAF as a wing commander and became Sector Controller at Hornchurch – the film firmly held Hitler responsible for causing the war, while emphasising that Britain's industry was prepared for war production, the excellence of our own bomber force, and, most importantly, that the RAF could defeat any German bomber attack. Indeed, this underpinned the entire film, the destruction of a German bomber (in this case a Focke-Wulf Condor long-range reconnaissance bomber) by Spitfires providing a climatic conclusion. The film was the top cinema attraction of November 1939, the British Film Institute reporting that the movie 'admirably fulfils its object – to inspire quiet confidence in the hearts of those who see it'. Indeed, the evidence available from Mass-Observation surveys indicates that the film definitely helped to assuage public anxiety, at least temporarily until the bombs began to rain down on Britain. For 'B' Flight, their contribution to the film's flying scenes was a welcome and light-hearted diversion, and there was no mistaking which squadron was involved – the 'The Tiger's Den' sign was visible on the Flight Commander's tent.

While 'B' Flight performed for the cameras, just a few hours after the 'Barking Creek' debacle, Flight Lieutenant Malan took off at 1440 hrs on a training flight with Sergeant E.A. 'Boy' Mould, a reservist who had joined 74 Squadron from FTS on 1 July 1939. At this time, conversion to operational types and operational training was provided by squadrons, and up to this point Mould had not flown operationally. It could be, therefore, that this sortie of fifty-five minutes was for the Flight Commander to check out the 'sprog' – after one more evening training flight, Mould flew his first patrol the following day, so had clearly satisfied Flight Lieutenant Malan. Already 74 Squadron had received an influx of new pilots, whom Sailor was keen to make combat-ready as soon as possible – but only if his exacting standards were met. Indeed, the whole squadron spent hours flying various training sorties, including formation practice, night-flying and Fighter Command attacks. By the month's end, however, there was still no sign of the 'knock-out blow'. There would, in fact, be no attempt by either side that year to deliver such a decisive air attack – because in reality neither were in a position to do so, and both sides were anxious not to be judged responsible for unleashing unrestricted aerial warfare. And so the so-called 'Phoney War' began, the '*Sitzkrieg*' of the war's first autumn and winter, as Hitler's next military move was patiently awaited.

On 22 October 1939, 74 Squadron was deployed to operate from Hornchurch's satellite airfield at Rochford, previously home to a civilian flying club. Over the next few months, 74 Squadron, along with Hornchurch's two other Spitfire squadrons, 54 and 65, would rotate between these two airfields, thereby ensuring that the sector's fighters were dispersed. But still the monotonous round of training sorties and routine patrols continued unabated – until 20 November 1939. On that date, at mid-day, Yellow Section of 74 Squadron was at readiness when scrambled from Hornchurch to intercept an X-Raid. At 27,000 feet over the sea, fifteen miles off Southend, Flying Officer Measures, Pilot Officer Temple-Harris and Sergeant Flinders intercepted an 'He 111', which was flying east, above and ahead. Opening fire at the raider from 400 yards, Yellow Section pressed home a Fighter Command Number 1 Attack, forcing the enemy reconnaissance bomber to dive to 6,000 feet and seek sanctuary in cloud. Yellow Section gave chase, firing intermittently until a small piece broke off from the target and Measures found himself buffeted by the bomber's slipstream. Breaking away, Yellow 1's place was taken by Temple-Harris, who fired a burst from long range, as did Flinders, after which the German disappeared into cloud. The following day it was confirmed that the enemy aircraft had crashed into the sea – in the process becoming 74 Squadron's first aerial victory of the Second World War. It was not in fact an 'He 111' but a Do 17 of 4(F)121, engaged on a photographic sortie of London and the Thames Estuary. The German crew, Leutnant Meyer, Feldwebel Rickertsen and Unteroffizier Steyrer, were captured bobbing about the North Sea in their dinghy. It was a landmark moment for 74 Squadron – but one again highlighting the difficulties of aircraft identification in combat, and that attacking from 400 yards was too far away.

As the winter wore on, what with heavy snow and fog, by February 1940 flying had all but ground to a halt. On 25 February 1940, Squadron Leader Francis Lawrence 'Droguer' White succeeded Squadron Leader G.E. Sampson. White was the embodiment of Trenchard's pre-war expansion plans, having begun his service as an Aircraft Apprentice – a 'Halton Brat' – passing out in 1924 as an engine fitter. Later, thanks to Trenchard's efforts to expand the RAF, he successfully applied to become a pilot. An indication of his standing and ability is that when a sergeant-pilot in 1931, White was given a Permanent Commission. He then enjoyed various appointments at home and abroad, before taking over the 'Tigers'. At this time, the primary fighting formation was the flight, not squadron as a whole, and so the two flights tended to operate largely autonomously, their respective flight commanders holding sway. White was determined to see 74 Squadron operate as a cohesive unit, and devoted himself to effecting this operational change. According to Tidy, this was eventually achieved, 'although initially it was somewhat tricky dealing with two such individualistic characters as Sailor and Paddy [Byrne]'.

Life for the Spitfire squadrons continued, focussing on training, as the apparently interminable Phoney War ground on. For the first three months of 1940 little happened. The Soviets finally overwhelmed the Finns, and U-Boats continued attacking Britain's North Atlantic shipping, but elsewhere the *Sitzkrieg* persisted. With the exception of the Czechs and Poles, few had thus far suffered unduly from the conflict. In early April, Hitler attacked Denmark and Norway, drawing Anglo-French forces into a hopeless campaign in Norway's inhospitable terrain. On 2 September 1939 the British Advanced Air Striking Force had flown to France, Fairey Battle light bombers preceding Blenheims and Hurricanes – but no Spitfires. Indeed, Air Chief Marshal Dowding had only sent Hurricanes for two reasons: due to political pressure he had no choice but to support the French by providing some fighters, and, that being so, only sent Hurricanes, the performance of which was inferior to the Spitfire, thus preserving his precious Spitfires for the defence of Britain. Although, like Spitfires back home, the Hurricanes engaged and destroyed the odd German reconnaissance bomber prowling about over France during the Phoney War, it was not until 26 March 1940 that 73 Squadron's Hurricane pilots engaged Me 109s over Saarlautern and Trier, claiming four destroyed and two unconfirmed. A few weeks later, Hitler's long-awaited assault on the West began – which changed everything.

Chapter Seven

Dunkirk

Abruptly, on 10 May 1940, the great storm finally broke when Hitler invaded Belgium, Holland, Luxembourg and France. Two days later Liège fell, and *Panzers* crossed the Meuse at Dinant and Sedan. Hitherto, in the naïve hope of remaining neutral, the Belgians had refused Lord Gort's British Expeditionary Force permission to fortify their border with Germany. Now the Belgian King called for help, the BEF pivoting forward from its prepared defences on the Belgian-French border. The British advanced for sixty miles over unfamiliar ground expecting to meet the German *Schwerpunkt* – point of main effort – which was expected to follow the same route as in the Great War. It did not. Holland was certainly attacked – the Dutch Air Force being wiped out on the first day – but the main enemy thrust was cleverly disguised. As Allied eyes were firmly focussed on the Belgian-Dutch border, *Panzergruppe* von Kleist achieved the supposedly impossible and successfully negotiated the Ardennes, much further south. German armour then poured out of the forest, bypassing the Maginot Line, rendering its concrete forts useless. The Panzers then punched upwards, towards the Channel coast – ten days later the Germans had reached Laon, Cambrai, Arras, Amiens and even Abbeville. Indeed, Erwin Rommel's 7th Panzer covered ground so quickly that it became known as the 'Ghost Division'. The effect on the Allies was virtual paralysis, so shocking was the assault, unprecedented in its speed and fury. Civilians in Britain were equally shocked – not least after the bombing of Rotterdam on 14 May reportedly caused 30,000 civilian fatalities (although post-war estimates put the death toll at nearer 3,000). Hard on the heels of Guernica and Warsaw, Rotterdam's fate was terrifying news indeed.

By 10 May 1940 there were six squadrons of Hurricanes in France. One week later the equivalent of six more had crossed the Channel and another four were operating from bases on the south-east coast of England, hopping over the Channel on a daily basis but returning to England – if they could –

at the end of each day. Losses in France rapidly stacked up. The Air Ministry acted as though these casualties were a complete surprise. Dowding's sharp riposte was 'What do you expect? When you get into a war you have to lose things, including precious aircraft. That's exactly what I've been warning you about!' His fears regarding the wastage of fighters were now being realised. The crux of the problem was that the more fighters Dowding sent to France, the further he weakened Britain's defences. Already Dowding had insisted that the minimum strength required to guarantee Britain's safety was fifty-two squadrons, and yet soon he was arguing a case to retain just thirty-six. Although Churchill later wrote that Dowding agreed with him the figure of twenty-five, the latter dismissed this statement as 'absurd'. With the French constantly clamouring for more fighters, and putting Churchill's War Cabinet under increasing pressure, things came to a head on 15 May.

On that day, Dowding joined Newall, the CAS, at a Cabinet meeting. As the BEF were poised to attack enemy communications near Brussels, both men spoke out against sending more fighters across the Channel. Dowding later commented, 'There had already been serious casualties in France, and they alone had been worrying me a very great deal. I had to know how much longer the drain was going on, and I had to ask for a figure at which they would shut the stable door and say no more squadrons would be sent to France.' Unable to request an interview with the Cabinet every time a new demand for fighters was received, on 16 May, Dowding sat and composed the strongest case he could to prevent further fighters being drained away in a battle already lost. The following is extracted from that letter:

'I must therefore request that as a matter of paramount urgency the Air Ministry will consider and decide what level of strength is to be left to the Fighter Command for the defence of this country, and will assure me that when this level has been reached not one fighter will be sent across the Channel however urgent and insistent appeals for help may be.

'I believe that, if an adequate fighter force is kept in this country, if the fleets remain in being, and if the Home Forces are suitably organized to resist invasion, we should be able to carry on the war single-handed for some time, if not indefinitely. But, if the Home Defence force is drained away in desperate attempts to remedy the situation in France, defeat in France will involve the final, complete and irremediable defeat of this country.'

On the very day that Dowding argued to stem the flow of British fighters to France, the Air Ministry required that a further eight half-squadrons be sent across the Channel. Worse, Churchill himself then flew to France, subsequently requesting a further six squadrons and a night attack by heavy bombers. By 19 May the situation on the continent had deteriorated further still. On that day, the War Office and Admiralty began considering the unthinkable possibility of evacuating the BEF from France, and Churchill finally saw sense. The Prime Minister's subsequent decision was recorded in a minute: 'No more squadrons of fighters will leave the country whatever the need of France.' By the following day, only three of Dowding's squadrons remained on the Continent. He considered that this 'converted a desperate into a serious situation'.

Squadron Leader 'Teddy' Donaldson, the commander of 151 Squadron, was amongst the Hurricane pilots fighting in France and remembered:

'The French bolted, including their air force. I have never seen so many people running so fast anywhere, as long as it were west. The British Tommies were marvellous, however, and fought their way to the sand dunes of Dunkirk. I was in command of 151 Squadron, and our Hurricanes were sent to reinforce the AASF, flying from Manston to France on a daily basis.

'In some respects the Germans were grossly over confident in the air, and so didn't have it all their own way. But every day we had damaged Hurricanes and no ground crews to mend them, dictating that we had to return to Manston every evening. In any event, our airfields in France were being heavily bombed, so had we stayed, although pilots could have got off the airfield to sleep, our aircraft would have taking a beating. 151 Squadron would fly up to seven sorties a day, against overwhelming odds, and on one occasion even stayed on patrol after expending our ammunition so as to prevent the Luftwaffe attacking defenceless British troops on the ground.'

Amongst those 'defenceless British troops' was Eric Wylam of the Royal Engineers:

'On we went, after ascertaining that the coast was clear, eventually reached the top of the "Mont-du-Chats" (Mount of Cats) without further interruptions and able to indulge in a short rest. This brief spell was soon broken by the ominous drone of many planes in the distance. Anti-aircraft fire soon warned us that these were enemy planes. We dived into the thickly wooded hillside more for camouflage than for shelter. These visitors evidently meant business for there were about thirty of them and the tactics they used were pretty frightening: the first five to ten planes released all their bombs at once, at least ten more dived and dropped their missiles singly – literally combing the hill with bombs. More and more arrived, and closer came the bombs. It seemed as though the raid would never end. The twelve and a half minutes they were bombing us seemed like an eternity, but once again we were relieved to hear of no casualties.

'…The planes were on their way: the ominous drone filled the sky. There was obviously a large number as the drone grew louder and louder. The wounded were moved against the walls of the building to afford them a little protection from the expected bombs that would be falling in a matter of minutes – poor devils.

'Ten, twenty, thirty – forty – fifty planes in all we counted, consisting of twenty-five Messerschmitts and twenty-five Heinkels – and more coming. Page, Jennings and myself were in the midst of making some tea and eats for the lads and we decided to carry on to the last minute, or until "bombs were dropping". This we did, and when they did start falling, we were too late to get any substantial shelter, so we parked ourselves under the lintel of a door leading to the cellar. There were women in that shelter…

'The first concussions of the bombs were soon felt, and they weren't far away. They appeared to be fairly small high-explosive bombs, but quite capable of causing a fair amount of damage should they have dropped closer. Fires clearly indicated where incendiary bombs had fallen.

'We clustered, somewhat scared and certainly with tense anticipation, expecting the very roof to collapse on us at any moment. CRASH! One heavy high-explosive bomb had landed in the garden, not thirty yards from us. Every pane of glass on that side of the building was blown into the room. The impact was horrifying. The very building shook from its foundations and we could see large cracks running the length of the room we were in. But alas! No masonry fell and the monastery remained erect – Thank God! Other high-explosive bombs crashed in the vicinity of the monastery. The building withstood the concussion and remained steady, much to our relief.

'The Messerschmitts were now fiercely attacking us with their machine guns: peppering the walls for all they were worth. They dived and turned with the most hair-raising stunts in accompaniment, and we could not help but marvel at the skill at which the German pilots handled their planes. What can we do? We were helpless against such "bloody" warfare! Again and again the fighters dived and splattered machine-gun fire at the building with even greater viciousness. But still everyone on the staff was unharmed. Once again it seemed as if we were all being protected by some invisible hand.'

The RAF in France was receiving a short sharp shock regarding the vital importance of fighters in achieving aerial superiority over the battlefield, enabling ground troops freedom of movement. According to John Terraine, 'The German fighters – over 1,200 of them, but above all the Me 109s – ruled the sky, and in doing so achieved, for the first time against a major enemy, the saturation of a battle area by air power, and that is what won the Battle of France. It was, in fact, won in six days… The Allies had lost the battle… to the achievement of complete air superiority by the German Air Force, enabling the Stukas to perform, the Panzers to roam where they willed; this was an achievement above all of the fighter arm, in particular the Messerschmitt 109.'

74 Squadron had been training hard, and flying the usual round of routine patrols and X-Raid interceptions from Hornchurch and Rochford, in addition to intensive air firing at Dengie Flats on the Essex coast. At 1550 hrs on 16 May 1940, Squadron Leader White led off nine other Spitfires from Hornchurch, the formation including Flight Lieutenant Malan, uneventfully patrolling the Belgian coast off Ostend. A similar 'Offensive Patrol' was flown in squadron strength over Ostend the following day, while on 19 May, Flight Lieutenant Malan led just 'A' Flight across the Channel to the Belgian coast, again returning to Hornchurch without incident. By 21 May, Amiens had fallen and German armour had reached Abbeville, with reconnaissance units on the Channel coast. This enemy thrust had effectively cut the Allied armies north of the Somme from those to the south, effectively trapping the BEF, three French armies and the battered remnants of the Belgian army. Clearly the BEF was now in great peril. On this day, Gort's divisions were lined up along the river Escaut, just across the Franco-Belgian border, determined to stop the German advance. A great battle was fought, Victoria Crosses won, and the enemy held off. The problem was that the position north and south of the BEF's sector made the BEF's position untenable, and so, in danger of envelopment, Gort had no choice but to continue withdrawing back to the French border.

Shortly after 1700 hrs that day, 21 May 1940, Flight Lieutenant Malan led 'A' Flight to patrol Dover at 20,000 feet. Sailor described the ensuing action in a subsequent interview with the American journalist Quentin Reynolds:

'There wasn't much hope of finding the enemy formation we had been sent up to intercept in these broken clouds. It was just another patrol by the look of it. I felt mad because I knew we were a good flight, but how good or bad we couldn't say. We'd never been tried. We'd been reading what Hurricanes could do in France against Messerschmitt 109s and Heinkels. We thought we had something better still in the Spit. But that still had to be *proved*...

'Anyhow, we came out of the clouds at 17,000 feet. There were six of us all told, and we came out in perfect formation. Johnny's (Pilot Officer Freeborn's) wing was tucked right inside mine, and on the left Bertie Aubert, who was half-American, had his wing-tip nestling close. I said through my intercom disc "Nice flying, boys", and then I looked towards France and saw something else.

'France was still our ally then, remember. I saw black puffs about 15,000 feet over Calais. The ack-ack guns kept firing and that meant there were Jerries about. I yelled "Tally Ho over Calais. Let's cut some cake!"

'We opened up fast, A Spit can cross the Channel about as quick as you can cross the street. There were more clouds between us and Calais. I was flying across the top of a great hummock when I nearly flew into a He 111. What happened next was done mainly by instinct. I was moving so fast that only by pulling the stick back and a quick swerve did I avoid ramming him. I was so afraid the German might drop down into the cloud a hundred feet below that I began firing as I did a steep banking turn on his tail. The bullets ripped into him from tail to nose. Pieces flew off. He belched heavy smoke, his undercart fell out and he dropped helplessly into the cloud. As I saw it breaking up I yelled through the intercom "Re-form, re-form".'

The historic moment was dramatically recorded by Sailor's cine-gun camera. The enemy aircraft of 1/LG1 force-landed at Groede, the crew of four being captured, one of whom died in hospital from wounds. Sailor continues:

'I'd tasted blood at last. The release from tension was terrific, the thrill enormous. I'd been wondering for so long – too long, how I'd react in my first show. Now I knew. Everything I had learnt had come right. There was hardly any time to feel even scared. After that I found a Ju 88. That was a much slower-moving target. It seemed easy, even though it carried rear-gunners. I got on its tail and fired when I was about 500 yards off. That was more or less according to regulations. It wasn't quite so simple, although I saw my bullets hammering against his starboard wing-root, where the wing meets the fuselage. In the next few moments I was more into position. At 150 yards my bullets burst all over him. There was no return fire. Then he fell into a dive, with flames showing. I turned to look for the other two in my flight.'

During the attack on the Ju 88, Pilot Officer Freeborn was immediately behind Malan, also attacking the same target successfully. Of Pilot Officer Aubert, however, there was no trace. Reported 'missing', fortunately news was later received that Aubert was safe. Having attacked two enemy bombers, short on fuel the American-born pilot force-landed on Berck-sur-Mer aerodrome. After unsuccessfully foraging for petrol in Boulogne, Aubert returned to find the airfield abandoned and German armour in the vicinity. Being left no choice, he had to reluctantly leave his undamaged Spitfire and head for Calais, returning home as a passenger in a Blenheim on 23 May. After the successful action on 21 May, notwithstanding Aubert being missing at that time, the 'Tigers' were naturally elated. In addition to the Ju 88 destroyed and He 111 'unconfirmed destroyed' claimed by Flight Lieutenant Malan, Pilot Officer Freeborn claimed a Ju 88, Pilot Officer Aubert an unconfirmed Ju 88 and He 111, and Flying Officer 'Tink' Measures an He 111 destroyed. That evening the Station Commander, Group Captain 'Daddy' Bouchier, sent champagne to the officers' mess at Hornchurch, where 74 Squadron celebrated its success. What was a historic combat is also of interest for two other reasons: clearly, in spite of 'Barking Creek' and the personal enmity arising, Malan and Freeborn maintained a professional relationship; secondly, at first sticking to the text book, Sailor opened fire at 500 yards – but noted how much more effective his shooting was at 150 yards. This undoubtedly gave Malan food for thought. Nonetheless, so far as the commander of 'A' Flight was concerned, the account of that first combat 'was not much of a story. Any other pilot remembering his first "kill" and engagement could tell you much the same.' But Sailor Malan was not just 'any other pilot'. He would become one of the most legendary fighter aces of the Second World War – and had now opened his account. From now on, there would be little respite.

On 22 May 1940, German armour continued advancing northwards, threatening Boulogne. Home-based Spitfire and Hurricane squadrons provided air cover for that port, Calais and Dunkirk, flying a total of 198 patrols. At dawn, Flight Lieutenant Malan and 'A' Flight were at Rochford on readiness, and scrambled shortly after 0500 hrs. Sailor's combat report describes events:

'I was leading three sections off Dover at 12,000 feet when I sighted a Ju 88 steering NE in a clearing in the clouds. Formed line astern with Red Section and cut enemy aircraft off from cloud. He dived for sea very steeply at 400 mph, IAS (Indicated Air Speed) and jettisoned four bombs. I delivered No 1 Attack at 250 yards range. After second two second burst, rear gunner stopped firing from twin guns in top blister. Enemy aircraft took avoiding action by skidding and turning. I saw incendiary entering port engine and all-around fuselage, while white vapour was emitted by both motors. At commencement of action IAS was 280 mph, but after my fifth burst speed suddenly reduced, and as my windscreen was covered in white vapour I broke off to port and observed results of action.

'No 3 (Sergeant Mould), whose R/T had failed, then attacked from 200 yards and expended all his ammunition and broke off. No 2 (Pilot Officer Freeborn) then attacked but after his first burst enemy aircraft suddenly lost height, as though both engines had stopped and broken up. There was nothing left after two seconds except the dinghy. Searched for crew but found none.'

The Ju 88 had been engaged at 0545 hrs, 'ten miles north of Calais', at 'sea level'. During this combat Flight Lieutenant Malan closed to 200 yards. This machine, which went down in the Channel, was an aircraft of 3/KG30 engaged on a reconnaissance sortie at first light – all aboard were lost. From Malan's perspective, it was a perfect example of team work. It was 74 Squadron's only engagement that day, the remainder of which was largely spent providing aerial protection to coastal convoys.

With an armoured wedge driven firmly between the Allied armies, those in the north were now focussed on retiring to the Channel coast. By 23 May 1940 however, Boulogne was besieged, Calais isolated, leaving Dunkirk as the only option. On this day, Fighter Command would fly 250 sorties providing air cover over the French coast; at 0600 hrs 74 Squadron was up from Rochford, the CO, Squadron Leader Laurie White, and Flying Officer Measures shooting down an Hs 126 reconnaissance aircraft of 1(H)/14 over Guines, killing the pilot and wounding the observer. The German observer's return fire, however, damaged White's radiator, forcing the CO to land at Calais-Marck airfield. Hornchurch's other Spitfire squadron, 54, had preceded 74 on patrol that morning but returned after yet another uneventful sortie, enviously eyeing the Tigers' lead section returning with gun patches blown. Pilot Officer Al Deere, a tough, no-nonsense Kiwi, of 54 Squadron, immediately drove over to 74 Squadron's dispersal to get the 'form'. First to land was Sailor. Air Commodore Deere, as he later became, recalled the conversation with Sailor:

'Hello, Al, I might have known you'd be sniffing around to find out the form. I always said that the "Tigers" would be first to get amongst them; aren't you envious?'

57

'You bet I am, Sailor! Tell me more…'

'Sorry, haven't got time. All I can say is that we were jumped, and all because some bloody fool would keep nattering on the R/T with the result that when Paddy Treacy gave a sighting report only one or two of the chaps heard it. On top of that the CO had engine trouble, and all in all it was a confusing and frustrating engagement. I think he finally made Calais/Marck airfield where he landed successfully.'

Little did he know it, but Al Deere would soon be caught up in high drama owing to Squadron Leader White's predicament.

Having force-landed, Squadron Leader White hitch-hiked to Calais, presented himself to the nearest Army Transport Officer and telephoned Fighter Command HQ requesting that a new engine be sent over for his Spitfire, which was a new aircraft and repairable, and an aircraft to collect him. The Hornchurch Station Commander was informed, and he, Group Captain 'Daddy' Bouchier, aware that 54 Squadron possessed a two-seater Miles Master, ordered Flight Lieutenant 'Prof' Leathart of that unit to fly over to Calais, escorted by two Spitfires, and collect 'Droguer' White. Understandably, when Sailor was told about the plan he insisted that the 'Tigers' were perfectly capable of rescuing their own CO, and requested that Sergeant Skinner of 74 Squadron should fly the Master, which he had once instructed on. For some unknown reason Bouchier refused – for which, according to Ira Jones, 'Malan never forgave him'. So Leathart flew to Calais-Marck, closely escorted by two 54 Squadron Spitfires, flown by Pilot Officers Al Deere and Johnny Allen, while Flight Lieutenant Malan – honour slightly restored – and 74 Squadron provided high cover. Over the French airfield, the Master was attacked by Me 109s of 1/JG1, Deere and Allen joining the fray and claiming three confirmed destroyed and three unconfirmed between them. Flight Lieutenant Leathart was then able to safely extract Squadron Leader White, for which feat 'Prof' received the DSO, while Deere and Allen were both awarded DFCs.

Another 'Tiger' had failed to return from the same patrol in which Squadron Leader White had been shot down: Flying Officer Paddy Byrne. On that dawn patrol, Sailor led his flight over British troops at just 300 feet, roaring over their heads and passing over Clamarais wood – which was German held. AA fire erupted from the trees, hitting Byrne's Spitfire and wounding him. He force-landed near St Omer and was captured.

On 24 May 1940 the situation in France was becoming graver by the minute. That afternoon a substantial German force bypassed Calais, heading towards the Belgian coastline, cutting off the gallant British garrison. Again, Fighter Command was heavily committed patrolling the coast and Pas-de-Calais inland to St Omer, losing ten aircraft and six pilots – 'Tigers' amongst them. Again operating out of Rochford, Flight Lieutenant Malan's combat report takes up the story of the mid-morning patrol:

'The Squadron was on offensive patrol of Calais. Sighted Do 17 five miles out to sea, below 8/10th cumulus. E/A made off towards cloud at very high speed. Delivered short bursts at E/A whenever opportunities occurred, i.e. when he emerged into clear air between clouds. Most of my bursts were delivered at 4-500 yards owing to difficulty of closing up quickly. Broke away after E/A dived below cloud-base and I had expended my remaining ammunition and had his starboard engine on fire. I then saw Red 2 and 3 firing from astern. The E/A burst into flames and crashed. I filmed the crash and wreck with my cine-gun. The pilot got out and dragged a wounded crew-member out. At one time I saw what appeared to be flaps falling off when I was firing.'

The Do 17 was very likely a machine of 1/KG77, which crashed near Fruges killing one crew-member. Unteroffizier Heilmann is known to have been wounded and was possibly the man Sailor saw dragged from the wreck. The victory was shared by Sailor with the two other members of Red Section. Another Do 17 was claimed by Flight Lieutenant Treacy and Pilot Officer Derek Dowding (son of Air Chief Marshal Dowding).

The afternoon patrol was hectic; Sailor's combat report:

'I was leading Yellow Section of four aircraft on offensive patrol Dunkirk – Calais – Boulogne. Spotted AA fire at 12,000 feet over Dunkirk when at 500 feet off coast west of Dunkirk. Climbed in line astern to investigate and saw three vics of mixed bombers (approx. 9 -12 - 9). Intercepted second vic at 12,000 feet and passed through very heavy and accurate AA barrage. Attacked starboard flank in echelon port from astern as Me 109 and Me 110 were observed above and into sun, turning onto our flank to attack. Observed about eight of these but probably many more about. Delivered three one second bursts at both engines and fuselage of He 111 on starboard flank, 250 – 150 yards. I was then hit on starboard mainplane and through fuselage by AA fire which severed electrical leads near my seat and extinguished reflector sight. As I broke off I observed one Me 110 coming up on starboard quarter and one 109 astern. I executed some very steep turns into sun and lost sight of the other two fighters. I changed bulb in reflector sight but as it failed to function I concluded that wiring had been cut and chipped spare ring for ring and bead sight. By this time the battle had gone out of sight and I hadn't enough petrol to give chase. While climbing into sun I observed crew of He 111 I had shot take to parachutes and aircraft gradually lose height on zig-zag course. While climbing up to the attack, I observed one bomber badly hit (presumably by AA) with port engine stopped and left wing well down, dropping out of formation.'

This is quite incredible: while under attack from two German fighters and executing violent evasive manoeuvres, Flight Lieutenant Malan – cool as you like – *changes the bulb in his gunsight – and even tries to replace the unserviceable electric unit with the spare ring and bead sight in his locker*! If ever evidence was required of the man's professionalism and self-control in a combat situation, that surely provides it in spades. The He 111 was claimed destroyed. During his interview with the American Quentin Reynolds, Sailor added more detail:

'They were the first parachutes I had seen open in the air… Bertie Aubert was killed, Johnny Freeborn was hit. Mungo-Park got one in the arm, and Paddy Treacy got it bad. At least his plane did. His engine was on fire, but he kept going till a bullet went through his windshield and he got a mouthful of glass. Then he baled out. On his way down a Messerschmitt kept circling and taking pot shots that peppered his 'chute and hastened his descent. As he got near the ground – it was just outside Dunkirk – French troops fired at him. He landed in a pigpen deep in mud. He didn't mind the mud, it broke his fall. He did mind the owner of the pen, a large boar which charged and caused him to twist his ankle!'

Flight Lieutenant Treacy had been shot down by Leutnant Hillecke, an Me 109 pilot of Stab II/JG26. Sergeant Tony 'Boy' Mould was also shot down in flames and baled out; both 'Tigers' returned home via Dunkirk. Also, Flying Officer D.S. Hoare's glycol system was hit, forcing him to land, as had Squadron Leader White the previous day, at Calais-Marck. Unfortunately, unlike his lucky CO, Hoare was captured. Finally, as Sailor mentioned, Pilot Officer R.D. Aubert – who only returned to 74 Squadron that morning after his previous escapade – was killed, shot down by Hauptmann Karl Ebbighausen, the Gruppenkommandeur of II/JG26. At this time, Fighter Command's squadrons, operating from 11 Group airfields, were patrolling singly – whereas the German fighters were sweeping the Channel coast in *Gruppe* strength (of three squadrons or *Staffeln*). As Sailor said, for the outnumbered Tigers 'it was a rough trip home.'

That Sailor mentions leading a section of four Spitfires in line astern, rather than the usual vic of three, is noteworthy. Al Deere, also to become a great ace, remembered:

'Sailor Malan was the first [RAF] fighter leader to appreciate the advantage of basing squadron tactics on sections of four aircraft, spaced in such a way that each of the three sections, although an integral part of the squadron, had freedom of action in combat. The element of two, on which this formation was based, was a direct copy of the tactics so effectively employed by the German fighter formations whose leaders must be given full credit for their foresight in introducing the pair as the best fighting unit.'

This development was an early indication of Sailor's tactical ability and 'foresight'. These combats were also highlighting issues such as the point at which machine guns needed to be 'harmonised', which is to say the point at which rounds from all eight guns should converge for maximum destructive effect. Al Deere remembered that Sailor – who he considered 'probably the best shot in Fighter Command' – believed 250 yards to be the optimum distance, and this was adopted as standard throughout the Command. Sailor also immediately recognised the advantage to sighting provided by De Wilde ammunition, an incendiary bullet which, unlike other varieties in use, did not generate a trace of smoke or flame in its wake but simply a flash upon impact. Consequently, with De Wilde rounds included at intervals in belts of bullets, the pilot could see by flashes on his target whether or not his rounds were hitting their mark or not. Sailor realised that if De Wilde was adopted as standard, Fighter Command's kill ratio would increase, and Deere also recalled Sailor encouraging other squadron commanders and fighter pilots to argue this point. Eventually the Command Armament Officer was persuaded and De Wilde ammunition was widely distributed. This is further evidence that Sailor Malan's thinking was far broader than the accumulation of a high personal score and reputation; he was thinking about tactics and other operational issues of benefit to the whole of Fighter Command, and sharing his experience and ideas.

In France things had gone from bad to worse. By 25 May 1940 the BEF was virtually surrounded, its back to the Channel port at Dunkirk. Already,

Reichsmarschall Hermann Göring, chief of the Luftwaffe, had recognised an opportunity: if General Guderian's Panzers were halted on the line Lens–Béthune–Aire–St Omer–Gravelines, his air force could annihilate the BEF. According to eyewitness testimony from General Walter Warlimont, Deputy Chief of Operations of the *Oberkommando der Wehrmacht* (Armed Forces High Command, OKW), Hitler agreed to Göring's proposal on 23 May, the controversial 'Halt Order' being formally approved by the Führer the following day. On 25 May the order was issued to German ground forces via the HQ of General von Rundstedt's Army Group A. There were, however, other considerations aside from the Luftwaffe's desire to deliver a knock-out blow. Von Rundstedt, for example, claimed post-war that Hitler was concerned that his armour was not strong enough, after two weeks of rapid advance and heavy fighting, to conclude the campaign, and that by allowing the BEF to escape, this may favourably dispose the British towards a negotiated peace. Whatever the truth, the fact remains that Guderian's tanks ground to a halt – and were denied the opportunity to take the ports of Calais and Dunkirk, cutting off Gort's access to the coast and completely surrounding the British force. That being so, Hitler's decision would be a deliverance, so far as the Allies were concerned. On this day, it was also clear to both Churchill and Gort that there was only one, unthinkable, option: the BEF must be evacuated via Dunkirk. On this momentous day, 74 Squadron patrolled without event.

On 26 May 1940, the decision was finally and reluctantly made for the BEF to retire upon and evacuate from Dunkirk. Consequently, Operation *Dynamo* was implemented by Vice-Admiral Bertram Ramsay, Flag Officer Commanding Dover, the intention of which was to return home up to 45,000 of Gort's troops within two days – by which time the rescue mission was expected to be halted by enemy intervention. Ramsay was to be responsible for embarkation, Air Vice-Marshal Keith Park, the commander of 11 Group, for tactical control of covering fighters. Park had already decided on these tactics, which he explained to 11 Group's controllers. Some squadrons had been brought south to make up the sixteen squadrons assigned for the task. These would operate from airfields near the coast, such as Hornchurch, Biggin Hill, and Manston. After their first patrol, however, squadrons would land at forward stations such as Hawkinge and Lympne, where the fighters would be quickly rearmed and refuelled before returning to their patrol lines. The force would be divided so that half worked mornings, the other half afternoons. After the day's second patrol, unless, as Orange wrote, 'the crisis was great', the squadrons were permitted to return to their home or adopted home base as appropriate. Dunkirk, however, was further from Park's coastal airfields than Calais or Boulogne, and therefore a difficult location to cover with short-range defensive fighters. As Sailor said, 'The only way we could fly to Dunkirk and have enough juice to spend a few minutes over the battle area was by coasting and flying at sea-level from Boulogne.' Moreover, it would not be possible to patrol the French coast from dawn to dusk, because the quantity of fighters available made it impossible to meet the demands of both continuity and strength. This is why, until now, Dowding had insisted upon squadrons patrolling individually, so as to extend the length of coverage provided. Experience, however, had already indicated the vulnerability of weak patrols. This historic day, though, passed without event for 74 Squadron – which would patrol alone from Rochford again the following day.

At 0745 hrs on 27 May 1940, Flight Lieutenant Malan led 74 Squadron back to the French coast, clashing with Me 109s of JG1 at 0900 hrs:

'I was Red 1. 74 Squadron (eleven aircraft) on offensive patrol over Calais – Dunkirk at varying heights, 2,000 – 15,000 feet, owing to cloud formation. AA fire was observed at 5,000 feet south of Dunkirk. Investigated round cumulus cloud but no E/A seen. On returning towards Dunkirk at 2,000 feet, various Me 109s were sighted above and behind. Red 1 and 3 attacked one E/A which was above Red 2. I ordered sections to break up into pairs. Red 3 and I climbed and observed one Me 109 directly above, pulled up my nose and gave two full deflection bursts at 100 yards range. E/A immediately dived towards cumulus. I followed and gave about four two second bursts at approximately 300 yards range, owing to difficulty of closing range in the time. Just before he entered cloud, heavy smoke poured out of the starboard side of engine, and I concluded he had been badly hit. I followed into cloud but lost him. Red 3 saw my tail was safe and attacked other 109s as stated in his combat report.'

This report is of interest. Previously we have read how Sailor was operating sections of four – not the usual three aircraft, and now advanced that concept further by instructing pilots to break into fighting pairs – remarkably similar to the enemy's *Schwarm* of four and *Rotte* tactic of leader and wingman. This is clear evidence that already Sailor Malan had recognised that the inflexible set-piece attacks and right formations recommended by the manual were impractical, especially when engaging similarly fast-moving and highly manoeuvrable fighters. Moreover, to conserve ammunition the optimum firing time is two-seconds a time – and consistently this is repeated in this air-fighting master's reports.

After the combat, Flight Lieutenant Malan paired up with Red 4, Pilot Officer P.C.F. 'Paddy' Stevenson, for the return flight to Rochford:

'Both aircraft very short of petrol. Sighted eight Do 215s in two vics (five and three). Attacked rear vic of three, leader right flank, No 4 left flank. Enemy opened fire at 800 yards and dived for cumulous layer and towards German AA fire. As we couldn't afford a long chase we closed rather rapidly and delivered four one second bursts from 300 – 100 yards at port engine and fuselage. I broke off to right and observed smoke from tail and port engine and fuselage. As I was returning for second quick attack from astern, I observed that Red 4 (whose first contact it was) had apparently been hit in the glycol feeder tank and would have to land very soon. I followed him up and called him on R/T with no reply. He suddenly changed his course from cross-Channel and dived towards direction of Dunkirk and I presumed he would attempt a landing on the beach there. I then had to return and landed with two gallons of petrol. Firing seen from E/A appeared to come from one top gun only.'

During the combat with the Me 109s, Pilot Officer Stevenson had fought alongside Pilot Officer Freeborn, firing at a 109 that attacked his comrade, leaving the enemy fighter in an 'obviously distressed condition'. Still covered by Stephenson, Freeborn also destroyed a 109. Stephenson later safely alighted on Dunkirk beach, returning home and to 74 Squadron a few days later. Other 'Tigers' were also successful in this combat: 40-year-old Warrant Officer Ernie Mayne blasted a 109 out of the sky from just fifty yards, and Pilot Officer H.M. 'Steve' Stephen and Flight Lieutenant 'Treacle' Tracey also despatched Messerschmitts.

That afternoon, Flight Lieutenant Malan was leading 74 Squadron over France once more, reporting that at 1600 hrs, 8,000 feet over St Omer:

'Sighted German bomber vics of five and three. Red Section broke up into pairs and approached a wide vic of five, which split up and dived on a SE course. Red 3 and 4 delivered No 1 Attacks on Do 17 at high speed from 250 – 50 yards range. Red 3 delivered last attack at *twenty-five feet height* and E/A had burning port engine and smoking tail. We experienced very severe and accurate light flak and returned to coast through continuous AA fire.'

The Do 17, probably from KG3, was claimed as 'badly crippled'. Having initially been ordered to patrol at a much higher altitude, finding no 'trade', Sailor had descended to a lower height, finding the enemy formation. Again, this is further evidence of his tactical intelligence and willingness to seek, locate and destroy the enemy. Pilot Officer Dowding also damaged a Dornier, Flight Lieutenant Measures and Pilot Officer St John sharing another. Flight Lieutenant Treacy and Pilot Officer Stephen pursued three bombers inland, setting both engines of one ablaze. Treacy, however, was hit by a German gunner, force-landing near Gravelines where he was captured. Although the pilots were not to know it, it would be the 'Tigers' last patrol during Operation *Dynamo*.

By this time, since 21 May 1940, 74 Squadron had lost four pilots, three of whom were prisoners, and another wounded. With fresh squadrons reinforcing 11 Group, it was time for the 'Tigers' to be withdrawn, to rebuild back to strength. According to Ira Jones, 'Both men and machines were fatigued. Malan told me that on one or two occasions, when making the last landings of the day on 27 May, his eyes were so tired that the aerodrome was in a sort of haze and he just "threw the old Spitfire on the ground". He said he did not know why he had not crashed.'

The 'Tigers' had collectively claimed the destruction of sixteen enemy aircraft, in addition to ten more probably destroyed and three damaged. Of that total, Flight Lieutenant Malan – who had often led the squadron on patrol – had personally destroyed at least four and shared two others (one a third share, the other a fifth), probably destroyed another, and damaged others. Like other Spitfire pilots and fighter leaders, he had gained essential combat experience – and confidence – during this intensive fighting over the French coast.

On 27 May 1940, HQ 11 Group signalled 74 Squadron ordering a move to 12 Group's Leconfield Sector Station in Yorkshire. That evening the squadron flew north and away from the blazing oil tanks of Dunkirk.

Chapter Eight

Night Victories

At Leconfield on 1 June 1940 good news was received: Flight Lieutenant Malan had been awarded the DFC for his efforts over the French coast. Published in the *London Gazette* ten days later, the citation read:

'During May 1940, this officer led his flight, and on certain occasions his Squadron, on ten offensive patrols in Northern France. He has personally shot down two enemy aircraft, and probably three others. Flight Lieutenant Malan has displayed great skill, courage and relentless determination in his attacks upon the enemy.'

So, there it was, in black and white: official recognition of Sailor's skill as both a fighter pilot and leader, and his personal courage. With the diagonally striped medal ribbon above his tunic's left breast pocket, Flight Lieutenant A.G. Malan DFC now belonged to a small and elite band of fighter pilots so decorated early on in the war.

Sergeant Bill Skinner had flown with Malan on those operations over the French coast (and afterwards):

'He was a born leader and natural pilot of the first order. Complete absence of balderdash. As far as he was concerned you either did your job properly or were on your way. He inspired his aircrews by his dynamic and forceful personality, and by the fact that he set a high standard in his flying. Weather never bothered him. He would frequently take off when the birds were grounded. On occasion, notably at Rochford, he would give a spontaneous display of aerobatics fully equal to the demonstration of Supermarine's own test pilots, which were acknowledged to be in a class of their own. Another example of Malan's supreme flying ability and powers of leadership was shown by the fact that when occasion presented itself at Hornchurch or Manston he would take off and land the whole Squadron in perfect formation. When it is realised that the twelve machines in vics of three occupied the whole width of the aerodrome, and the complicated cockpit drill allied to the high landing speed of the Spitfires, it will be appreciated that, to put it mildly, a very good sense of judgement and timing was involved... Malan weighed up every position before going into attack... he was cool and calculating.'

Another rising 'Tiger' who had been successful over Dunkirk was Flying Officer John Mungo-Park:

'What I like about Sailor is his quiet, firm manner and cold courage. He is gifted with uncanny eyesight and is a natural fighter pilot. When he calls over the R/T "Let 'em have it! Let 'em have it!" there's no messing, the bastards are in for it, particularly the one he has in his own reflector sight. Mannock [the First World War ace] and Malan have made 74. Up the "Tigers"!'

According to Pilot Officer Harborne MacKay Stephen, Sailor was 'probably the best pilot and shot on the station. I was a very junior officer, he the senior flight commander and an imposing figure, already of great reputation. He was a strict disciplinarian and expected 100 per cent from everyone – 150 per cent from himself. He set a great example to us all.'

Reg Howard was an engine fitter posted to 74 Squadron at Rochford, after completion of technical training at RAF Cosford, and recalls an example of true leadership, reflecting Sailor's personality, which is contrary to the popular narrative of a martinet:

'I eventually found the Airmen's Dining Room and soon made myself known to other 74 Squadron people, and immediately felt comfortable. They told me to report to the Orderly Sergeant, and he in turn showed me the ropes regarding daily routine, pointing to a Spitfire standing in a bay and saying "Give it a good DI" (Daily Inspection). Fortunately, my recent training had provided a good insight into the procedure. I reported back to the sergeant in charge upon completion, confirming that the job had been carried out satisfactorily. Shortly after this I saw a pilot walk towards the Spitfire, and a member of the groundcrew stood on a wing and helped the pilot do up his harness; the groundcrew chap patted the pilot on his shoulder, and stepped down, the engine roaring into action. I felt so proud of what was known as the finest squadron in Fighter Command. A while later a fellow airman told me that the Sergeant wanted to see me "At once". I reported to him immediately and my world of pride at being a member of this illustrious Squadron was completely shattered. I was shouted at and called an "idiot", plus a few other shattering descriptions. Apparently, the pilot had reported that the top of the anti-freeze compartment had not been tightened, which I had overlooked in my excitement at doing the DI. Consequently, in flight the fluid leaked, and it was lucky that the pilot decided to land, otherwise his windscreen would have been covered in glycol, making it impossible to see anything.

'The fact that Flight Lieutenant Sailor Malan was the pilot made my confidence and pride evaporate completely… but a miracle, well, almost a miracle, came to my rescue because later in the day I was told to report in person to the great man himself. I will never forget the way he spoke to me, like a father figure, talking about the comradeship and care each member of the Squadron should have for each other, so in future I should not forget this fact and remember that each action we take means that somebody else's life may depend upon it. I have always recalled this interview with this outstanding man. From that time on, he ordered the Sergeant to let me, AC1 Howard, service his aeroplane, which I did for many weeks'.

While 74 Squadron began a monotonous programme of routine training flights, Operation *Dynamo* continued until 3 June 1940. Ultimately the evacuation, having originally been expected to last just two days before being closed down by enemy action, lasted nine – and rescued a staggering 338,226 men. The BEF, however, left behind 68,000 men, 40,000 of whom were prisoners, and all heavy equipment. Whereas the German fighters had undoubtedly dominated the battlefield since 10 May 1940, Air Vice-Marshal Park reported that his fighters had achieved 'total ascendency' over the German bombers, the advantage only resting with the Luftwaffe on 27 May and 1 June. Importantly, Park acknowledged that 'the RAF's tactical doctrine, techniques and procedures had been found wanting and many of them were changed – just in time.' During *Dynamo*, Fighter Command flew 101 patrols over the beaches, destroying 258 enemy aircraft and damaging 119 more – for the loss of 141 RAF machines. Because of the limited number of fighters available to Air Vice-Marshal Park, and their comparatively short range, as previously discussed, it was impossible to provide standing patrols from dawn to dusk. Consequently there were occasions when enemy aircraft penetrated to attack defenceless troops on the beaches, and Allied shipping. Moreover, many of the aerial combats occurred unseen by those on the ground, either at high altitude, above cloud, or away from the actual beaches. Many would therefore ask, 'Where is the RAF?', the RN, having lost 228 vessels, being most vociferous in criticising Fighter Command. Clearly, however, the RAF was there and achieved local aerial superiority overall, without the advantages of radio-telephony enabling communication between squadrons in the air, or advance warning of the enemy's location and approach via radar. That being so, the record indicates that Air Vice-Marshal Park's Spitfire pilots actually achieved a small miracle within the wider context of the 'Miracle of Dunkirk'.

After the exertions of both sides during the Fall of France and Operation *Dynamo*, there was a brief lull in aerial activity. After a rest at Leconfield, on 6 June 1940, 74 Squadron returned to Rochford, from where it would resume interception patrols in response to X-Raids and genuine Luftwaffe incursions, provide convoy protection, and continue training.

On 13 June 1940, Flight Lieutenant Malan flew Spitfire Mk IA K9953 to the Aircraft & Armament Experimental Establishment at Farnborough for comparison trials with a captured Me 109E. Various Spitfires – including examples fitted with the new Rotol Constant Speed propeller – were pitted against the German fighter, with varying results, all eagerly analysed by the 'boffins'. The RAF fighter pilots were also provided the opportunity to fly the 109 – which must have been a highly beneficial experience.

By now it was all over in France. The personal diary of Pilot Officer David Scott-Malden, learning to fly Spitfires at 5 OTU, near Stroud, captures those dramatic times:

Wednesday 12 June 1940: Had a test at 1.15 pm on a Harvard and passed successfully into Spitfire flight. First solo an indescribable thrill. Felt a pretty king man!

Friday 14 June 1940: Paris falls. Astonishing to think of it in the hands of the Germans. Reynaud declares 'will fight on even if driven out of France'. Marvellous days doing aerobatics in Spitfires.

Monday 17 June 1940: The French give up hostilities. Cannot yet conceive the enormity of it. I suppose it will not be long before we start defending England in earnest.

On that day, the French sued for peace.

Churchill addressed the House on 18 June 1940, concluding with these powerful and prophetic words:

'What General Weygand called the Battle of France is over. I expect that the Battle of Britain is about to begin. Upon this battle depends the survival of Christian civilization. Upon it depends our own British life, and the long continuity of our institutions and our Empire. The whole fury and might of the enemy must very soon be turned on us. Hitler knows that he will have to break us in this island or lose the war. If we can stand up to him, all Europe may be free and the life of the world may move forward into broad, sunlit uplands. But if we fail, then the whole world, including the United States, including all that we have known and cared for, will sink into the abyss of a new Dark Age made more sinister, and perhaps more protracted, by the lights of perverted science. Let us therefore brace ourselves to our duties and so bear ourselves that, if the British Empire should last a thousand years, men will still say, "This was their finest hour".'

Amidst the gloomy war news, there was personal joy for Sailor and Lynda Malan, when on 11 June 1940 their first child, Jonathan Winston Fraser Malan, was born in a nursing home at Westcliffe-on-Sea, near Southend. There would be no respite from the war though, not even for new fathers.

After Dunkirk, although aerial activity was reduced by day, the Luftwaffe kept up the pressure on Fighter Command by prowling over England at night, lone raiders dropping bombs and causing such a general nuisance that the defenders were compelled to react. The problem was that Britain's nocturnal aerial defences remained primitive; advanced airborne interception radar and dedicated night-fighting aircraft had yet to be developed and integrated into the System. There was no option but to deploy day fighters, including the Spitfire, after dark. On the night of 18/19 June 1940, German bombers launched the largest attack on England so far, some seventy raiders attacking a wide range of targets. The enemy was particularly active over East Anglia, 'red' air-raid warnings being issued to Peterborough, Cambridge, Norwich, King's Lynn, Ipswich, Bury St Edmunds, Colchester and Chelmsford. Oil installations were bombed at Canvey Island, breaching a pipeline which blazed for two hours, and nine civilians were killed and ten injured when a row of terraced homes were hit in Cambridge. At Southend, residential property was damaged in addition to the local boys' high school, and fourteen casualties were sustained. At Rochford, Flight Lieutenant Malan was wide awake and becoming increasingly concerned as the crump of exploding bombs could be heard from a direction of Southend – uncomfortably close to his wife and new-born son in Westcliffe. It was too much for the 'Tiger' to bear: Sailor requested permission to scramble. An anonymous eyewitness described the scene on that clear, moonlit, night:

'Without waiting to dress, Sailor's rigger and fitter, who had already turned in, pushed their feet into gum boots, slung their rifles over their shoulders, put on their tin hats, and reported for duty in their striped pyjamas. Then they rushed out to the dispersal post. While the mechanics worked swiftly to start up the Spitfire, Sailor methodically buckled on the harness of the parachute. By the time he had got his gear on, the engine had started, so he climbed into the cockpit and strapped himself in before opening up the throttle to warm the engine up a bit. Meanwhile, he looked up and tried to pick out a target ahead and saw a He 111 at 6,000 feet being held by searchlights. It was making a straight run directly across him. A second glance at the approaching bomber made him decide that the engine was quite capable of warming itself up. Leaping out of the cockpit with his parachute on, he made a dive for a little trench close at hand. The last time he saw the trench it was only about eighteen inches deep, but unbeknown to him the men had continued to dig until it was five feet deep. He dived in just as the bomber appeared slap overhead, and landed on his face at the bottom.'

Immediately the raider had passed overhead, Sailor jumped out of the trench, back into his Spitfire, and hastened off in pursuit; his personal combat report describes events:

'I climbed towards E/A which was making for the coast and held in searchlight beams at 8,000 feet. I positioned myself astern and opened fire at 200 yards, closing to fifty yards with one burst. Observed bullets entering E/A and had my windscreen covered in oil. Broke off to the left and immediately below as E/A spiralled out of beam.'

This attack – incredibly delivered from as close as fifty yards *at night* – occurred between '0020 hrs to 0030 hrs (approximately)', 'off Foulness'. According to local records, this He 111 of Stab/KG4 crashed into the Bishop of Chelmsford's garden in Springfield Road, Chelmsford, at 0030 hrs. The crew of four baled out and were captured. This was a historic occasion: it was the Spitfire's first nocturnal 'kill'.

The night's action was not yet over, as Sailor:

'Climbed to 12,000 feet towards another E/A held by searchlights on northerly course. Opened fire at 250 yards, taking good care not to overshoot this time. Gave five two-second bursts and observed bullets entering all over E/A with slight deflection as he was turning to port. E/A emitted heavy smoke and I saw one parachute open very close. E/A went down in spiral dive. Searchlights and I following him right down until he crashed in flames near Chelmsford. As I approached target in each case I flashed succession of dots on downward recognition light before moving into attack. I did not notice AA gunfire after I had done this. When following second E/A down I switched on navigation lights for a short time to help establish identity. Gave letter of period only once when returning at 3,000 feet from Chelmsford when one searchlight searched for me.'

This was incredible – and the switching on of navigation lights, thereby illuminating the Spitfire and making it a target for German gunners, 'to help establish identity', is completely consistent with the careful professional fighter pilot the record proves he was – as opposed to accusations levelled at him over 'Barking Creek'. The second He 111 destroyed by Sailor belonged to 4/KG4 and was attacked between Wickford and Chelmsford at 12,000 feet; the Cork Light Vessel, anchored off Felixstowe reported seeing the enemy bomber crash into the sea at 0115 hrs, killing all aboard, including the Staffelkapitän, Oberleutnant H. Prochnow. To destroy one enemy aircraft in one night was a feat enough in itself – but two was a huge achievement. That night, Blenheim pilot Flight Lieutenant Miles Duke-Woolley also destroyed a Heinkel, as did Spitfire pilots Pilot Officer John Petre and Flying Officer Eric Ball of Duxford-based 19 Squadron. It was certainly a successful night for Fighter Command – one which, as it transpired, baby Jonathan Malan and mother slept through, blissfully unaware of the drama unfolding above their heads.

Three days after Sailor's historic night-time achievement, the French formally surrendered. The Fall of France was a catastrophe, the enormity of which for the western democracies is perhaps difficult for people to grasp today. In June 1940, the British people were in no doubt of their perilous position – facing the undefeated Germans across just twenty-two miles of English Channel. A version of Churchill's speech made on 18 June was broadcast to the nation – leaving the British people in no doubt that fighting on, alone, for their very survival now lay ahead.

On 28 June 1940, King George VI visited RAF Hornchurch, holding an investiture in the presence of Air Chief Marshal Dowding. Flight Lieutenant Malan of 74 Squadron and Flight Lieutenant Bob Stanford Tuck of 92 received the DFC for their efforts over Dunkirk, while 54 Squadron's Pilot Officers Al Deere and Johnny Allen theirs for the escort flight rescuing Squadron Leader White. For flying the aircraft effecting that epic rescue, Squadron Leader 'Prof' Leathart of 54 Squadron was appointed to the DSO.

Sailor Malan was now officially an 'ace', with seven enemy aircraft destroyed to his credit, and a leading figure in Fighter Command.

Chapter Nine

Battle of Britain

At a time when the British should have been enjoying their annual vacations at such south-east Victorian coastal resorts as Brighton, Eastbourne and Hove, the nation braced itself for a German seaborne invasion. At London's railway stations, lists appeared of hundreds of coastal locations that could no longer be visited for 'holiday, recreation or pleasure'. Large tracts of the coastline became 'Defence Areas', entry forbidden to those without special permits. Sea-front hotels were requisitioned, beaches were criss-crossed with barbed wire, and machine guns sprouted from pill boxes everywhere. A curfew was imposed. The great British novelist and broadcaster J.B. Priestley visited Margate, observing, 'The few signs of life only made the place seem more unreal and spectral.' The British were in no mood, however, for summer holidays.

On 1 July 1940 the Luftwaffe began attacking Britain in daylight as the precursor to a whole new phase of aerial warfare. These initial raids were made on Wick, in Scotland, and various north-eastern ports, where nineteen people were killed. Significantly, on this day the OKW ordered all three services to begin preliminary planning for a seaborne invasion of southern England. This opportunity was as unprecedented as it was unexpected – because no-one, not even Hitler, could have predicted how overwhelmingly successful – and lightning-fast – the campaign against the west would be. In short order, the Germans had bludgeoned their way westwards – now holding the Channel ports, and French airfields putting London within even the Me 109's range. Although the OKW lacked experience and, in truth, the resources required to mount such a huge joint operation, Hitler rightly had occasion to consider that the unthinkable could become reality – providing aerial superiority could first be achieved over southern England. With his Luftwaffe's unchecked success to date, Göring was sublimely confident and predicted that the objective would be achieved in three weeks. What Churchill had already called the 'Battle of Britain' was 'about to begin' – and increasingly the nation looked to Fighter Command's young aircrews for salvation.

2 July 1940 saw a distinct change in the fighting when shipping was attacked in the Channel, in an attempt to draw Fighter Command into battle for destruction *en masse*. Air Vice-Marshal Park reacted cautiously, preserving his fighters by responding to these raids economically, by flights or single squadrons, moving a number of units to airfields on the south coast, reducing response time. Fighting over the sea was fraught with danger, and a higher rate of loss was expected because there was no properly organised system for rescuing shot-down airman – who had to rely on passing ships.

For 74 Squadron the beginning of July was largely uneventful – except when Sergeant White's Spitfire was hit by lightning on the afternoon of 3 July while on a 'Air Drill' exercise, the pilot being killed when his stricken machine crashed near Margate. Other flights included routine patrols over the coast and convoys, and training sorties. There was more excitement on 6 July, however, when Flight Lieutenant Measures and Pilot Officer Dowding intercepted two He 111s near Dover, destroying one and damaging another. Although Sailor did not fly between 7 and 11 July, 74 Squadron found action again on 8 July, on the morning of which Measures and Dowding destroyed another He 111. During the afternoon, Sergeants Mould and Stevenson patrolled Manston, sighting and attacking a *Schwarm* of four Me 109s, one of which Mould forced to land at Elham while Stevenson destroyed another. Things were hotting up.

On 10 July 1940, eight convoys were at sea around Britain's coastline, requiring Fighter Command to provide protection to shipping from Exeter to Wick. At 1037 hrs that day, Pilot Officer Freeborn was leading 'A' Flight in his Flight Commander's absence, intercepting a whole *Gruppe* of Me 109s escorting a reconnaissance bomber shadowing Convoy BREAD off Deal. Freeborn 'dropped' a 109 but was himself shot up, force-landing at Manston, his wingman, Sergeant Mould, likewise crash-landing a damaged Spitfire. Pilot Officer Stevenson 'crippled one and destroyed a second Me 109', with other pilots claiming 109s as damaged. At 1345 hrs, Flying Officer Mungo-Park led six 74 Squadron Spitfires to patrol the Dover–Deal line, meeting '20 Do 17s escorted by 40 Me 110s and 40 Me 109s' heading for the same convoy, 9,000 feet over Dover at 1050 hrs. In the ensuing 'general dogfight', the 'Tigers' claimed a number of the enemy destroyed or damaged, for no loss. These were historic combats – because later, the Air Ministry decreed that it was on this date that the Battle of Britain officially began.

Since 2 July 1940, Fighter Command had intercepted over a dozen raids by enemy formations in excess of fifty aircraft, losing eighteen pilots with thirteen of them killed and six wounded, so it is difficult to fathom why 10 July 1940 – and not 2 July 1940 – was chosen as the start-date. This is important, because when it was decided to recognise aircrew who had fought in the Battle of Britain with the award of a clasp to the 1939-45 Star, a certain criterion had to be met: that at least one operational patrol had to have been flown with one of the accredited Fighter Command and appended units deemed to have participated between 10 July 1940 and 31 October 1940. It is a travesty, therefore, that those killed or incapacitated in these convoy battles between 2 and 9 July 1940 inclusive are ineligible for the clasp and are not, therefore, included in the nominal roll of the 'Few'. From the 74 Squadron Operations Record Book we know that Flight Lieutenant Malan made his first operational flight, a convoy patrol, to qualify for the Battle of Britain Clasp between 1430 and 1615 hrs on 11 July 1940 in Spitfire K9953; the sortie was uneventful, but, again, was a significant one because Sailor Malan was now one of the Few.

According to the 74 Squadron Form 540 (monthly summary of events, day-by-day) for 12 July 1940:

'At 1630 hrs, Red Section left (Hornchurch) to investigate a raid fifteen miles off Margate. AA fire was sighted from a ship which was being bombed by a He 111. Flight Lieutenant Malan DFC, leading Red Section, gave order to attack in line astern and opened attack, closing to 300 yards range. Heavy fire from the aircraft's rear gunner was silenced by Red Leader. Sergeant Mould and Pilot Officer Stevenson also attacked in turn and enemy aircraft seen to crash into the sea.'

This apparent combat is problematic. According to virtually all secondary sources consulted, the pilots of Red Section were each credited with a third share in the destruction of this He 111. However, the 74 Squadron Form 541 (daily record of flights) does not record any such flight for Malan, Mould or Stevenson that day. Moreover, no Fighter Command Form 'F' (pilot's personal combat report) can be found relating to this combat. Finally, none of the He 111s recorded by the Luftwaffe quartermaster as having been destroyed or damaged on this day relate to this time or location, although Mason (see Bibliography) states that the bomber concerned belonged to 'II/KG53' but does not identify the actual aircraft or provide a source for this information. So, whether or not this combat claim is accurate, and was Sailor Malan's first Battle of Britain victory, is for the reader to decide – but it does appear doubtful, and administrative errors did happen.

'SAILOR' MALAN – FREEDOM FIGHTER

On 16 July 1940 the OKW issued Führer Directive Number 16 – leaving no doubt as to Hitler's intentions:

'As England, despite her hopeless military situation, still shows no sign of willingness to come to terms, I have decided to prepare, and if necessary to carry out, a landing operation against her... The aim of this operation is to eliminate the English motherland as a base from which war against Germany can be continued and if necessary to occupy the country completely.'

19 July 1940 dawned a day of fine weather – and with nine convoys steaming around Britain, in anticipation of heavy fighting, controllers moved more fighter squadrons than usual to operate from forward airfields – which for 74 Squadron meant flying to and operating from Manston. At lunchtime the hapless Defiants of 141 Squadron were massacred off Folkestone by Me 109s of JG2, five of the turret-fighters destroyed in less time than it takes to tell. The Hurricanes of Squadron Leader John Thompson's 111 Squadron came to the rescue. Had they not intervened, the likelihood is that all of the Defiants would have been lost. Further combats followed as the day wore on. This fighting took place in circumstances almost always unfavourable to the defenders, the Luftwaffe holding the initiative and able to dictate when and where battles were fought – consequently enjoying the advantage of already being at height. During this phase of fighting, the German fighters tended to arrive over the combat area at 15,000 feet, the bombers some 5,000 feet below, while scrambling RAF fighters had to climb flat-out to get up to them. Sailor's combat report on this day describes a typical Channel combat:

'I was leader of 74 Squadron when at about 1545 hrs the Squadron was sent off to Deal to intercept enemy bombers at 6,000 feet, and layers of fighters at 10,000 feet and 12,000 feet. I saw salvoes of bombs falling in Dover harbour at the same time as information was received that the raid had turned south. Squadron climbed towards Dover, in sections astern, towards numerous groups of fighters above.

'Red Section, with me leading, broke off towards the left and onto a group of three at 13,000 feet which proved to be two Me 109s and a Hurricane in a tight circle. I delivered one two second burst at a 109 at 100 yards range, which was trying to turn onto the tail of the Hurricane. After my first burst the Hurricane immediately broke off and I applied full starboard bank and turned onto the 109's tail. I got in two two second bursts at 75 yards range. E/A emitted smoke from starboard side and straightened up into a staggering dive. I then climbed steeply to starboard as the other 109 was turning into my starboard quarter, and met groups of fighters above me which in all cases proved to be Hurricanes. During my climb I noticed the second 109 being pursued at close range by a Spitfire, which proved to be Red 3 (Pilot Officer Stevenson). The remainder of the Squadron were not engaged as all remaining fighters in the vicinity proved to be Hurricanes.'

Pilot Officer Hastings, Yellow 3:

'At approx. 1550 hrs I saw Red 1 attack one Me 109 and fire two bursts while climbing. I saw smoke pouring from the E/A which was diving steeply towards the sea, his wings rocking laterally as if out of control. Camouflage and markings appeared to be normal. I was then obliged to turn sharply to the right to avoid a Hurricane. When I had avoided the friendly fighter I turned to the left and looked for the E/A but only saw a round white patch of foam in the sea where previously there had been no such disturbance.'

The Me 109 attacked by Sailor was accredited as a 'probable'. Pilot Officer Stevenson likewise claimed a 109 probably destroyed, last seen descending towards the French coast trailing smoke. According to German loss records, which were for internal audit and not propaganda purposes, the only 109 listed on this day was a machine of II/JG51 which 'crashed near Chartres'. Because the Me 109 had a fuel-injected engine and was therefore able to lose a Spitfire or Hurricane in the dive, diving away when attacked by an RAF fighter became the enemy's standard evasive tactic. Diving vertically with the throttle rammed forward for maximum power generated a substantial emission of black smoke from the 109's exhausts – giving the appearance that the enemy aircraft was fatally hit and going to crash. Owing to the presence of other enemy fighters and heights involved, rarely could a pilot watch his victim all the way down to confirm whether or not the machine crashed. In reality and all too often the German fighter was not so badly damaged, and levelled out, unseen, returning safely to base. These claims were made in good faith by RAF pilots, as in this case, where both Malan and Stevenson were credited with a 'probable'. In this way, however, a single German casualty could become exaggerated on the scorecard, as the same aircraft could be claimed and accredited to multiple pilots, thereby providing a false impression of combat successes. This also emphasises the gulf of difference between a combat claim and an actual enemy loss. It is worth adding that a 109 streaming a plume of white smoke, however, was a different matter, and more likely to result in the damaged machine not making it home, because this was coolant, without which the engine would overheat and seize. In this case, unfortunately, neither Sailor nor Hastings mention the colour of the smoke emitting from Sailor's target. Whether the 109 which crashed at Chartres with a wounded pilot aboard was that claimed by Sailor or Stevenson we will never know, and likewise what had crashed into the sea cannot be confirmed.

At 1721 hrs on 24 July 1940, Sailor led 'A' Flight up from Manston to patrol the Channel. Four minutes later Dysoe Leader was ordered to intercept 'Raid 45 near Dover'. Pilot Officer Hastings reported:

'I was Red 3 of 74 Squadron on patrol with Yellow Section over the Channel at 2,000 feet. Three Do 215s were sighted flying at sea level. They immediately turned towards the French coast upon sighting us and were flying very fast.

'I was flying practically line abreast to Red 1 and closing on the 215s. They climbed towards the cloud and as I thought it may have been a big cloud I gave the starboard 215 a three second burst at about 350 – 300 yards. I then climbed above and to the right of the cloud and the 215s were again headed for cloud. I gave the second 215 three bursts of about four seconds and saw my bullets entering the 215. As I broke away I saw that his starboard motor was emitting black smoke. The 215s kept a fairly tight vic formation, with No 2 doing a fair amount of rotation. All three enemy aircraft opened fire when I was a long way away and out of their range, and their fire was ineffective in that my machine was not hit.'

Hastings was credited with a damaged Do 215. Sailor submitted no claim, possibly having held his fire on account of the range, preferring as he did to get in close.

At mid-day on 25 July 1940, a large westbound convoy negotiated the narrow and dangerous Dover Strait, provoking heavy fighting. Heavily escorted Stukas forced two destroyers back to Dover and the convoy was forced to scatter when attacked by E-Boats. That afternoon, Sailor led 'A' Flight to intercept enemy aircraft over Dover. On arrival, various groups of friendly fighters were sighted, until Sailor investigated a formation flying towards Calais. Giving chase, these were identified as Me 109s, and when three miles off the French coast, at 1610 hrs, Sailor got off a quick burst at one of the fleeting enemy fighters, hitting it in the fuselage. 74 Squadron, the ORB bemoaned, had been 'detailed to intercept a few minutes too late'.

On 28 July 1940, so Battle of Britain folklore has it, Flight Lieutenant Sailor Malan DFC and Major Werner Mölders – the 'Father of Modern Air Fighting' himself – met in combat over the Channel. In recent times, commentators have challenged this, accrediting Mölders' discomfort that day to Flight Lieutenant Terry Webster of 41 Squadron. Clearly, this requires further analysis.

The day in question dawned fine, after the previous day's storms, and in anticipation of heavy enemy air activity the Sector Controllers at Biggin Hill, Hornchurch and North Weald moved eight fighter squadrons to operate from forward coastal airfields at Hawkinge, Manston and Martlesham Heath. At 0940 hrs Sailor led 'A' Flight of 74 Squadron to Manston, 'B' Flight following an hour or so later. There the 'Tigers' awaited events. Two days previously, Squadron Leader Robin Hood's 41 Squadron had arrived at Hornchurch from Catterick, and also spent the morning of 28 July 1940 at Manston. At lunchtime, Hood's Spitfires returned to Hornchurch, remaining at readiness. The morning passed surprisingly quietly, the only action being when 234 Squadron destroyed a Ju 88 reconnaissance bomber off Plymouth. Then, at 1330 hrs, Flight Lieutenant Malan's 'A' Flight, comprising Pilot Officers Freeborn, Draper, Hastings and St John, was scrambled to intercept a large raid approaching Dover. At the same time, according to the ORB, a section of three 257 Squadron Hurricanes, Pilot Officers Coke and Hunt, led by Flight Lieutenant Hugh Beresford, were scrambled – although unrecorded is that Sergeant Ron Forward also flew on this sortie, again indicating how incomplete and inaccurate records often are. Further confusion is caused by the 74 Squadron ORB, which states that at 1350 hrs, also scrambled from Manston were Pilot Officers Hastings, Stevenson and Freeborn, and Sergeant Mould – somewhat remarkable considering that Freeborn and Hastings were already supposed to be in the air with Malan! This is clearly incorrect, as evidenced by the following combat reports ('significant statements' in italics):

According to Sailor's personal combat report, a total of 'thirty-six' Me 109s were engaged at 1400 hrs – this being a fighter sweep in *Gruppe* strength:

'I was Dysoe Leader on interception patrol on reported enemy raid on Dover. Climbed to 18,000 feet having been ordered to engage enemy fighters and leave bombers to the Hurricanes. Met up with six or nine Me 109s at 18,000 feet, coming from sun towards Dover to attack some Hurricanes. Turned onto their tails without being observed and led Red Section into attack. *Gave one enemy aircraft about six two second bursts from 250 yards closing in to 100 yards. He attempted no evasive tactics except a gentle right turn, and decreasing speed, by which I concluded he had at least had his controls hit (shot away). I then turned onto another Me 109 which had turned past my nose and delivered three deflection bursts at 100 yards range. He went down in spiral.* I then returned as my ammunition had run out.'

The first 109 was credited as a 'probable', the second as damaged.

Sailor's wingman was Pilot Officer Peter Stevenson:

'I was Red 2 when 74 Squadron was ordered to patrol from Manston. At 18,000 feet over Dover Red Leader engaged one of two Me 109s flying abreast, going east. I broke off and engaged the Me 109 on the port side. *I gave him two two second bursts, closing from 250 – 200 yards. He dived and turned for the French coast. I saw smoke start coming from the port side of the engine.*

'*I engaged another single 109 and gave a three second burst (deflection) at 300 yards range. I saw my De Wilde (tracer ammunition) enter his fuselage and he wobbled when I fired, as though he had been hit.*

'*I saw a section of three Me 109s at 15,000 feet, diving in line astern formation towards French coast. I dived after number three and gave him a five second burst from fully line astern. I saw he was hit hard. He slowed down and dropped below his formation as though he was out of control.*

'I saw a stream of lead pass below me. I immediately broke off and climbed. There were glycol and cordite fumes in the cockpit. My engine began to run roughly. I was at 20,000 feet, half way across the Channel. I glided down towards Manston. At 2,000 feet my engine was just about to seize up, so I lowered the retractable engine-driven undercarriage.

'I force-landed at Manston with the wheels and flaps down, with the engine seized solid. There were two bullets in my oil tank. My elevator and rudder had been hit.

'I noticed two formations of three Me 109s in line astern diving into the attack.

'I noticed that the manoeuvrability of the Me 109s was considerably better at height (20,000 feet) than when they flew at 10,000 feet and below.'

Stevenson was credited with one Me 109 probably destroyed and two more damaged.

Pilot Officer D.P. Kelly of 'B' Flight, who is not even mentioned in the 74 Squadron ORB, also reported engaging thirty-six Me 109s at 1400 hrs, 17,000 feet over Dover:

'I was Blue 1 of 74 Squadron and flying about 300 yards astern and to port of Red Leader (Malan) when we saw some Me 109s a little below us (we were at 18,000 feet).' This evidences the fact that, contrary to the ORB, Sailor was leading the whole of 74 Squadron, not just 'A' Flight. Kelly continues:

'Red Section turned and dived down to port. I likewise turned to port but found a formation in vic of three Me 109s pass across my nose. I took a snap shot at them but noticed no effect. Immediately after this I saw three Me 109s to port, diving down very fast. I found it necessary to use boost cut-out and dived down on the leading one, whom I managed to get on the tail of by diving steeply and turning left. *I closed to 250 yards and opened fire with slight deflection and saw after a few seconds the machine turn left, dive, and a tongue of flame appeared on port side. It then dived down into the sea, burning.*

'Blue 2 confirms that he saw smoke and glycol coming from enemy aircraft before he broke away to engage the second enemy aircraft.'

There is no doubt that Kelly's 109 was destroyed, and he was credited with a 'confirmed'.

Pilot Officer Harborne 'Steve' Stephen:

'I was Blue 2 of 74 Squadron and on patrol over Dover at 1500 hrs approx. when we engaged several Me 109s. *Three Me 109s started to dive towards the French coast when Blue Leader and myself dived after them. The Leader got in at least two long bursts and I saw smoke and glycol pouring out of enemy aircraft, which was diving very steeply towards the sea when I engaged the second one. The second enemy aircraft appeared to be hit in the tail and rudder.* The burst of fire was about five seconds – range about 300 yards.'

Having confirmed Kelly's 'kill', Stephen was awarded a 'damaged'.

Pilot Officer Harold Gunn:

'I was Green Leader of 74 Squadron and flying in the box behind Red Leader with sections line astern. On sighting six Me 109s at 18,000 feet, Red Leader turned to port to engage. I began to turn my Section to follow when I sighted another squadron of Me 109s, normal squadron formation, above, coming down sun. I immediately turned to starboard and climbed to engage – height 23,000 feet to 25,000 feet.

'In the ensuing dogfight I found I was isolated. I engaged several Me 109s (about nine) and on several occasions was fired upon by enemy aircraft from the beam, quarter and head-on. *One enemy aircraft I fired on for approximately seven seconds from dead astern, range 300 – 150 yards – while he was diving on a straight course, he turned slowly on his back and was last seen going down steeply. This aircraft would probably crash five to ten miles north-east of Dover.*

'One enemy aircraft I attacked head-on, opened fire at 500 yards. I opened fire at approximately 400 yards. I observed smoke tracings from his guns passing overhead. He broke away straight down underneath me, missing my aircraft by only a few feet. No damage was observed as he passed from view beneath me, but I believe some damage must have been done to him while he broke as I was still firing.'

Gunn, who would be shot down and killed a few days later, was credited with an 'unconfirmed'.

Pilot Officer Freeborn:

'I was flying as Yellow Leader when we intercepted approximately nine Me 109s at 18,000 feet. Red Leader turned to attack enemy aircraft about 1,000 feet below us. As Red Leader attacked, I observed approximately thirty Me 109s above and behind us. I climbed up and behind them. *I attacked one and did a slight deflection attack from above and behind. After a burst of about two to four seconds at a range of approximately 200 yards, enemy aircraft burst into flames.* I was then attacked by enemy aircraft and returned to base.'

Freeborn was credited with the Me 109 'destroyed, unconfirmed'.

Pilot Officer Peter St John:

'I was Yellow 3 when I saw eight Me 109s. We climbed to the attack and I attacked an enemy aircraft which had broken away. *I got onto his tail and he went into a very steep dive. I followed him and gave him a burst, firing 70 rounds per gun, at 250 yards range. I saw my shots going in* and I looked behind me to see if there were any enemy aircraft on my tail. I saw four Me 109s diving onto my tail. I increased my dive and went into cloud. I came out of cloud into the middle of a squadron of Hurricanes. After coming out of the dive I could see neither Hurricanes nor Me 109s. I climbed to 10,000 feet and endeavoured to find my Squadron but was unable to. I heard over the R/T the order to land, so I then returned to Manston and landed.'

St John was credited with a 109 damaged.

During this engagement, the Spitfires of Freeborn and Stevenson were damaged but both pilots returned safely to base. Sergeant Tony Mould was shot down, baling out wounded, and Pilot Officer James Young was shot down over the Goodwin Sands and killed, both 'Tiger' losses recorded as 1420 hrs. The Hurricane pilots of 257 Squadron made no combat claims, but one of their number, Sergeant Forward, was shot up and at 1400 hrs, crash-landed at Hawkinge. This combat therefore took place over Dover and the Channel between 1400 and 1420 hrs.

According to the 41 Squadron ORB, Hood's Spitfires were not scrambled until 1430 hrs, to carry out an 'interception patrol over Dover'. The following combat claims arose, timed at 1500 hrs, 20,000-22,000 feet, between Dover and Calais:

Flight Lieutenant Terry Webster, OC 'B' Flight:

'I was leading Green Section over to orbit Dover at 20,000 feet. While the Squadron was turning into the coast, I sighted two E/A about 2,000 feet above me. I warned Blue Leader (Squadron Leader Hood) but received no reply. The E/A then turned to attack Blue Section.

'I told Green 3 to come into a No 2 Attack position. I opened fire at the outside aircraft, which I then identified as a Me 109, just as he opened fire on Blue 2. *I fired a five second burst from the quarter, closing to dead-astern, opening at 200 yards and closing to 100 yards. I saw the E/A pull up and fall into a spin. It spun away very flat, out of sight.*

'I then dived down after another E/A (He 113). *On the way down I was passed by another E/A (He 113). I chased this down to sea level and out to sea. I fired short bursts, closing from 100 to 50 yards. I then saw thick black smoke coming from the cowling over the windscreen.* I broke off the engagement as I saw five or six further enemy fighters about 2,000 feet above me.

'I returned home at 0 feet, 12 boost, and landed at Hornchurch.'

Webster was credited with an 'He 113' damaged and an Me 109 'probable'. The He 113, however, was a prototype German fighter which never saw operational service – although the German propaganda machine made believe it did.

Pilot Officer George 'Ben' Bennions:

'Yellow Section of 41 Squadron were detailed to act as rear-guard for the Squadron, which was climbing to engage the enemy at 20,000 feet, when

I sighted two E/A diving onto the leading Section from above. At that moment, Red 3 sighted the enemy and called a warning to the leading Section over the R/T.

'The leading Section then took avoiding action by turning to port. One of the enemy aircraft turned to port and closed with Mitor Leader. While this was happening I ordered Yellow Section to carry out a Number One Attack on this aircraft. *Using the emergency boost I closed right in using full deflection and firing at the enemy from 200 yards to 100 yards. The enemy turned over on its side and went almost vertically downwards. I followed using full boost and gave two more bursts of about four seconds each from a position slightly left of astern, and after the second burst the whole of the enemy fuselage was enveloped in thick black smoke.* I pulled out at 3,000 feet to see what was happening, and looking in the mirror found two aircraft on my tail. I called to ascertain if they were Yellow Section but received no reply. Since practically all my ammunition was exhausted, I evaded these aircraft and returned to base at sea level, from a position about fifteen miles south of Dover.'

Bennions was credited with an Me 109 'unconfirmed'.

Pilot Officer R.W. 'Wally' Wallens:

'I was No 2 aircraft in Green Section, 41 Squadron, ordered to orbit Dover at 20,000 feet. I saw two E/A 2,000 feet above as Green Leader warned Blue Leader. I was left behind by Green Leader and Green 3, and was unable to catch up. While still 1,000 feet below I saw one E/A attack Blue Leader. One aircraft of Yellow Section then attacked this E/A (Pilot Officer Bennions). *The E/A turned over and dived vertically for several thousand feet, giving off a trail of thick blue smoke. The E/A then levelled off for a few seconds and then dived again, giving off black smoke.* I did not see this E/A crash but saw it last at approx. 5,000 feet, diving steeply.'

During this combat, Flying Officer Tony Lovell of 41 Squadron was shot up and wounded, crash-landing at Manston.

Major Mölders had been appointed Kommodore of JG51 only the previous day, and wrote an account of this action:

'My first flight against England will remain in my memory forever. I was flying with my Adjutant, Oberleutnant Kirchless. North of Dover we saw three Spitfires below us and more machines appeared out of the mist. We attacked the first three and I shot down one of them. However, by this time I was flying in the middle of eight or ten Englishmen and they seemed to be mad at me. They all dived towards me and was that my lucky break. Endeavouring to gain laurels at the expense of the solitary German, each hindered the other. I flew about furiously and confused them even more. By then it was only a matter of time before I was hit. My machine rattled wildly. The radiator and fuel tank were damaged and all I could do was dive away to the Channel at 700kmh. The whole gang followed me like a waterfall. Oberleutnant Leppl had seen what was happening and succeeded in shooting down the Spitfire that was nearest to me. The pressure was off. 'Luckily the engine kept going until I reached the French coast. Then it began spluttering. When I wanted to land, the undercarriage would not lower; I had to land with it retracted – which I managed successfully. When I wanted to clamber out of my machine my legs felt singularly weak. Examining them I saw large bloodstains. My visit to hospital proved that I had three splinters in my upper thigh, one in my knee joint and one in my left foot. In the heat of battle I had not felt a thing – the splinter in my kneecap is still there. On this occasion I experienced the fatherly solicitude of our Reichsmarschall once more; he had me flown to the *Luftwaffenlazaret* (air force hospital) in Berlin. The eleven days in the Lazaret were a wonderful convalescence. I believe I was something of the "showpiece" of the hospital and the sisters looked after me in a way that my own mother could not have bettered. Later on I sent the good people a sack of coffee.'

What else is known of the German side? As usual, comparatively little, that is reliable, anyway, because so many Luftwaffe records were destroyed in 1945. The most reliable source is Caldwell (see Bibliography), owing to painstaking day-by-day reconstructions of combats involving JG26 from various primary sources, Allied and German. According to Caldwell, 74 Squadron met I and II/JG51 (this was Major Mölders' 129th combat mission and his first as Geschwaderkommodore). 41 Squadron, arriving on the scene after the 'Tigers', were attacked by Major Adolf Galland's III/JG26, which suffered no loss in the exchange. JG51 lost one Me 109 shot down into the sea, the pilot killed; another killed crash-landed at Wissant; Mölders himself was shot up, wounded, and made an emergency landing on the French coast. 74 and 41 Squadrons claimed four Me 109s destroyed, three probably destroyed, and six more damaged. In total the RAF lost two Spitfires destroyed, one pilot killed, and three more aircraft damaged in addition to a single Hurricane which force-landed. The German combat claims are remarkably accurate (Continental time, so an hour ahead of GMT):

Major Adolf Galland, Stab III/JG26: Hurricane, 10 km NNE Dover, 6,000 metres, 1514 hrs.

Oblt Joachim Müncheberg, Stab III/JG26: Hurricane, 15 km NE Dover, 1515 hrs.

Müncheberg shot up Sergeant Forward and was credited with having destroyed his Hurricane, which was seen to crash-land at Hawkinge.

Fw Konrad Carl, 9/JG26: Spitfire,	NE Dover, 1525 hrs.
Major Werner Mölders: Stab/JG51,	Spitfire, Dover, 1530 hrs.
Ofw Karl Schmid, 1/JG 51, Spitfire,	Dover 1515hrs.
Oblt Richard Leppl, 1/JG 51, Spitfire,	Dover, 1530hrs.

Having read the RAF combat reports, the reader will appreciate the difficulty of confirming who shot down who. That said, while two great aces meeting in combat makes for a great story, it is impossible to conclude from Sailor's combat report that it was he who shot up Mölders. Likewise it cannot be said with any certainty whatsoever that Webster of 41 Squadron was responsible, taking aside any ambiguity over timings, and in fact I would suggest he was not. The most likely scenario, I would argue, is that it was Sailor's Red 2, Pilot Officer Peter Stevenson, who actually pursued the enemy across the Channel, hitting a 109 'hard' before getting shot up himself – quite possibly by Oberleutnant Leppl. Whatever the truth, *Vati* Mölders certainly had a lucky escape that day – as did several others on both sides. In the summer of 1941, aged 28, Mölders would become the first *General der Jagdflieger* – but luck deserted him on 22 November 1941 when he was killed in a flying accident.

On the last day of July 1940, 74 Squadron was in action again. Sailor and 'A' Flight were up from Manston but unable to catch the Me 109s sighted over the Channel. 'B' Flight, however, became embroiled with 109s of II/JG51 over 'Hellfire Corner'. Hauptmann Horst Tietzen, Staffelkapitän of 5/JG51, shot down Sergeant Fred Eley, who crashed into Folkestone harbour and was killed, while Oberleutnant 'Joschko' Fözö, Staffelkapitän of 4/JG51, killed Pilot Officer Harold Gunn. More fortunate was Flight Lieutenant Piers Kelly, who survived being badly shot up by another 4/JG51 *experte*, Leutnant Erich Hohagen. In response, Sergeant Bill Skinner claimed a 109 destroyed, but with two pilots missing on return to Manston, the 'Tigers' needed a morale-boosting lift – and got one: Sailor was awarded a Bar to his DFC, and Pilot Officer John Freeborn – now an ace with five confirmed victories – was awarded a well-deserved DFC.

According to an anonymous 74 Squadron fitter:

'Having spent many hours patching up his (Sailor's) Spitfire ready for the next trip I could well realize the marvellous escapes he must have had. Although his Spitfire came back battered each time he would not part with it in exchange for a new and more modern one. His instructions to his crew were "My machine has got to be serviceable. There is no excuse." His engine had to go first time, the radio-telephone just had to function even if his junior pilots' radios failed at times. And his guns weren't allowed to have stoppages. On one occasion it was my job to work out in the open all night with a hand torch to renew his battered tailplane. I don't quite know how I managed it: but I knew it just had to be done by 0400 hrs. Flight Lieutenant Malan got in his cockpit and said "Contact", without asking if I had finished. In fact I was struggling with the last stubborn split pin. The day came when we were shown films of his combats which was a tonic to us all after eight months of terrible waiting, but always ready. The greatest thrill of all was the night of the first raids when Flight Lieutenant Malan went up alone through intense gunfire and shot down two German machines in what seemed like less than ten minutes. In my heart, I knew that this was another award for my Flight Commander.'

He was right. The citation for Sailor's Bar, gazetted on 13 August 1940, read,

'Since the end of May 1940, this officer has continued to lead his flight and on many occasions the Squadron, in numerous successful engagements against the enemy. During the Dunkirk operations he shot down three enemy aircraft and assisted in destroying a further three. In June 1940, during a night attack by enemy aircraft, he shot down two Heinkel 111s. His magnificent leadership, skill and courage have been largely responsible for the many successes obtained by his Squadron.'

It was far from one-sided however. There were now seven 'Tigers' who had failed to return, although two were known to be prisoners, and Sergeant

Mould remained in Dover Military Hospital after baling out three days previously. Even the increasingly legendary Sailor had narrow escapes:

'The sky's very small when you want to hide… I did everything but fall into the sea to dodge them. I was partly shot up. I had glass from a broken windscreen in my eyes. Each time I could see one coming down I swung round to face it. They only left me when I reached our coast. I still don't know how I got down on the deck safely. When I went into interrogation, the Station Commander said: "This looks like a man who could use a tot of brandy, Doctor". I said "I'd like two of those. I always thought it was coloured water you kept in those bottles anyway!"'

The next few days were quiet, at least so far as 74 Squadron was concerned. 8 August 1940, however, was a significant day, for two reasons.

Firstly, the Battle of Britain entered its second phase, and indeed for some years after the war officialdom considered this to be the conflict's start-date. That said, the pattern of enemy attacks would not change significantly until 12 August 1940, when heavy attacks were made against radar installations as a prelude to the great *Adlerangriff* (Eagle Attack) planned for the following day – the objective of which was the destruction of Fighter Command. This second phase, according to the official account, would last until 18 August 1940. The first few days continued to see skirmishing over the Channel and very heavy fighting revolving around Convoy CW9, better known as PEEWIT.

Secondly, on 8 August 1940, Squadron Leader White was posted to Fighter Command HQ at Bentley Priory as a staff officer. In command of the 'Tigers', White was succeeded by Sailor, now promoted to Acting Squadron Leader – another landmark and quite a moment for 'Angel Face', the '*Botha* Boy'. It was a natural progression. Sailor was now amongst Fighter Command's most decorated and celebrated pilots, and had led 74 Squadron in the air on innumerable occasions since May 1940. That experience well-placed him to take over the squadron, which was a natural progression. Squadron Leader A.G. Malan DFC and Bar would lead the 'Tigers' into action for the first time as CO on 11 August 1940 – a day remembered with pride by 74 Squadron as 'Sailor's August Eleventh'.

There was no significant enemy activity on 11 August 1940 until 0730 hrs, when a hostile plot appeared in the radar screen approaching a northbound convoy off Southend. A section of 56 Squadron's Hurricanes were up from North Weald and patrolling over the convoy but saw no trace of the enemy machine owing to thick cloud – but the Germans spotted and reported the convoy's position, of that there can be no doubt, given subsequent events. Five minutes later, two enemy formations, each of over thirty aircraft, were identified by radar approaching Dover, seven miles east of South Foreland. The only RAF fighters airborne in this area at that time were just four Spitfires of 64 Squadron, which were vectored towards the hostiles, and 32 Squadron's Hurricanes were scrambled from Hawkinge to patrol that vulnerable coastal airfield. At 0750 hrs, 74 Squadron – the new CO leading – was scrambled from Manston. Squadron Leader Malan's personal combat report: -

'I was Dysoe Leader when Squadron was sent off to intercept bandits approaching Dover at a reported height of 13,000 feet. I climbed on a ENE course to 20,000 feet into the sun, and then turned down-sun towards Dover, and surprised eight Me 109s at 20,000 feet, flying in pairs, staggered in line astern, towards Dover.

'I ordered the Squadron to attack. Some of them adopted the usual German fighter evasive tactics – i.e. quick half-roll and dive. On this occasion, as the air seemed clear of German aircraft above us, I followed one down and overtook him after he had dived 2,000 feet – opening fire during the dive at 200 yards range with deflection. He levelled out at about 12,000 feet when I gave him two two second bursts at 200 yards range. He was in a quick half-roll and dived towards the French coast. I closed again to 100 yards range and gave him another two or three two second bursts, when he suddenly burst into flames and was obscured by heavy smoke. This was at 4,000 feet, one-mile NW of Cap Gris Nez. I did not watch him go in but flew back as fast as I could. I did not see the engagement of the rest of the Squadron.

'Normally I have strongly advised all pilots in the Squadron not to follow 109s on the half-roll and dive because in most cases we are outnumbered, and generally at least one layer of enemy fighters is some thousands of feet above. It was found that even at high altitudes there was no difficulty in overtaking E/A on diving, apart from the physical strain imposed on the body when pulling out.'

Sailor was credited with an 'unconfirmed destroyed'.

It was a hectic and confused combat, once more fought against elements of JG51, with various *staffel*-strength formations sweeping over the Channel. The 'Tigers', having attacked out of the sun and achieved complete surprise, also claimed seven other Me 109s destroyed, a probable and three damaged. Only one of these destroyed claims was confirmed however, and just one Me 109, in fact, is known not to have returned to France, that being Feldwebel Walz of 5/JG51, who remains missing and was very likely Sailor's victim. 74 Squadron also suffered a loss, although Pilot Officer Stevenson baled out of his Spitfire over the Channel and, having drifted eleven miles out to sea, was luckily rescued by a Motor Torpedo Boat. This was the only Spitfire down in this engagement, although between 0803 and 0810 hrs, three JG51 pilots each claimed a Spitfire destroyed over Dover.

A lull then followed, until 0900 hrs when nine enemy aircraft stooged around the Dover Strait for thirty minutes before being reinforced. Ten minutes later, thirty more 'bandits' approached Dover, but all of this harassment was a feint, drawing attention away from the main Luftwaffe effort, which was building up for a huge attack on Portland. Nonetheless, at 0932 hrs, 64 Squadron's Spitfires were scrambled from Kenley, Dover-bound, followed at 0950 hrs by those of 74 Squadron from Manston, and at 1100 hrs 32 Squadron's Hurricanes from Biggin Hill. At 0951 hrs, 64 Squadron sighted twenty Me 109s over Dover, but being 9,000 feet below the Germans it was another ten minutes before the Kenley Spitfires engaged. Indeed, by the time both 64 and 74 Squadrons came into action, the Germans were already retiring. Again, Sailor's personal combat report describes the action:

'I was Dysoe Leader ordered to intercept enemy fighters approaching Dover. I climbed on a north-easterly course to 24,000 feet and did a sweep to the right, approaching Dover from the sea. I saw a number of small groups of Me 109s in mid-Channel at about 24,000 feet and we approached most of them, diving towards the French coast.

'I intercepted two Me 109s, dived onto their tails with Red Section. I delivered two two second bursts at 150 yards, but as I was overshooting I went off and the remainder of the Section continued the attack. I immediately climbed back towards where Blue and Green Sections were waiting above and tried to attract their attention, but owing to R/T difficulties did not manage to get them to form up on me.

'I proceeded towards Dover by myself. I attacked two Me 109s at 25,000 feet about mid-Channel, delivered two two second bursts with deflection at the rearmost one, and saw my bullets entering the fuselage with about 15° deflection. He immediately flicked off to the left and I delivered two long bursts at the leading one. He poured out quite a quantity of white vapour. Eight 109s, who had previously escaped my attention, dived towards me and I climbed in right-hand spiral, and they made no attempt to follow. I proceeded towards Dover on the climb and saw ten Me 109s at 27,000 feet in line astern with one straggler, which I tried to pick off but was unable to close the range without being turned on by the leader of the formation. I circled on a wide sweep with them for about ten minutes while I attempted to notify the remainder of the Squadron by R/T. This proved to be impossible, owing to heavy atmospherics, and in the end I gave up and returned to Manston.'

The Me 109 was claimed as damaged. Warrant Officer Mayne also damaged a 109 and claimed another destroyed (unconfirmed), as did Pilot Officer Freeborn. The enemy fighters belonged to III/JG26, which had been balloon-busting at Dover harbour; Leutnant Bürschgens' Me 109E-1 was damaged and force-landed near his base at Caffiers.

Some of 74 Squadron's combats had occurred at 27,000 feet, Sailor adding to his report that 'It seemed to me that at 27,000 feet I had no superior speed or manoeuvrability over the 109.' In previous combats 74 Squadron's pilots had reported their Spitfires outfighting the 109 at heights of up to 20,000 feet – but the German fighter was found to excel at high altitude, 25,000 feet and above, being slightly superior to the Spitfire and considerably better than the Hurricane. In fighter combat, height is everything – so this performance advantage was a very definite plus for the enemy.

To the west, the great attack on Portland was barely over before more raids were made further east. Soon, 74 Squadron, this time led by Pilot Officer Freeborn, was in action over Convoy BOOTY, off Clacton, along with the Hurricanes of 17 and 85 Squadrons engaging some forty Me 110s of the crack precision bombing unit *Erprobungsgruppe* 210 and ZG26. In the resulting combat, the 'Tigers' claimed ten enemy aircraft destroyed, one probable and five damaged, but lost Pilot Officers Denis Smith (unusually a veteran of the Spanish Civil War, having flown against Franco in the Republican Air Force) and Donald Cobden (a New Zealander), both of whom were killed – undoubtedly by Oberleutnant Heinz Schoenfeldt and Feldwebel Otto Rückert, both of 3/ Erprobungsgruppe 210, who each claimed a Spitfire destroyed.

Squadron Leader Malan led the next scramble, the CO reporting:

'I was Dysoe Leader and told to patrol Manston at 10,000 feet. I climbed through 10/10 cloud with the eight machines in two sections of four. On emerging through cloud, I spotted about thirty Ju 87s in a long line of small vic formations, about fifteen Me 109s about 2,000 feet above and half a mile astern. On sighting us, the bombers dived towards a gap in the cloud while the 109s closed their range with the bombers.

'I ordered Blue Leader to attack the bombers while I attacked the fighters with Red Section. I closed the range with the fighters and attacked an Me 109 as he dived through a gap. I opened up with 30° deflection at

200 yards and closed to 100 yards dead astern. After the third two second burst he burst into flames and went into the sea approximately off Margate.

I immediately climbed towards the cloud and then dived towards another group of four Me 109s and delivered 30° deflection bursts of about three seconds at about 20 yards. I saw no results. As my ammunition was now expended I returned to Manston.'

This 109 was credited as destroyed but unconfirmed, although there can be no doubting that the enemy fighter was destroyed. In this action, 3/JG3 lost two Me 109E-1s, with both pilots killed. Pilot Officer Freeborn claimed a 109 destroyed and another damaged, and both Flying Officer Mungo-Park and Pilot Officer Stephen a destroyed each.

It was the fourth time the 'Tigers' had seen action that day – and an indication of what lay ahead. The following day was uneventful, providing a brief respite for the exhausted pilots and groundcrews.

Between 0530 and 0540 hrs on 13 August 1940 the radar screens showed the first signs of a big build-up of enemy aircraft over Amiens. At 0610 hrs these two formations, each of thirty plus, struck northwards, towards England. Simultaneously, a formation of over 100 enemy aircraft was detected near Dieppe, and another of forty plus over Cherbourg. This was it: *Adlertag*.

Early warning from radar had given sector controllers time to order a substantial number of squadrons to intercept. By 0615 hrs, 151 Squadron was patrolling over a convoy in the Thames Estuary, 111 was up over Hawkinge, and Squadron Leader Malan led 74 Squadron to patrol Manston. Furthermore, sections of three other squadrons were airborne and patrolling their bases. 74 would be the first RAF squadron to engage the raiders. A German formation of four unescorted sections of ten Do 17s in line astern emerged from cloud near Whitstable – to find Sailor and his 'Tigers' ready and waiting.

Squadron Leader Malan:

'While leading the Squadron into attack against enemy bombers in the Estuary I came across them in a vic formation on my beam.

'I closed to within 100 yards and raked them with machine-gun fire. I then swung into line astern and fired at No 3 of the formation. I fired at 150 yards, using four two second bursts. This machine burst into flame in mid-air and was last seen heading for the sea.

'I then attacked the leader of the formation and gave him a three second burst at 150 yards, and one of the engines was put out of action and bits and pieces fell off. This machine cannot possibly have reached home.

'I attacked the third of the Section and used the last of my ammunition but did not see any result.

'No evasive action was taken by these machines.'

Sailor was credited with one Do 17 destroyed and a probable. Every Dornier in the rearmost KG2 section was hit and six were definitely destroyed. The remainder, however, continued to bomb Eastchurch airfield on the Isle of Sheppey, a Coastal Command airfield unconnected to Fighter Command's System of Air Defence. Coincidentally, the previous day a flight of both 19 and 266 Squadrons had arrived at Eastchurch, from where it was proposed the 12 Group Spitfires would strafe the Channel ports and E-Boats. The attack on Eastchurch lasted twenty minutes, some 300 bombs being dropped on the airfield, according to 19 Squadron's CO, Squadron Leader Philip Pinkham. While 19 Squadron survived the traumatic experience unscathed, 266 lost a Spitfire destroyed on the ground, and five Coastal Command Blenheims were likewise written off. Because Eastchurch was not a Fighter Command sector station however, the results were of limited value to the enemy effort – which throughout the Battle of Britain suffered from faulty or poor intelligence, leading to indiscriminate target selection failing to focus specifically upon Fighter Command. It was also an example of what lay in store for German bomber formations foolish enough to venture over southern England without fighter escort. It would be 74 Squadron's only combat on *Aldertag* – which failed to achieve the decisive result Reichsmarschall Göring intended.

The following day, 14 August 1940, 74 Squadron was withdrawn from Hornchurch to rest and refit at Wittering, on the boundary of Cambridgeshire and Northamptonshire, away from the southern combat zone. It was the end of an intensive period of active operations, including the air fighting over Dunkirk and opening stages of the Battle of Britain, which had seen Sailor open his account, achieve the Spitfire's first nocturnal kill, and become a decorated ace and squadron commander. His early experience of growing up on the farm, followed by training for sea and eight years on the ocean waves had provided Sailor with life experience and a maturity far beyond his years. Moreover, Sailor happened to be an exceptional fighter pilot, tactician and leader – and since May 1940 it had all come together.

If Squadron Leader Malan led 74 Squadron to Wittering feeling satisfied with life, he had every reason to.

Chapter Ten

Big Wing

74 Squadron's stay at Wittering was brief. On 21 August 1940 the 'Tigers' moved to Kirton-in-Lindsey, North Lincolnshire, also in 12 Group, there to receive and train replacement pilots. As the squadron arrived at Kirton, three new pilots reported for duty, Flying Officer Walter Franklin and Pilot Officers Alan Ricalton and Roger Boulding. All three had previously flown Fairey Battle light bombers with 142 Squadron during the Fall of France, which suffered heavy losses in that ill-fated campaign. Afterwards 142 operated from Eastchurch, dive-bombing the Channel ports and disrupting German invasion preparations. Years later Wing Commander Boulding recalled:

'Operationally, I first flew Fairey Battles with 52 Squadron at Upwood, Kidlington and Benson, then with 98 Squadron at Hucknall before going to France with 142 Squadron as part of the AASF. When things turned a bit sour over there I managed to escape, flying back to England from Dieppe in a Tiger Moth, landing at Hawkinge on 22 May 1940. I remember that on that day, 22 May 1940, Boulogne Harbour was being heavily dive-bombed.

'Of course, during the summer of 1940, the RAF needed fighter pilots, to make good losses suffered in France and already during the Battle of Britain, which started in July. I therefore answered the call and, much to my delight, converted to Spitfires... I was posted to 74 Squadron, the famous 'Tigers', at Kirton-in-Lindsey, where the Squadron was re-forming after involvement in the Dunkirk air fighting and early stage of the Battle of Britain. Our CO was the highly successful fighter pilot and leader 'Sailor' Malan. I first flew a Spitfire the day after my arrival on the Squadron.'

Having already accumulated a substantial number of flying hours and operational experience, these three new pilots were more fortunate than most – but survival was never guaranteed.

Also joining the 'Tigers' that day, from 7 OTU at Hawarden, were two young New Zealanders, Pilot Officers Wally Churches, from Auckland, and Wanganui's Bob Spurdle. Years later Spurdle would write in his superb memoir *The Blue Arena* (see bibliography):

'Wally and I stood before Sailor Malan and gazed at our new CO with deep respect. "You pilots will be trained hard in the next few weeks. Your life expectancy will be in direct ratio to your ability to learn… This is a famous Squadron and I expect you both to remember it. In the last war, Major Mannock won the VC flying for 74. He shot down seventy-three enemy aircraft. Soon you too will have plenty of targets. I'm sure you'll do well!"'

As Spurdle commented: 'We couldn't have joined a better squadron.'

Spurdle also recorded, however, how he and fellow colonial Wally Churches were referred to by certain of the British 'Tigers' as 'coloured troops'. This derogatory moniker was also used by the socially elite Auxiliary Air Force officers of 601 Squadron, the so-called 'Millionaire's Mob', when referring to regular RAF officers. Again, this is clear evidence of the attitude towards people of colour, who were seen as inferior. Ironically, as a South African, in this context, 74's increasingly revered commander was amongst the 'coloured troops'. Spurdle also noted that their fellow 'newbies', namely Boulding, Franklin and Ricalton, all being British, were 'more readily assimilated' into 74 Squadron. Clearly, divisions within the service were not simply aligned to colour or social class, but even between the white nationalities. Interestingly, Spurdle also observed that while 74 Squadron had 'a tremendous élan in the air', it was 'a curiously divided and unhappy unit on the ground. With Malan we would have flown anywhere against anything, but 74's curse was, in my opinion, the presence of several Auxiliary Air Force types, who affected longer than regulation hair and who tended to treat menials and pilot officers as they must have treated fags at their public schools [younger boys used as servants]… In a subtle way we "Colonials" and the new young British recruits, unless "well connected", were largely excluded from this kind of old boys' club and felt it keenly.' Unfortunately, one of the primary protagonists in this bullying culture was the 'stooge' of Spurdle's Flight Commander, Flight Lieutenant Freeborn (who had recently been promoted and succeeded Sailor as commander of 'A' Flight) and was therefore untouchable.

By now Sailor was a leading light and known throughout Fighter Command – and beyond. On 27 August 1940, an official Air Ministry war artist, the celebrated painter John Mansbridge RA, visited Kirton and began work on a portrait of the great man, wearing his iconic Irvin flying jacket and parachute, climbing into his Spitfire. On completion the work was hung in the art gallery of South Africa House in Trafalgar Square, London (now in the possession of Sailor's daughter, Valerie).

As the 'Tigers' trained hard, on 3 September 1940, the first anniversary of the declaration of war, Squadron Leader Malan and Flight Lieutenant Freeborn attended an investiture in the air raid shelter of Buckingham Palace, receiving their decorations from the King. The citation for Freeborn's DFC read:

'This officer has taken part in nearly all offensive patrols carried out by his Squadron since the commencement of the war, including operations over the Low Countries and Dunkirk, and, more recently, engagements over the Channel and SE of England. During this intensive period of air warfare he has destroyed four enemy aircraft. His high courage and exceptional abilities as a leader have materially contributed to the notable successes and high standard of efficiency maintained by his Squadron.'

The award had been recommended by Sailor.

On 6 September 1940, Squadron Leader Malan visited 12 Group HQ at Hucknall, accompanied by another 'Tiger' ace, Pilot Officer Harbourne Mackay Stephen DFC, for an interview with the AOC, Air Vice-Marshal Leigh-Mallory. The purpose of the interview is unknown.

On 9 September 1940, the 'Tigers' were on the move again, this time to Coltishall, just north of Norwich in Norfolk – where 242 (Canadian) Squadron was commanded by another RAF legend, Squadron Leader Douglas Bader. A Cranwell graduate and gifted aerobatic pilot with an irrepressible spirit, Bader, a talented and highly competitive sportsman, had to be the best at everything he did. In 1931 the headstrong 23 Squadron pilot had crashed his biplane Bulldog fighter, showing off at a civilian flying club near Reading, resulting in the amputation of both legs. A lesser man would have died, but incredibly Bader mastered artificial legs and returned to the service. The problem was that King's Regulations failed to provide for disabled pilots. Finding this unacceptable, and unable to contemplate a chairborne role, he left the RAF. Working in the Petroleum Company's home-based aviation section, for Bader – the man of action – the tedium was unbearable. Instead of aerobatics, Bader found his thrills behind the wheel of his MG, negotiating the Great West Road at high speed. With the rise of Hitler and the threat Germany posed to Britain's security he saw salvation, a means to escape the wilderness and return to the cockpit.

Cutting a long story short, after war was declared Douglas Bader passed a flying test and by February 1940 was flying Spitfires with 19 Squadron at Duxford. His CO though was his old Cranwell and 23 Squadron contemporary Geoffrey Stephenson, now a squadron leader, and the 30-year-old Flying Officer Bader found it difficult serving under his old friend – once an equal – and taking orders from younger men. Again cutting another long story short, Bader persuaded another Cranwell pal, Squadron Leader H.W. 'Tubby' Mermagen, to have him as a flight commander in his 222 Squadron. Elevated to flight lieutenant, the legless fighter pilot scored his first victories over Dunkirk, naturally attracting publicity. During the Battle of France, 242 Squadron had suffered from poor leadership and had returned home battered. Morale was low. Bader's exceptional achievements, coupled with his charismatic and forceful personality, had already impressed both Duxford's Station Commander, Wing Commander A.B. 'Woody' Woodhall, and his AOC, Air Vice-Marshal Leigh-Mallory. Consequently the swashbuckling Bader was their first choice to command and restore 242 Squadron to an effective fighting unit – which Squadron Leader Bader achieved, at Coltishall, when his unit was declared fully operational on 9 July 1940 – the Battle of Britain officially began the following day.

The role of 12 Group, however, was to defend the industrial Midlands and the north, provide protection to shipping off the east coast, and defend 11 Group's airfields when Air Vice-Marshal Park's fighters were engaged further forward. Whereas it was initially assumed that any air attacks on England would approach the east coast across the North Sea, from bases in Germany, making 12 Group the front line, Hitler's rapid advance to the Channel coast changed everything. Instead of operating from their homeland, the Luftwaffe now enjoyed the benefit of bases in north-west France, putting London even within range of the single-engined Me 109. This completely shifted the fighting's focus, the main assault now falling upon the south-east, and the brunt, therefore, borne by 11 Group. The Germans, ideally, needed to lure Dowding into basing most of his strength in 11 Group, within range of escorted bombers, for destruction on the ground and in the air – en masse. This, however, is exactly what the Commander-in-Chief did not do. Instead Dowding maintained a spread of strength nationwide, conscious of the threat to the north from the Luftwaffe based in Norway, and commitment to defend multiple targets. Squadrons were therefore rotated, taking a turn in the hot zone before withdrawing to rest and refit, as 74 Squadron was currently doing, their place in the line taken by a rebuilt squadron, and so on. In this way strength was both maintained and preserved, without falling into the trap of concentration in the south-east.

Air Vice-Marshal Park was fighting the battle in such a way as to further preserve strength – while concurrently providing flexibility and a rapid reaction. This dictated using small formations, of either a flight or single squadron. Furthermore, the Me 109 had demonstrated its excellent high-altitude ability, matched only by the Spitfire, while the Hurricane performed better lower down and was therefore more effectively deployed, when possible, against bombers with a protective umbrella of Spitfires. So while the pilots of 11 Group were busy, often in action several times daily, those of 12 Group largely stood by, monotonously stooging around over convoys, chasing lone German reconnaissance aircraft, and awaiting the call to reinforce 11 Group – which never came. For Squadron Leader Bader – to whom action was life-blood – this was intolerable. Another wilderness. It was a frustration shared by his AOC, Air Vice-Marshal Leigh-Mallory, who equally craved a share of the action and deeply resented 11 Group taking the limelight – which became a festering sore. 30 August 1940, however, had been a significant day for Squadron Leader Douglas Bader's Coltishall-based 242 Squadron – which would have ramifications not just for 242 but equally 12 Group and ultimately Fighter Command as a whole.

On that day, Air Vice-Marshal Leigh-Mallory sent 242 Squadron south, to operate from Duxford, there to await events closer to the action. At 1600 hrs, 300-plus bandits were reported incoming over Kent and the Thames Estuary, splitting into two formations and attacking airfields in 11 Group. At 1620 hrs, sixty He 111s and their Me 110 escorts were approaching north of the Thames. Anticipating attacks on North Weald and Hornchurch, 11 Group requested assistance from 12 Group via Fighter Command HQ. At 1623 hrs, Wing Commander Woodhall scrambled 242 to patrol North Weald at Angels 15. As Squadron Leader Bader led fourteen Hurricanes south, the incoming threat separated and headed for two different targets: I/KG1 struck out towards the Vauxhall Motor Works and aerodrome at Luton, while II/KG53, the larger of the two formations, fought its way to the Handley Page Aircraft Factory at Radlett. In response 11 Group scrambled further squadrons. In *Reach for the Sky*, author Paul Brickhill claimed that Bader contradicted the Controller's instructions, knowing better, flying contrary to the ordered course and consequently intercepting the Radlett raiders. This is not so. Primary evidence confirms that 242 Squadron was guided to what was a successful interception by the Controller. The vast enemy formation travelling east, the like of which none of 242 Squadron's pilots had seen before, was, according to their leader 'awe-inspiring'. Up-sun and with the advantage of height, 242 Squadron was perfectly positioned for a surprise attack. After the ensuing combat, an elated 242 Squadron returned to Duxford, claiming eight Me 110s destroyed and another damaged, and five He 111s destroyed for no loss. All were confirmed – although today it is impossible to corroborate more than two Me 110s and an He 111; this is because of the high level of confusion in air fighting involving so many aircraft, with pilots simultaneously attacking the same target, oblivious to each other's presence, meaning that one enemy machine could be multiplied many times on the balance sheet. Nonetheless, there appears to have been little or no effort to more appropriately scrutinise 242's claims, which were accepted in their entirety.

242 Squadron's apparent success inspired various congratulatory signals from Air Vice-Marshal Leigh-Mallory and even the CAS. The experience confirmed in Bader's mind that, contrary to the System, 12 Group should be operating mass formations of fighters, able to either roam over the aerial battlefield for deployment at their leader's direction, or be scrambled and vectored en masse towards the trouble. Bader immediately submitted his report 'Fighter Tactics v Escort & Bomber Formations', promoting his theories. The truth was, though, that 11 Group's smaller formations, in action daily, did not over-claim to the extent that the comparatively inexperienced 242 Squadron demonstrably did on 30 August 1940. Moreover, 242 had been perfectly positioned by the Controller, not the leader in the air as later claimed by Bader's first biographer, the journalist Paul Brickhill. Furthermore, and fortunately for Bader's Hurricanes, there was no high-flying Me 109 escort ready to pounce. Bader, however, firmly believed that had he had more fighters under his direction, even more damage could have been done to the enemy. Bader, in the heat of the moment, was unaware that there were actually 11 Group Hurricanes and Spitfires – a total of fifty fighters – attacking the Germans simultaneously with his pilots, a fact confirmed through an analysis of combat reports by all involved – meaning that Bader's mass formation theory was flawed from the outset. Nonetheless, Air Vice-Marshal Leigh-Mallory agreed with Bader, recognising that here, patrolling and intercepting with a wing of multiple squadrons as opposed to a single unit, was a means of getting 12 Group into action – and the AOC set about making this happen. The following day, 31 August 1940, Duxford was bombed, 19 Squadron losing several Spitfires in the ensuing fighting, including one pilot killed and another badly wounded. On 1 September 1940, 242 Squadron reinforced the Duxford Sector and again operated from that airfield, patrolling uneventfully. Squadron Leader Bader, though, was at 12 Group HQ, expounding his mass fighter formation theories to his AOC.

Immediately after 74 Squadron left 11 Group, the Luftwaffe had started pounding Air Vice-Marshal Park's all-important sector airfields, the resulting air fighting being hitherto unprecedented in its scale and ferocity. The situation soon became critical: on 7 September 1940, Codename 'CROMWELL' was broadcast – imminent. Having now concentrated scores of fighter aircraft in the Pas-de-Calais, Reichsmarschall Göring's aim of luring Fighter Command to battle to be destroyed en masse was constantly frustrated by Air Vice-Marshal Park's careful preservation of his force. Instead of doing exactly what the Germans wanted and committing large numbers of fighters to battle, the strategy steadfastly pursued by 11 Group was to keep aircraft well dispersed on the ground and attack in penny-packet formations. The Luftwaffe, due to over-confidence and faulty intelligence, continued to fight an ill-directed campaign contravening that fundamental principle – maintenance of aim. That 'aim' had already changed several times. At what was a vital moment, considering the battering 11 Group's airfields had taken these past few weeks, thanks to Bomber Command the Germans again changed tack. On the night of 24 August 1940, RAF bombers had attacked Berlin – Hitler immediately seizing upon this as justification for ordering an all-out assault on London. In previous campaigns, the Poles and Dutch had both surrendered after the bombing of their main centres of population, and the Danes did so at merely the threat. Moreover, Göring believed that round-the-clock bombing of London would exhaust Fighter Command and was the only target capable of forcing Dowding to commit his entire force to battle. So it was, then, that on this date the Battle of Britain entered another phase: *Unternehmen Loge* – target London – named after the Nordic fire god.

At 1635 hrs that afternoon, Göring and his staff stood on the cliffs at Cap Gris-Nez marvelling at Germany's aerial might – as 348 bombers and 617 fighters roared overhead towards south-east England. Anxiously monitoring the approach of this huge armada – the largest unleashed against Britain so far – the 11 Group Controller naturally assumed that sector stations in the south-east were again the target. At 1617 hrs, eleven squadrons were scrambled, and by 1630 hrs all of Air Vice-Marshal Park's twenty-one squadrons were airborne. Assistance was called for from both 10 and 12 Groups. On that day, Air Vice-Marshal Leigh-Mallory had ordered the Hurricane-equipped 242 and 310 (Czech) Squadrons to operate from Duxford with the Spitfires of 19 Squadron, which were based at nearby Fowlmere. Naturally, what became known as the 'Duxford Wing', or 'Big Wing', was led by Squadron Leader Bader, although in the air this was actually problematic, as Sir Douglas, as he later became, explained:

'Only the squadron commanders were on the same frequency. We had four buttons on the VHF in those days, which we had received just before the Battle of Britain. It was ridiculous anyway, trying to tune this thing with someone shooting-up your backside! Anyway, the other pilots each had their own squadron frequency. The Controller would talk to me on my frequency, but to talk to the chaps I would have to keep changing frequency from squadron to squadron. Later, of course, we got it so that we were all on the same frequency… My objective was to get the Wing into the right position, then say "Attacking now", after which it was up to them. They awaited my order, every man knew what he had to do, but the Wing was impossible for me to control after that point.'

At 1645 hrs, the Duxford Wing was scrambled to patrol North Weald at 10,000 feet. Given that height is everything, it is impossible to understand, however, why all three squadrons of the Wing were ordered to patrol at such a low height. Squadron Leader Bader, sensibly, climbed the Wing 5,000 feet higher over North Weald – sighting a phalanx of bombers 5,000 feet above his formation and the German fighter escort a further 5,000 feet above their charges. The enemy was attacking Thameshaven, south of Squadron Leader Bader's position. London, not airfields, was being bombed – catching Fighter Command wrong-footed. Squadron Leader Bader informed the 12 Group Controller that he had the enemy in sight and requested permission to engage, which was duly granted. Climbing at full throttle to at least get level with the enemy meant that the element of surprise had been lost. Furthermore, owing to the difference in performance between the Spitfire and Hurricane, the Wing became 'straggled out so that the full weight could not be pressed home'. Inevitably, the German fighter escort pounced.

Squadron Leader Douglas Bader:

'To be attacked by an enemy fighter when you are climbing is fatal if your opponent is experienced. You are flying slowly and are thus virtually un-manoeuvrable, as well as being a sitting target for an opponent flying above you and flying faster. It was windy work, let there be no mistake. On landing I rang the Operations Room in a fury, to be told that we had been sent off as soon as 11 Group had called for us.'

Although the Duxford Wing's first action on 7 September had been 'windy work' provoking Squadron Leader Bader's 'fury', for the loss of one pilot the Wing claimed twenty enemy aircraft destroyed, five probables and six damaged. The Luftwaffe lost forty aircraft on operations this date – seventeen of which either crashed in England or close enough to the coast for their crews to be captured or bodies recovered. From the evidence available it is difficult to confirm more than six kills by 242 Squadron, suggesting an over-claiming ratio of 3:1. Once more, though, the claims of Douglas Bader and his pilots appear to have been accepted without question. The issue of verifying combat claims would vex both sides throughout the Battle of Britain. Accurate intelligence regarding losses and claims was crucial to both evaluating enemy strength and the success of one's own tactics. Inevitably, the Duxford Wing's tally attracted further congratulatory signals from both Air Vice-Marshal Leigh-Mallory and the Secretary of State for Air, Sir Archibald Sinclair. The claims submitted suggested that, in spite of the late call to scramble and the absurdly low height at which the Wing had been ordered to patrol, it had actually fought a successful action. Air Vice-Marshal Leigh-Mallory, Wing Commander Woodhall and Squadron Leader Bader were convinced that with some fine-tuning the Duxford Wing would positively contribute to the battle being fought over 11 Group.

As a result of the 'Black Saturday' attack on the capital, 1,800 Londoners were killed or seriously injured. That night, the relentless Luftwaffe returned, guided to their target by the fires still burning from the earlier attacks, and rained down more death and destruction between 2210 and 0430 hrs. That day, Fighter Command lost a further twenty-eight aircraft, the Luftwaffe forty.

For Air Vice-Marshal Park, however, the change in target was a blessing: -

'It was burning all down the river. It was a horrid sight. But I looked down and said "Thank God for that," because I knew that the Nazis had switched their attack from our fighter stations, thinking they were knocked out. They weren't, but they were pretty groggy.'

The following day was thankfully quiet, but on 9 September 1940, the day 74 Squadron arrived at Coltishall, 242 Squadron was again operating from Duxford, patrolling with three other squadrons. South of London, battle was joined, the Wing claiming twenty destroyed and two shared, plus six probables and two more damaged. Again, these claims were accepted, but more recent research suggests an overclaiming factor of 5:1.

This then was the 12 Group situation when Squadron Leader Sailor Malan arrived at Coltishall. 74 Squadron's combat experience had previously been with 11 Group, fighting over Dunkirk, and for the first part of the Battle of Britain frequently operating from the forward coastal base of Manston, either as a flight or squadron. The 'Big Wing' concept was contrary to Air Chief Marshal Dowding's strategy, in reality flawed from the outset, and the brainchild of Squadron Leader Douglas Bader who, for all his other attributes, was only recently returned to the modern RAF, with comparatively little combat experience. Nonetheless, as ever, Bader, backed up by his influential AOC, knew best, or so he thought. It would be illuminating to know what Sailor's view was of 242 Squadron's buccaneering CO and his 'Big Wing' ideas – which would shortly involve the 'Tigers'.

On 10 September 1940, no less than fourteen 74 Squadron Spitfires left Coltishall for Duxford, to operate with the 12 Group Wing, although there would be no action. The same day, Squadron Leader Bader flew to 12 Group HQ for an hour-long interview with Air Vice-Marshal Leigh-Mallory. The AOC listened while the legless squadron commander explained his belief that it was the formation leader who should decide when and where to attack – not the controller – on the grounds that height information received from RDF was frequently inaccurate and that, in any case, the controller could not see the enemy personally. This, however, was absolutely and completely contrary to Fighter Command's System. Leigh-Mallory agreed and said, 'I'll put this to the right people, and in the meantime you might as well carry on with your theory. It seems to work.' So convinced was Leigh-Mallory that 12 Group knew better than both Air Chief Marshal Dowding and Air Vice-Marshal Park that he added two more squadrons to the Duxford Wing. This was now not just a wing, but a *big* wing of five squadrons – a 12 Group *corps d'élite* indeed. Nothing could have been more contrary to how Dowding had expressly ordered the battle to be fought. Even the CAS, a confirmed 'Big Wing' supporter, was surprised.

On this day, 74 Squadron started re-equipping with the new Spitfire Mk II. This new Spitfire enjoyed several benefits over the Mk IA currently in operational service. The Spitfire Mk II was powered by the Merlin XII, which produced 1,175 hp, as opposed to the Mk IA's Merlin III's 1,030 hp. The Mk II's top speed was 370 mph – 15 mph faster than the Mk IA; its rate of climb was 2,600 feet a minute, 473 feet a minute more than the Mk IA. The new engine was fitted with a Coffman automatic starter, which reduced starting time, and, most importantly, all of the new Spitfires were fitted with the Rotol constant speed propeller. Concurrently the Hurricane was also being improved. On 4 September Fighter Command received the first deliveries of the Hurricane Mk II. Hawker's improved fighter was powered by the Merlin XX, which produced ten hp more than the Spitfire Mk II's Merlin XII; the Hurricane Mk II was also fitted with the Rotol CS propeller as standard. These improvements increased the Hurricane's top speed to 342 mph – but this was 28 mph slower than the new Spitfires, and 12 mph slower than the Me 109E-3. The Spitfire, therefore, remained the superior RAF fighter – but still had no 20mm cannon.

On 11 September 1940, poor weather again delayed the enemy's main assault until afternoon. 242 Squadron had remained at Coltishall, instead of flying down to and operating from Duxford. 611 Squadron's Spitfires had flown from Digby to join those of 19 Squadron at Fowlmere – as had one flight of both 74 Squadron and the Wittering-based 266 Squadron. At 1500 hrs, the He 111s of I and II/KG26 left their French bases, bound for England. After rendezvousing with their 200-strong fighter escort, the bombers headed east over the Thames Estuary towards London. From 1530 hrs onwards, 11 Group squadrons attacked the enemy formation but failed to reach the bombers until after their bombs exploded in the docklands below. At 1530 hrs, this all-Spitfire 12 Group Fowlmere Wing was scrambled, led south by 19 Squadron's CO, Squadron Leader Brian Lane.

Squadron Leader Malan reported engaging up to fifty 'Ju 88s' (actually KG26 He 111s) over London at 1630 hrs:

'I was Dysoe Leader operating from Duxford aerodrome as rear squadron of three-squadron wing led by 19 Squadron, with 611 Squadron in the middle. Detailed to intercept raids over London at 20,000 feet. It was arranged that the two leading squadrons should keep fighter escort at bay while I attack bombers with 74 Squadron.

'We intercepted long rectangle of bombers at 20,000 feet over London at approximately 1630 hrs. We were flying in three fours, sections line astern. I gave order for head-on attack but before I could get far enough ahead I saw He 113s coming down onto us and turned towards bombers immediately, in order to deliver some form of attack before engaging fighters. I could not turn in the space and quite accidentally delivered a very effective beam attack at close range by turning across bows of formation and opening fire at 150 yards, closing to 50 yards.

'I saw my ammunition pouring into two E/A as I raked across formation, which was tightly packed and, because of close pursuit of enemy fighters, continued down in fast spiral to 13,000 feet and climbed into sun at 20,000 feet. Proceeded towards one turning onto southerly course but spotted a Ju 88 at 20,000 feet which had either engine trouble or was observing results of bombing. I delivered a head-on attack and blew large pieces from port engine. I turned and delivered beam attack at 100 yards as enemy fighter dived down onto me. I continued down but saw port engine well on fire and aircraft going down in gentle dive. Also thought I saw one parachute open close to the E/A.

'The enemy fighter, which appeared to be He 113, followed me down to 10,000 feet where I did a steep left-hand turn, blacking myself out, and shook him off.

'As my ammunition was expended, I returned to Duxford. Position of last engagement was about over Biggin Hill.'

The first enemy aircraft was credited as 'damaged', the second destroyed. In total, the Duxford Wing claimed eleven Me 110s and bombers destroyed, in addition to various 'probables' and damaged. After the action, Squadron Leader Malan led 74 Squadron back to Coltishall. It would be the last time that the 'Tigers' would fly with the controversial Duxford Wing. Interestingly, at this time, Air Vice-Marshal Park was deploying Spitfire squadrons from Hornchurch and Biggin Hill, both sector stations located half way between the coast and London, in pairs, to engage the high-flying enemy fighter escorts, while the Hurricanes attacked the close escorts and bombers. Park later reported that 'Fighter squadrons from Debden, Tangmere and sometimes Northolt were employed in wings or three squadrons in pairs to form a screen south-east of London... Experience shows that even small wings of three squadrons were not effective against high fighter patrols, and the Spitfire squadrons were therefore used in pairs.' This clearly demonstrates Air Vice-Marshal Park's flexible approach and ability to respond to changing tactical scenarios – effectively.

Sailor:

'How did we feel? Of course we had our tails up. At that time the Luftwaffe seemed to be running on an endless belt – the fellow you knocked down yesterday seemed to be back next day, asking for another wallop. We were not without fear. The fellow who wasn't didn't live long. And taking a Spitfire into the sky in September 1940 often corresponded to entering a dark room with a madman weaving a knife behind your back. We could see behind us and the Hun was everywhere, ready to spit his guns.

'There was a spirit of exaltation in the pilots, that spirit which made one of them insist that his CO write a chit: "IOU one show"; the spirit that sent one pilot up on seven fights in one day so that he fell asleep getting out of his cockpit and fell asleep for twenty-four hours.'

Churchill visited 11 Group's underground Operations Room at Uxbridge, watching the high drama unfold in person. After one such visit, deeply moved, the Prime Minister evolved his defining phrase: 'Never in the field of human conflict has so much been owed, by so many, to so few.' It was an inspired choice of words, directly connecting RAF aircrews with Henry V's heavily outnumbered and disease-ridden army, which routed the cream of French nobility at Agincourt, immortalized by Shakespeare in the King's St Crispin's Day speech: 'We few, we happy few, we band of brothers.' Churchill's inspirational words were included in a long speech made to the House of Commons on 20 August 1940, which must surely be the Battle of Britain's greatest eulogy.

On 14 September 1940, 74 Squadron was again in action, this time mainly over the east coast, although Sailor did not fly. Down south, the Battle of Britain was about to reach its climax. In the enemy camp, frustrations were mounting at the Luftwaffe's apparent inability to score a decisive victory over Fighter Command. The German invasion fleet was due to sail five days later, and there was neither any sign of Fighter Command throwing in the towel or being down to its last fifty Spitfires and Hurricanes, as Göring insisted was the case. The Reichsmarschall was determined not to lose either face or his Fuhrer's confidence however, and so on 15 September 1940 unleashed another day of massive air attacks against London. Time and time again the enemy assaulted the capital, wave after wave of bombers escorted by fighters.

Sailor:

'We were never in desperate straits… My Squadron was pulled out of the line, with others, when we were in top form and with very few losses, in order to form a reserve that could be flung into the breach – if there was a breach.... Many of us were tired. We had been pulled out for a second breather. Older sweats like Mungo-Park, Steve [Stephen] and Johnny Freeborn and I were using a few hours' rest to train new pilots and snatch an odd half pint of the local brew at Coltishall, on the east coast. Sharing our airfield was 242, a Canadian squadron commanded by Douglas Bader. As far as I remember – I don't believe in diaries – it was a quiet day [14 September 1940]. Bader and I, and, for that matter, all the fellows in the squadrons at Coltishall, knew that Göring's nut still had to be cracked. The fact that at that moment the Luftwaffe was being assembled for its greatest bid only a hundred or so miles from us across the Channel, was unknown to us as we played our game of billiards, drank a glass of beer or lay on our beds in the dispersal huts at readiness.

By now 12 Group's Duxford Wing comprised five squadrons, and made its greatest contribution to the battle when Squadron Leader Douglas Bader bludgeoned his way over London on 15 September 1940 at the head of fifty fighters – putting heart and hope into the hard-pressed defenders, and dealing a crushing blow to the Luftwaffe airmen's morale, who just could not believe what they were seeing. This would be Göring's last attempt to destroy Fighter Command en-masse. At the end of the day, the British press trumpeted that 185 enemy aircraft had been destroyed for the loss of only thirty friendly fighters and ten pilots. In reality, the Germans had lost fifty-six machines, less than on 15 August 1940 (seventy-five) and 18 August 1940 (sixty-nine). Such an ongoing scale of loss, however, was unsustainable, and the defenders sensed that this day was a significant turning point – celebrated ever since as 'Battle of Britain Day'. Two days later, Hitler postponed the proposed invasion of southern England, Operation *Seelöwe*, indefinitely.

After more losses, on 30 September 1940 the Luftwaffe had no choice but to withdraw the He 111 from daylight operations. By then, a *staffel* of Me 109s in each *gruppe* had been converted to fighter-bombers, meaning that Fighter Command Controllers were unable to differentiate between pure high-altitude fighter sweeps and those including fighter-bombers, and so had to react to every incursion. Bombing operations now changed tack once more, focusing, too late, on the British aircraft industry. By day, in addition to the nuisance attacks, raids were either made by lone, fast, Ju 88s, or comparatively small formations of same, heavily escorted by fighters. The main enemy assault shifted to Britain's night skies, trading accuracy for safety, given that night-fighting remained in its infancy.

This, then, was the picture when on 15 October 1940, on which day Squadron Leader Malan led sixteen Spitfires of the replenished and rested 74 Squadron to re-join 11 Group – this time at that most famous of fighter stations, Biggin Hill. As the squadron's diarist recorded, 'Should now get back into our stride again!' Indeed, as Spurdle wrote, 'We were a strong, well-trained and competent Squadron and led by the best' – Sailor Malan.

Chapter Eleven

'Snappers' over Biggin Hill

When 74 Squadron landed at 'Biggin on the Bump' on 15 October 1940, the Battle of Britain was in its final – and most exhausting – phase.

The current German bombing policy primarily concerned the progressive destruction of London, mainly after dark; disrupting armament production in the Midlands, again mainly at night, and harassing factories by day, that effort focused on the aircraft industry. It was clear that a seaborne invasion attempt was not imminent, and indeed intelligence from various sources confirmed that the plan had now been completely abandoned. The enemy's aim was now about conserving its bomber force while concurrently achieving small gains which, over time, would represent substantial damage to industrial and domestic property, ultimately assisting invasion plans by reducing production and lowering public morale.

Most importantly, the Luftwaffe was now pressurizing Fighter Command through fighter and fighter-bomber sweeps penetrating to London. Unshackled from their close bomber escort role, the lethal German fighters were now able to intrude at an even greater height – literally holding all the aces. Unable to identify which incursions included fighter-bombers, controllers had to react to every sweep – a huge commitment, dawn to dusk, for 11 Group's Spitfire squadrons, based at Hornchurch and Biggin Hill, which Air Vice-Marshal Park was now using in pairs. The paired squadrons would patrol further back, then engage the enemy fighters at 30,000 feet, half way between London and the south-east coast. The Spitfires were also at height to protect Hurricane squadrons climbing and while they engaged any incoming bombers. 74 would relieve 72 Squadron at Biggin Hill, pairing with 92 Squadron; Squadron Leader Geoffrey 'Boy' Wellum DFC of the latter unit recalled years later that during this final phase of battle, 'Me 109s were always in the Biggin Hill Sector and caused problems. I recall that they were always above us as we never seemed to be scrambled in time to get enough height. Our climb was always a desperate, full-throttle affair, but we never quite got up to them.' Clearly, plenty more air-fighting awaited Sailor and his 'Tigers'.

'SNAPPERS' OVER BIGGIN HILL

On 15 October 1940, over 500 enemy fighters and fighter-bombers flew five sweeps over south-east England, penetrating as far as Hornchurch and central London, where railway lines were damaged at Waterloo and Vauxhall, and factories hit in West Ham along with the King George V Dock. At 0845 hrs, 92 Squadron took off from Biggin Hill and rendezvoused over base with the Gravesend-based Spitfires of 66 Squadron. Climbing over London, the Spitfires ran into fifty Me 109s, which were pursued and engaged over the Channel, half way between Dover and Cap Gris-Nez. In the ensuing combat, Sergeant Fokes claimed a 109 destroyed, along with a stray He 111, and Sergeant Don Kingaby shot down another German fighter – but Sergeant Ken Parker was killed. At 1120 hrs, 92 were up again, patrolling Sevenoaks, intercepting more Me 109s over Kent; Sergeant Fokes was again successful, shooting a 109 down in flames, while Pilot Officer 'Dutch' Holland claimed a probable. Pilot Officer Tommy Lund, however, was shot down, crashing in the Channel, fortunately being rescued by HMS *Nysan*. Ten minutes before 92 Squadron returned to Biggin Hill at 1330 hrs, Squadron Leader Malan and 74 Squadron had landed on what was already another busy day. Almost immediately, Squadron Leader Malan was leading 74 Squadron on a patrol of the Maidstone line. According to Pilot Officer Bob Spurdle, the 'Tigers' were 'led by the best'; he described that first sortie from Biggin Hill – his first in the combat zone – in his superb memoir, *The Blue Arena* (see Bibliography):

'We taxied to our new dispersal points and immediately the petrol bowsers started pumping fuel to top up our tanks. The CO was being briefed by a "Spy" [author's note: intelligence officer] who crouched on his wing and gesticulated at the pilots now clambering out of their machines. A runner came tearing over. "Get back in – you're off as soon as re-fuelled!" and away he went to the next kite and the next. Groundcrew collected the small toilet bags that the pilots had with them, and in a few minutes, we taxied out and formed up for take-off. Hell, that was quick, I thought. Whacko!

'Malan looked right and left at the Spits on either side, raising his gloved hand. Thumbs up! We acknowledged in the same way. The CO lowered his arm and with exaggerated nods of his head indicated to open throttles. As one, our flight of four aircraft rolled forward, faster and faster, with marker boards zipping past and clouds of grass particles and dust billowing behind us. "A" Flight and "B" Flight followed to form up on us as we climbed towards the north-west.

'"Angels 20 Maidstone," the R/T crackled, and Malan's laconic "Dysoe on the way" brought things into perspective.

'This was it! The real thing! I felt sick with excitement. Far off in the cold blue to the south we could see tiny white contrails heading our way. My palms grew slippery with sweat and I wiped them on my Sidcot suit. I wouldn't wear gloves as they inhibited me – I'd take my chances if the plane caught fire.

'Now we settled down in 74's standard formation of three sections of four aircraft flying in line-astern, forming a vic on the leader.

'Up, up we flew, radiator flaps wide open, temperatures reaching danger levels. Oxygen on at 13,000 feet. Now the CO turned back towards Maidstone. Short snatches of information came through.

"Fifty snappers [enemy fighters] to your starboard, Angels 20."

"Forty plus snappers Angels 26 over Dungeness coming your way."

'But all we could see was our twelve Spits alone under the blazing sun. Far below, green and brown fields slowly shrank as we climbed still higher, and to the south the Channel curved around in a great green arc.

"Blue Leader here. I think I see them two o' clock below."

"Hurricanes."

"Okay."

'On and up; now each aircraft trailed white streamers which appeared as if by magic. Water vapour from the hot exhaust gases was condensing and giving our position away. Malan dipped the Squadron until the "tadpoles" disappeared, then levelled us off. The Jerries' smoke trails had disappeared – they too had dived below the condensation level and hoped to hide their presence as we had. But all the time our directions kept coming through – the magnificent Observer Corps and radar stations all feeding sightings into underground operations rooms. Here the reports were correlated and interceptions planned.

"Tally Ho! Bandits at one o'clock above!" and with that a cloud of silver arrows appeared, each tipped with a little black speck. The Jerries had seen us and were climbing to gain height advantage.

"Dysoe aircraft through the gate."'

'Through the gate' referred to using the Merlin's emergency boost – which could only be used for about five minutes, so as not to overstrain the engine; Spurdle continues:

'Good! I'd always wanted to do it! I pushed the throttle around past its notched slide, breaking the sealing wire. The Merlins' heavy purr became a harsh roar and brown smoke poured from the exhausts. The Spitfires leapt forward.

The *General Botha* training ship.

The *Sandown Castle.*

'Sailor' Malan, right, while serving as a junior officer aboard the *Sandown Castle*.

An He 111 under fire from Flight Lieutenant Malan – the best shot in the RAF.

On the night of 18/19 June 1940, Flight Lieutenant Malan achieved the Spitfire's first nocturnal kill, destroying two He 111s. This was how a war artist envisioned the crash of one of them.

Squadron Leader Malan with his dog 'Peter' at Biggin Hill in 1940 with two 'Tigers', namely Draper and Stephen.

Above left: An official portrait of Wing Commander Malan, at the time the RAF's top-scoring fighter pilot.

Above right: The blonde knight: Group Captain Sailor Malan.

Detail of the Mansbridge portrait.

Above left: Sailor Malan sketched during the Battle of Britain by Cuthbert Orde.

Above right: Group Captain Sailor Malan.

Group Captain Sailor Malan while commanding Biggin Hill in May 1943.

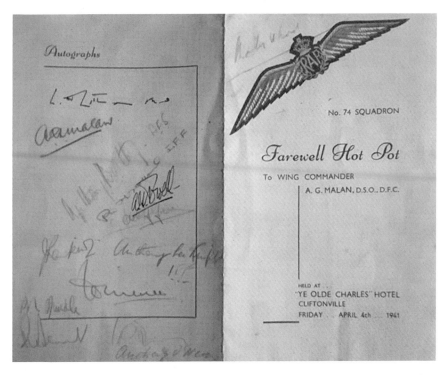

The menu from the dinner celebrating Sailor's promotion to Wing Commander, now in the author's archive. Amongst the pilots' signatures are those of Sailor Malan himself, Jamie Rankin, Anthony Bartley, Anthony Lee Knight, Bob Spurdle and Roland Beamont.

TEN of MY RULES for AIR FIGHTING.

1 Wait until you see the whites of his eyes.
    Fire short bursts of 1 to 2 seconds and only when your
sights are definitely 'ON'.

2 Whilst shooting think of nothing else, brace the whole of the
    body; have both hands on the stick, concentrate on your
ring sight.

3 Always keep a sharp lookout. "Keep your finger out"!

4 Height gives You the initiative.

5 Always turn and face the attack.

6 Make your decisions promptly. It is better to act quickly
    even though your tactics are not the best.

7 Never fly straight and level for more than 30 seconds in
    the combat area.

8 When diving to attack always leave a proportion of your
    formation above to act as top guard.

9 INITIATIVE, AGGRESSION, AIR DISCIPLINE, and
    TEAM WORK are words that MEAN something in
    Air Fighting.

10 Go in quickly – Punch hard – Get out!

Sailor Malan's 'Ten Rules for Air Fighting'.

Group Captain Malan
in his 'Super Spitfire' at
Biggin Hill.

Wing Commander Malan (fifth from left) and his New Zealander fighter ace friend
Squadron Leader Al Deere (to Sailor's left), with Lord Dowding and other Battle
of Britain survivors pictured in 1942 at what is believed to have been the first such
reunion dinner.

Group Captain Malan, cosy in woollen stockings for high altitude flying, in his personal Spitfire 'AGM' at Biggin Hill.

Group Captain Malan with his wife, Lynda, at the christening of their son, Jonathan, with Major John Churchill, brother of Winston, who was godfather.

Group Captain Malan at Biggin Hill in conversation with Squadron Leader Jack Charles (centre) and the Wing Leader, Wing Commander Al Deere.

Group Captain Malan, and 'Peter', with Wing Commander Dickie Milne, then Wing Leader, and Squadron Leader Bill Igoe.

Proud moment: Biggin Hill's 1,000th aerial victory. Group Captain Malan, the Station Commander, poses with pilots from the Wing, including the Wing Leader, Al Deere (to Sailor's left), and Squadron Leader Jack Charles (fifth from left) and Commandant René Mouchotte, who shared the historic kill.

Group Captain Malan in conversation with the Jamaican Flight Sergeant Vincent Bunting of 72 Squadron at Biggin Hill.

Group Captain Malan conferring with Squadron Leader 'Sinker' Armstrong, who would not survive the war.

D-Day: Group Captain Malan, looking cool in RAF sunglasses, with pilots of 145 Wing at Merston, including the ace Wing Commander Bill Crawford-Compton (extreme right in the group).

Group Captain Malan with Lynda and the children, Jonathan and Valerie, on return to Capetown in 1946.

Group Captain Malan, complete with iconic Irving flying jacket and medals, President of the Torch Commando.

Sailor Malan speaking at a Torch Commando rally.

The war hero speaks: Torch Commando.

Sailor Malan, the sheep farmer.

Above left, above right and below: The civic funeral of Group Captain Malan in Kimberley, 1963.

"Spread out and good hunting!"

'I saw the flight on either side of us slide away and each flight split into two pairs. Stephen and his No 2 lifted from below and behind me and climbed out to our port. I rechecked that my gun's safety catch was off. The gun-sight graticule glowed clearly and I lowered my seat a notch. Malan curved to meet the Huns head on and all at once we were into them.

'Yellow spinners, stiff square-tipped wings with sparkles of light flickering. I tried to follow my leader around but, being fascinated by the enemy aircraft, somehow I lost him. All at once I felt alone and frenzied with excitement. I couldn't find a single Jerry. Twisting and turning, I couldn't see a damned aircraft! Nothing! The sky was clean and bare. Far off, white contrails curved lazily this way and that. But I couldn't watch them. Where had everyone gone? It was no use horsing around up here, twisting from side to side, looking up, back and around, frantic with disappointment. I dived for the deck – orders were to go straight back if separated and there was no fight in one's vicinity.

'At 10,000 feet I formated alongside a Spit with its gun patches gone and smoke-stained wings. It was the CO! He looked at me and shook his fist. Automatically I lowered the undercarriage and, as the plane humped nose-down, Malan just turned away and slowly shook his head. I felt an awful fool but the clenched fist shaken (slowly and regularly) meant wheels down. Oh, we were well trained and obedient! Back at Biggin I was on the mat.

"Where the hell did you get to?"

"Sorry sir, I lost you in a turn."

"Clot! There were lots of targets! Better pull your finger out!"'

Spurdle's account provides a rare and atmospheric glimpse of one of those interceptions of high-flying Me 109s – and the confusion and excitement experienced by young pilots fresh to the fray. It is also evidence of Malan's uncompromising expectation of the required standards for 74 Squadron.

The following day was a quiet one, with only lone enemy aircraft intruding, and the 'Tigers' saw no action. On 17 October 1940, however, the enemy fighters and fighter-bombers swept over Kent, a total of 300 aircraft, in four waves. At 1510 hrs, the third of these raids, comprising four formations totalling around eighty aircraft, approached East London, Biggin Hill and Kenley, and Central London. 74 Squadron was scrambled at that time, as Sailor reported, and the enemy were met north of Ashford:

'I was leading Dysoe Squadron from Biggin Hill and took off at 1510 hrs to intercept fighter raids heading towards London.

111

'I climbed mostly on an up-sun course to 26,000 feet and flew towards AA bursts over the Thames Estuary.

'At approximately 1530 hrs, we suddenly saw two yellow noses (Me 109s) crossing our bows and surprised them from the sun. I gave the righthand one a two second burst with quarter deflection from 200 yards and closed to 150 yards astern, and delivered another two second burst. I then closed to 100 yards and delivered a four second burst which appeared to damage elevator controls as his nose went vertically downwards very suddenly, instead of the usual half-roll.

'My engine naturally stopped when I followed suit but it picked up again and I closed to 150 yards on half-roll and gave another four second burst.

'I found myself doing an aileron turn to keep direction and delivered another four second burst. He then started to smoke but I blacked out completely and lost consciousness for a couple of seconds, and eventually pulled out at 9,000 feet above 10/10ths cloud.

'My port guns failed to fire during the whole engagement.'

The 109 was claimed as a probable. The 'Tigers' also claimed three more German fighters destroyed and another probable – but Flying Officer Alan Ricalton had been shot down and killed, his Spitfire crashing at Hollingbourne, possibly the victim of Feldwebel Eduard Koslowski of 8/JG53, the 26-year old officer was buried at Sittingbourne. Flying Officer Ricalton – another Battle veteran of the Fall of France – had been amongst the first batch of replacement pilots posted to 74 Squadron at Wittering, and had sadly been lost in his first combat. As Wing Commander Roger Boulding said, who joined the 'Tigers' with Ricalton, 'There but for the grace of God...' Flying Officer Ricalton was 74 Squadron's first casualty during this tour of duty at Biggin Hill – but not the last.

The 17th of October 1940 also proved significant owing to a particular meeting held that day at Fighter Command HQ.

Owing to the fuss made by Air Vice-Marshal Leigh-Mallory and his subordinate Squadron Leader Douglas Bader regarding the supposed superiority and effectiveness of 'Big Wing' formations, certain high-ranking officers and politicians had been persuaded that the tactics employed for Air Chief Marshal Dowding and Air Vice-Marshal Park were inferior. On 14 October 1940, Air Vice-Marshal D.F. Stevenson, Deputy Director of Home Operations, prepared an 'Air Staff Note on the Operation of Fighter Wings' for the Deputy CAS, Air Vice-Marshal Sholto Douglas. Based on Air Vice-Marshal Leigh-Mallory's report of 17 September 1940, this amounted to a critique of the tactics employed by 11 Group. The fact is, however, that Air Vice-Marshal Park was not averse to using wing formations – in the right circumstances. His experience, though, had confirmed that these large formations had only proved successful in intercepting the enemy when a third wave of enemy fighters was incoming, and only if the squadrons involved climbed to height independently before joining up. Moreover, Park pointed out to Stevenson that his Air Staff Note was 'based upon the experience of 12 Group on the five occasions in which they have reinforced my Group. We in 11 Group used wings of three squadrons in May, June, July, August and September, and are still using them when conditions of time, space and weather make them effective.' The 11 Group commander also emphasized that 'Duxford roving wings caused considerable confusion to London defences and prolonged Air Raid Warnings through wandering uninvited and unannounced over East Kent after retreat of enemy.' The problem was that the Duxford Wing's combat claims had been accepted, surely with little scrutiny, providing the impression that the 'Big Wing' was infinitely more successful than 11 Group's generally – but not exclusively – much smaller formations. We know now, of course, following years of painstaking analysis by post-war researchers, that the Duxford Wing's claims were wildly exaggerated and that 11 Group had in fact got it right. What was happening now, however, was a determined assault by Leigh-Mallory and his influential supporters to push through wing formations as standard operating procedure.

On 17 October 1940, a meeting took place in the Air Council room, attended by Air Chief Marshal Dowding, his 10, 11 and 12 Group commanders, the DCAS, and a host of officers of air rank. Also present was Squadron Leader Douglas Bader – much to his AOC's astonishment. It immediately became clear to Dowding and Park that the purpose of the meeting was to push through the use of wings as standard, regardless of their evidenced argument in favour of flexibility. Beforehand, Dowding had placed little importance on the meeting, feeling that the enemy's tactics had changed so much as to make pointless the use of big wings in defence. It must have rapidly dawned on Dowding that the meeting's aim was not looking ahead – but a post mortem on Fighter Command tactics and that both he and Park were being called to account. Squadron Leader Bader related his experience of leading the Duxford Wing – but neither Air Vice-Marshals Park nor Brand, the latter AOC 10 Group, which had cooperated perfectly with neighbouring 11 Group, had been invited to bring one of their squadron commanders.

Although 74 Squadron had been resting in 12 Group for a few weeks, Squadron Leader Malan would have been an obvious choice to share his experience of fighting in 11 Group. That neither Park or Brand were invited to bring a squadron commander, and indeed not even Dowding knew that Bader would be present, tells us all we need to know about that infamous meeting. Interestingly, Sailor was invited, around that time, to join Air Chief Marshal Dowding on two lunches at Chartwell, Churchill's home close to Biggin Hill. According to Walker, the conversation largely concerned beating the German night offensive, although Sailor recalled that 'most of the time I let the others talk… just sitting gulping and sipping according to whether the Prime Minister looked my way or not.' Churchill had requested that Dowding bring along 'one of your able lieutenants who will talk freely'. It can be assumed, I feel sure, that Squadron Leader Malan would also have spoken 'freely' in the Air Council Room.

As it turned out, various comments on the subsequent minutes by Dowding, Park and Brand were not added to the record. There is no question, then, that Air Vice-Marshals Douglas and Leigh-Mallory had orchestrated the meeting purely to cement, going forward, mass fighter formations as Fighter Command's standard defensive and offensive method. Very soon this would have direct consequences for every pilot in Fighter Command – not least Squadron Leader Sailor Malan.

Five days later, Sailor was back in action. On 22 October 1940, after the usual morning reconnaissance incursions, two fighter sweeps were incoming, one over Kent, the other heading towards south-east London and the Thames Estuary. Sailor reported:

'At 1340 hrs I led Dysoe (74) Squadron with nine aircraft to 15,000 feet over Maidstone.

'We were then given various vectors for single high raiders but did not connect.

'We were then told to join 92 Squadron at 32,000 feet over Maidstone and intercept raids approaching from south and south-east.

'I stayed at 30,000 feet for a while in order to push out exhaust condensation trail to frighten the bomb carriers.

'I then connected with 92 Squadron over Maidstone and came down to 28,000 feet to stop exhaust trail.

'Over Ashford at 28,000 feet, 92 gave a "Tally Ho" below and circled, but I could see nothing. I then proceeded on vector 270° as ordered but did not connect and came back towards Ashford to join 92 Squadron.

'Suddenly, at approximately 1410 hrs I saw six Me 109s just below at 26,000 feet, steering SE and attacked with my five remaining aircraft

(Yellow Leader had gone down with oxygen leak and Yellow 2 had followed him), Yellow 3 and Red 2 having dropped back earlier as they could not keep up and told to land.

'I attacked a leading Me 109 in a fast dive at ranges from 200 to 50 yards. He started to smoke heavily after second burst but levelled out at 8,000 feet on south westerly course. I continued to fire at him intermittently because he wouldn't go down, and I had to break off unexpectedly to wipe ice layer off armour windscreen.

'Eventually he crossed the coast on southerly course at Hastings. I patrolled coast and watched smoke trail.

'About one mile off coast smoke trail suddenly went down and I saw a splash. I returned through lack of petrol and bad visibility.'

This Me 109 was credited as destroyed. This aircraft belonged to 3/JG51 and was flown by Leutnant Kurt Müller, who baled-out and was rescued by the Hastings lifeboat, spending the rest of the war as a prisoner. Malan's No 2, the comparatively inexperienced Pilot Officer Bob Spurdle, also survived being shot down and baling out, but sadly the popular Flying Officer Peter St John was killed. Interestingly, the only enemy victory claims that afternoon were by JG51's famous Kommodore, Major Werner Mölders, who claimed three 'Hurricanes' north-west of Maidstone, one minute apart. Without doubt, the '*Oberkanone*'s' victims were Spurdle and St John.

The patrols countering the high-altitude fighter-bomber threat went on, relentlessly, but, beyond doubt, especially with the turning weather, it was obvious that the threat of invasion had passed. The home team had won the critical contest by keeping Britain's shores free of the would-be invader and thereby maintaining the island as a base from which war could continue to be waged against Hitler's Germany. Ultimately, with American help, the liberation of enemy-occupied Europe was eventually launched.

According to officialdom, the Battle of Britain concluded, after sixteen weeks, on 31 October 1940 – not that Fighter Command noticed, because there was no abrupt end to the fighting (as films like the 1969 epic *Battle of Britain* would have us believe). Indeed the clashes between the opposing fighter forces continued unabated, as we will see, for some time yet, as did the night-bombing. Nonetheless, during that summer and autumn of infinite stakes and immense drama, 544 of these young airmen lost their lives in action – amongst them twelve 'Tigers'.

Sailor:

'Fear and intense physical danger and the discomfort of battle was more than compensated by the very positive feelings nearly all of us had of satisfaction at being the only human beings able to stand between Hitler and world freedom. We knew that any day we might be shot down to death, but I will swear this feeling of being the only spearhead, the only instrument between German domination and democracy, was the one that kept us going and beat the Luftwaffe. It gave us an elation that transcended all else.'

By the Battle of Britain's official end, Sailor's personal score stood at fourteen destroyed, six probables and another half-dozen damaged. This was important. The measure of a fighter pilot, at least to the public and as a propaganda tool, was how many aircraft he had destroyed. Up there in the burning blue, as Sailor himself said, it was RAF aircrews who were able to fight back – and were very much centre stage. The Germans were a formidable and unbeaten foe – and the propagandists sought to give public morale hope and heart by continually emphasizing that the RAF was shooting down more aircraft than it was losing. Churchill himself argued that the enemy's prowess should be praised, exaggerated even, to make the British effort appear an even greater achievement. Back then, the newspapers reported the daily score similarly to a cricket test match, although radio was the greatest medium for sharing news. The public saw the RAF fighter pilots and aircrews as glamorous heroes, and the BBC – central to British propaganda – lost no time in broadcasting accounts from fighter pilots. During this early war period, those newspaper reports and broadcasts were anonymous, the Air Ministry's policy being not to promote individuals, except when naming decorations or casualties, wishing to avoid a situation whereby morale could unduly suffer if reports concentrated on one or two fighter 'aces', the rest overlooked. Indeed, Sir Kingsley Wood, Secretary of State for Air, was clear that fighter pilots were part of the RAF, and the service as a whole is what was important to promote. The fighter ace, then, was a weapon in combat and in the propaganda war, tales of pilots' derring-do bolstering pubic confidence and morale. And Squadron Leader Sailor Malan, a squadron commander with a double DFC, was a well-known figure throughout the RAF – and to the public a star, albeit an anonymous South African one.

Chapter Twelve

'Reaching Out'

On 1 November 1940, 74 Squadron was again in action, this time losing two Spitfires badly shot up and both pilots wounded, and, worse, Flying Officer Nelson DFC killed by JG26's high-flying Me 109s. Sailor was not flying that day, but led 74 Squadron the following day, in company with 92 Squadron, again meeting German fighters over Kent and the Channel; four 109s were subsequently claimed destroyed by the 'Tigers', for no loss, but the CO was not amongst those making combat claims. Having taken some well-earned leave, Sailor also missed out on 14 November 1940, when 74 Squadron, in the CO's absence, engaged Me 109s of JG26 and III/JG51 escorting Ju 87s attacking a convoy off Dover; the 'Tigers' subsequently claimed the destruction of fourteen Stukas, provoking a barbed congratulatory telegram: 'Congratulations you rats – Sailor.' In reality, only two StG1 Stukas were destroyed, and in response the escorting enemy fighters shot down Pilot Officer Armstrong of 74 Squadron, who baled out over the coast.

On 23 November 1940, Sailor scored again, when, having pursued his quarry back to the French coast, he destroyed another 109, emptying all his ammunition into the target from just fifty yards. Four days later Sailor attacked another from very close range, blowing that 109 literally out of the sky, shot down another and damaged a third, leaving Squadron Leader Wilson (on secondment to the 'Tigers' from the Royal Aircraft Establishment, Farnborough) to finish the job – further evidence of Sailor focusing on the bigger picture and not selfishly on his personal score. Sailor commented:

'It's a nice after dinner story. That's all. I did once chase a Jerry down who was doing a terrific power dive after I had given him what I thought was a fatal burst. I followed him down so hard and fast it wasn't till he hit the water with a smack that I realized the pilot was dead, and I had to straighten out if I didn't want to join him very suddenly.'

Significantly, while acknowledging that the RAF was 'never short of publicity', of tactics Sailor said, 'Fighting is all teamwork. It's a good idea that we don't have ballyhoo'ed aces now. All we want is to ground Jerry – and that can't be done by individuals.' Geoffrey Flavell, who knew Sailor and other 74 Squadron pilots while a surgeon at Southend, recalled a conversation with Squadron Leader Malan:

'"Tell me Sailor, as a matter of technical interest, how exactly do you go about shooting down a bomber?"

"I try not to now."

"Whatever do you mean?"

"Well, I think it's a bad thing."

"Now, come on, Sailor, I really want to know. Don't trifle with me."

"I mean it. I think it's a thoroughly bad thing. You see, if you shoot them down they don't get back and no-one in Germany is a whit the wiser. So I figure the right thing to do is let them get back. With a dead rear gunner; a dead navigator, and the pilot coughing his lungs up in his hands… I think if you do that it has a better effect on their morale… That's what I want to aim at now. Of course, if you just mean to shoot them down, well what I generally do when I get on their tail is flick her port and starboard, with a burst each way, and knock out port and starboard engines. But, honestly, Doc, the other way is best."'

As Sailor said, 'They called me a cold, ruthless, calculating killer.' Of course, firing at a machine, not a man, high in the 'sunlit silence', Sailor never saw the men he killed.

In one interview, Sailor explained:

'There are certain qualities a fighter pilot must have, or he won't get away with it. In the First World War fighting in the air was largely a matter of individual courage. Flying ability and good shooting helped, but usually the aces were men who waited until they got in close and took terrific chances. It is different now. Courage these days is a minor talent. No man is braver than the next. The civilian fighters in London – the air raid wardens in Coventry or Plymouth – these men do things under fire which we fighter pilots can only regard with awe. A fighter pilot doesn't have to show that kind of courage. Unreasoning, unintelligent blind courage is, in fact, a tremendous handicap to him. He has to be cold when he's fighting. He fights with his head, not his heart. There are three things a first-class fighter pilot must have. First, he must have an aggressive nature. He must at all times be the attacker. It is against the nature of a Spitfire to run away. Second, both his mind and body must be alert and both must react instinctively to any tactical situation. When you are fighting you have no time to think. Third, he must have good eyes and clean hands and feet. His hands and feet control his plane and they must be sensitive. He can't be ham-handed. When your Spitfire is ambling along at 390 mph a too-heavy hand on the stick or a too-heavy foot on the rudder will send you into an inadvertent and very embarrassing spin. Your hands, your feet, your mind, your instinct must function as well whether you're right side up or upside down.'

To Basil Cardew of the *Daily Express*, Sailor said:

'We don't have much time to think. A scrap lasts, at the outside, two minutes. When you are up there, you're in another world. You see England, and bits of France stretching down below. You hear a roar and you know someone's gone down, or there are fireworks about. Knocking down the Hun is a foxy business. You've got to let 'em go sometimes, and get 'em the next day. The Hun won't always fight. He swoops down from a height, gives you a burst, and puts his nose down hard for home. He goes for stragglers. He won't join in a dog-fight.

'In the last five weeks we have pushed them back about thirty miles. They used to come all over Kent. Now they stop and are stopped over the coast. Their tactics now seem daft to us. Their Me 109s scamper over with a few light bombs and drop them anywhere – most times in the fields. Their fighters make their way across flying as high as they can like lost sheep. We would leave them alone for all the damage they do. But if we did, the artful devils might try to come down and machine-gun the ground.'

Sailor Malan was a consummate professional, totally dedicated to his mission as a fighter pilot and leader. According to 92 Squadron, which shared Biggin Hill with the 'Tigers', Malan kept 'his boys in order at the point of a pistol'. Malan's response was that given how casual and ill-disciplined 92 was, 74 Squadron could beat both Galland and Mölders' fighter groups 'single-handedly'. Indeed, according to Sailor, all he had to do was 'Kick their arses once a day and I have the toughest bunch in Fighter Command' – but he acknowledged that compared to 92, 74 Squadron was 'more mediocre... but made fewer mistakes'. Of the air-fighting at this time, he wrote: 'We reckon that for each sortie we make, each man should bring down four planes. That's our target. We don't do it, of course, but it's no use going for only one man then coming home. Nor is it any use firing all your ammunition into one Jerry. We are not so hard-pushed now. Jerry had his tail up once. Now he's got it well down. We don't think he has a chance of putting it up again.'

Change at the top in Fighter Command was very much in the air, now that the Battle of Britain crisis had passed. On 25 November 1940, Air Chief Marshal Dowding was succeeded by Air Chief Marshal William Sholto Douglas – a primary supporter of the Big Wing. More change would soon follow.

On 30 November 1940 there was cause for celebration at Biggin Hill: in bad weather, Flight Lieutenant John Mungo-Park and Pilot Officer 'Steve' Steven shot down an Me 109 of 5/JG53, which crashed at Ham Street, Kent – becoming the famous fighter station's 600th kill. During November 1940 alone, 74 Squadron had contributed twenty-six enemy aircraft to 11 Group's tally, according to the ORB, and 'topped the list'. This is clear evidence of the morale and efficiency of 'Tiger' Squadron – for which Squadron Leader Malan was largely responsible.

Still, however, in spite of worsening winter weather, while the night bombers pulverized British cities, by day the enemy's fighter sweeps continued. On 2 December 1940, Sailor scored again, reporting that at 1210 hrs:

'I was "Knockout Leader" and following 66 Squadron on patrol of Maidstone at 15,000 feet.

'Patrol proceeded to Dover – Dungeness to intercept thirty enemy aircraft at 24,000 feet. Crossed coast Dover – Dungeness. 66 Squadron at 24,000 feet, 74 Squadron at 27,000 feet. 66 Squadron turned north, but I led my Squadron to the south on sighting groups of Me 109s flying northwards onto our starboard quarter. Enemy aircraft continued past in fast dive as we met them almost head-on. I ordered Yellow Section to attack the leading groups and turned onto one of the later groups with Red Section. I glued onto tail of one E/A which turned SE, into sun, going flat-out. Opened fire during dive at 300 yards, closing to 100 yards and he started to smoke heavily. He flattened out at 1,000 feet and pulled up into sun, slowing down. At 5,000 feet I gave a long burst at 50 yards from port quarter and astern and was covered in oil as E/A continued in gentle dive. I saw the hood and what appeared to be the dinghy flash by to starboard. I flew behind for another 30 seconds when E/A slowly turned on its back and went in inverted. I do not believe the pilot got out. Position approximately 10-15 miles 160° from Dungeness.'

On 18 December 1940, Air Vice-Marshal Park was replaced as AOC 11 Group by Air Vice-Marshal Leigh-Mallory, previously AOC 12 Group and, with Squadron Leader Bader and Duxford's Station Commander, Wing Commander A.B. 'Woody' Woodhall, cause of the Big Wing trouble. Eighty years on, historians remain divided over the treatment of both Dowding and Park, the true victors of our 'Finest Hour'. Some argue that both Dowding and Park had made political enemies, and that the Big Wing controversy provided a means of removing them, others that their replacement was simply because Dowding's retirement was already overdue and Park, unsurprisingly, was tired. Another view is that Dowding's inability to deal with German night attacks was his downfall, and that with the Battle of Britain over a change in command – ready to fight a more offensive battle – was naturally required. The truth, very likely, includes elements of all these things – but whatever the actual facts, mass fighter formations would soon become standard, and a significant reorganisation of Fighter Command would soon take place. On 20 December 1940, Flight Lieutenant Christie and Pilot Officer Bodie of 66 Squadron crossed the Channel at low level and attacked the enemy airfield at either Berck or Le Touquet – a inconsequential operation but which set the scene for the New Year; 1941 would see a drastic change in policy: instead of continuing to fight a defensive battle, Fighter Command would soon be going on the offensive. Air Chief Marshal Douglas reported on these far-reaching plans:

'Broadly speaking the plan, which we now adopted, visualized two kinds of offensive operations. In cloudy weather, small numbers of fighters would cross the Channel under cover of the clouds, dart out of them to attack any German aircraft they could find, and return similarly protected. In good weather fighter forces amounting to several squadrons at a time, and sometimes accompanied by bombers, would sweep over Northern France. The codenames chosen for these operations were respectively "Mosquito" (later changed to "Rhubarb" to avoid confusion with the aircraft of that name) and "Circus"; but in practice it was necessary to restrict the name "Circus" to operations with bombers, and fulfilling certain other conditions…

'Rhubarb patrols began on 20 December 1940, and provided valuable experience alike for pilots, operational commanders, and the staffs of the formations concerned. I encouraged the delegation of responsibility for the planning of these patrols to lower formations, and many patrols were planned by the pilots themselves with the help of their Squadron Intelligence Officers.'

'SAILOR' MALAN – FREEDOM FIGHTER

On 21 December 1940, Fighter Command published a list naming its highest-scoring fighter pilots – Squadron Leader Malan being seventh, with eighteen destroyed. This was clearly a change in policy, in that the aces were no longer anonymous, although the legless Douglas Bader had been named in the press as early on as 15 July 1940. Vital to maintaining the morale of a population subjected to air attack was news of enemy losses – to which, of course, the fighter pilot, already glamourised by Great War exploits, was key. The fighter boys were now heroes of the hour – and the aces public property. On the same day Fighter Command's list was published, for example, Flight Lieutenant Mungo-Park and Pilot Officer Stephen – the latter fifth on Fighter Command's list, with twenty kills – made a morale-boosting visit to the Castle Bromwich Aircraft Factory, talking to workers building Spitfires. For Squadron Leader Malan, a special gift arrived that day, a Javanese statuette from the Dutch East Indies. Sailor too was now a household name. The following day, two leading war artists, Eric Kennington and Cuthbert Orde, were commissioned to produce portraits of Malan, Mungo-Park and Stephen. Of Sailor, Orde wrote:

'All would agree that Sailor is the outstanding pilot fighter of the war… I have seldom been more impressed by anyone than by him the first time I saw him. A very strong face, a very quiet manner and an air of authority made it obvious that here was a leader of great determination and ability… He is married and has a son… I mention this because when I was painting him he told me that having a wife and son had been the greatest moral help to him during the Battle of Britain; that it had been an absolute defining thing to fight for and defend and that this was his constant thought.

'I do not think Malan could join a squadron without improving it, no matter how good it was. Not by sword-waving but by strength of mind and integrity that are at once recognizable and effective. Don't imagine from this that he never laughs; but he has a serious mind and is intent on winning the war.'

Orde's appraisal is a great accolade – because he drew and painted virtually all of Fighter Command's leading lights.

On 24 December 1940, Squadron Leader Malan was appointed to the DSO; his citation read:

'This officer has commanded his Squadron with outstanding success over an intensive period of air operations and, by his brilliant leadership, skill and determination has contributed largely to the success obtained. Since early August 1940, the Squadron has destroyed at least eighty-four enemy aircraft and damaged many more. Squadron Leader Malan has himself destroyed at least eighteen hostile aircraft and possibly another six.'

Back home in Cape Town, Sailor's parents attended the unveiling of John Mansbridge's portrait of their famous son, the Mayor's speech urging Afrikaners to support the war effort – on which subject there were divisions, so deep did hatred and resentment of the British still go in some quarters. Also present at the prestigious ceremony were Sailor's brothers, both sergeants at the time, Stanley in the South African Union Army, and Ralph in the South African Air Force; brother Francis was in England, training to be a fighter pilot, while Pieter was too young to enlist. Little wonder that the press dubbed the serving brothers 'The Fighting Malans'. Their father, Willie, made clear the Malans' stance: 'We are proud of them all. Proud of the successes they gain; proud of the distinction, if any, that is theirs but prouder still that they have seen what they consider to be their duty, and, in this light, are doing it.' While fighter aces were essential to maintaining the morale of a people being bombed, Sailor was equally an instrument in South Africa's internal propaganda war.

Not all Afrikaners felt the same call however. On 4 February 1939, anti-British and pro-German Boer militants had founded the *Ossewabrandwag*, opposing South African participation in any war on British side, the ultimate aim of which was achieving, by force if necessary, an Afrikaner-controlled republic in South Africa. Membership of the 'OB' peaked in 1941 at hundreds of thousands of mainly young Afrikaner males, who refused to enlist and openly harassed servicemen, culminating in a large-scale riot occurring in Johannesburg in 1941. The embodiment of Afrikaner nationalism, though, which was not necessarily or entirely pro-Hitler, pro-Nazi, anti-Semitic or pro-German victory, was the 'Purified National Party', led by Daniel Francois Malan – a distant relation of Sailor's family. The OB went too far, however, in forming a paramilitary unit actively engaged in sabotage against the Union government, leading to D.F. Malan distancing his Nationalist Party in 1942. That said, within the Nationalist Party was a splinter movement called 'New Order', calling for South African society to be remodelled along Nazi lines. To some Afrikaners, sympathetic to Britain, the 'Fighting Malans' were therefore patriotic heroes – to others, traitors. Nonetheless, at no time did this vexing schism in their own society prevent the Malans from doing what they firmly believed was their duty – come what may and whatever the cost.

Far away, Squadron Leader Malan was poised to lead the 'Tigers' back into action – but was not without reservations about Fighter Command's new policy. Air Vice-Marshal Leigh-Mallory called a meeting of his squadron commanders at 11 Group HQ, impressing upon them the new policy of 'Leaning into France' and taking the war to the enemy. Sailor interrupted the AOC, pointing out that this plan of luring the enemy fighters up for destruction en-masse – which the Germans themselves had failed to do to Fighter Command the previous summer – was 'trying to achieve the impossible'. This, Leigh-Mallory – who had no personal fighter experience whatsoever and was obsessed with the Big Wing concept – did not want to hear from a fighter leader of Sailor's stature. After the meeting the AOC took the South African ace aside, rebuking him for his outspoken opinion and blaming operational fatigue as the cause. No effort was made at this time to actually rest Sailor, who pressed on. Of this time, Air Chief Marshal Douglas wrote:

'It was a tough job as the Germans had a very powerful fighter force in the Pas-de-Calais… and we were deliberately choosing to take them on their own ground. Sailor Malan's tactical ability and advice were invaluable to his Group Commander, Leigh-Mallory, and to myself in planning the tactics of these fighter sweeps. In fact, I would say that apart from his great courage, tactical ability and judgement were his outstanding characteristics. These allied to a cheerful and charming personality, made him perhaps the best of our fighter leaders in the early part of the war.'

On 10 January, 74 Squadron participated in 11 Group's first 'Circus'. These were complex operations. Whereas a 'Mosquito'/'Rhubarb' could be planned at squadron level, because of the large number of aircraft involved from various groups, a Circus had to be organised by Fighter Command. The object was that a swarm of fighters would escort a small number of medium bombers to attack a target in Northern France. The fighter squadrons would be deployed thus:

Close Escort: Surrounding and remaining with the bombers at all times.

Escort Cover: Protecting the Close Escort fighters.

High Cover: Preventing enemy fighters getting between the Close and Escort wings.

Target Support: Independently routed fighters flying directly to and covering the target area.

Withdrawal Cover: Fighters supporting the return flight, by which time escorting fighters would be running short of fuel and ammunition.

Fighter Diversion: A wing, or even wings, eventually, creating a diversionary sweep to keep hostile aircraft from the target area during 'Ramrod' operations, this being similar to a Circus but involving the destruction of a specific target.

Circus No 1 was despatched against ammunition supplies hidden in the Forêt de Guines. Blenheims of 114 Squadron were closely escorted by the Hurricanes of 56 Squadron, forward support being provided by the North Weald Hurricane squadrons: 242 and 249. 302 Squadron's Hurricanes and 610 Squadron's Spitfires flew target support; the Spitfires of 41, 64 and 611 Squadrons were high cover, and finally 74 and 92 Squadrons' Spitfires brought up the rear. This represented some 120 fighters and six bombers, and was a complete reversal of the defensive role previously undertaken by Fighter Command – and was an offensive one for which Hurricanes and Spitfires, intended as short-range interceptors, were not designed or intended. It was Fighter Command's pilots who now faced a two-way Channel crossing on a single engine with limited fuel, and combat either over the sea or enemy-occupied territory. On this initial operation, I and II/JG 53 responded and engaged the RAF fighters: one Hurricane and a Spitfire were destroyed for no German loss – rather setting the scene for the 'season' ahead. On this historic operation, Sailor had led 74 Squadron on a sweep of Cap Gris-Nez and Calais, diving on but failing to catch several Me 109s flying singly. Perhaps ominously, back at Biggin Hill a Captain Bennett of MI9 lectured the 'Tiger' Squadron pilots on 'escaping'.

While mass formations were now being employed in an offensive capacity, Air Vice-Marshal Leigh-Mallory remained determined to prove their worth in a defensive role. On 29 January 1941 he conducted a paper exercise. Using the circumstances of an actual attack made on the sector stations of Kenley and Biggin Hill on 6 September 1940, the new AOC 11 Group orchestrated an experiment to prove the great worth of large fighter formations in defence. The enemy 'raid', however, was not intercepted while inbound and bombed both target airfields. Leigh-Mallory's fighters never even got off the ground.

Circus No 2 went ahead on 2 February 1941, Blenheims of 139 Squadron targeting Boulogne docks. The Intelligence Report from the Biggin Hill Squadrons relates events:

'12 Spitfires of 66 Squadron and 12 Spitfires of 74 Squadron took off from Biggin Hill at 1325 hrs to meet 92 Squadron over West Malling at 10,000 feet before sweeping from Dungeness to Boulogne.

'66 Squadron, after making the indicated rendezvous ran into the cloud at 15,000 feet in mid-Channel and Blue Section became detached. They made three sweeps from Boulogne to Cap Gris-Nez and back, then patrolled Calais-Dunkirk and back at 19,000 feet but saw no E/A. Flak seen in Calais area and light flak bursting at 6-10,000 feet was seen. No balloons were seen. 66 Squadron landed at Biggin Hill by 1450 hrs.

'74 Squadron swept Boulogne at 19,000 feet and sighted six Me 109s in that area, slightly beneath them flying north-east. Squadron Leader Malan dived to attack 4 Me 109s which he sighted at 12,000 feet flying north, opening fire from astern and above at 300 yards, closing to 200 yards, he delivered two 4 second bursts. The E/A had dived and Squadron Leader Malan broke away at 4,000 feet, watching the Me 109 dive into the sea just outside Boulogne Harbour. His engine developed a glycol leak, but he nursed it back to Hawkinge, landing at 1430 hrs.

'Meanwhile, Sergeant Payne, Red 1, made a quarter attack on one E/A with a 3 second burst from 600 yards, resulting in the E/A diving steeply emitting blue smoke from the engine. Red 1 dived after him, giving a further 6 second burst, and closing to 50 yards he saw some bullets striking the water and then pulled out to avoid hitting the sea. P/O Chesters confirms that this E/A crashed into the sea in flames about five miles NW Boulogne. P/O Smith turned after an Me 109 which had passed under Red Section, going North, whereupon the enemy aircraft turned steeply to starboard. P/O Smith was inside his turn and opened fire at about 200 yards, continuing to fire until he had closed right up. He last saw the Me 109 at a height of 1,000 feet, diving steeply towards the sea. P/O Spurdle, Yellow 3, reports that he saw a large splash and a cloud of brownish smoke in the area in approximately this position, so a probably destroyed casualty is claimed by P/O Smith.'

Squadron Leader E.J.C. Michelmore, attached to 74 Squadron as supernumerary and flying as Sailor's No 2, was missing.

At 1320 hrs the following day, Sailor led two sections to patrol Dover at 10,000 feet:

'I was Knockout Red Leader… when one bandit was reported to be approaching coast between Dover and Folkestone at 4,000 feet. I dived inland to below 10/10ths cloud with base at 3,000 feet and spotted Do 215 at 2,000 feet, turning South off Dover.

'E/A made no attempt to enter cloud and was much slower than other Do 215s I have previously attacked. I approached from below on zig-zag course and closed to 150 yards before opening fire from below with deflection. Rear gunner opened fire at 400 yards and I received hit in spinner and port mainplane. Delivered several bursts from 150 yards to 50 yards and saw rounds pouring into engines and fuselage and chunks flying off. I broke away and delivered beam to quarter attack as No 2 attacked from astern. I finished up in astern position at 50 yards as my ammunition ran out.

'Yellow Section then attacked and E/A dived into sea on course for Calais.

'NB: I got the impression that this E/A was sent out specially to test new armour plating which appeared to be very effective from rear fire. I believe the rear gunner remained unharmed when I broke away as Yellow Leader was also fired upon.'

Little did the enemy gunner know that his rounds had hit a Spitfire flown by the RAF's greatest fighter leader of the period. Although unknown to Squadron Leader Malan, this would actually be the last German bomber he would engage, and his final kill as a 'Tiger', the victory being shared equally between the four pilots involved.

By this time, plans were afoot for all sector stations to accommodate a wing of three fighter squadrons. The Big Wing experience had indicated that such a formation required an overall leader, so it was therefore decided to create a new post: Wing Commander (Flying). In this new role, the wing leader was cut loose from day-to-day administration and able to concentrate purely on operational flying. Air Vice-Marshal Johnnie Johnson, officially the RAF's top-scoring fighter pilot of the Second World War, commented:

'The appointment "Wing Commander (Flying)" was every fighter pilot's dread job. Cut loose from administration and all the other ground-borne onerous tasks associated with command, the Wing Leader could just get on with leading his wing in action. Wing leaders' aircraft had their initials painted on the fuselage, for ease of identification in the air, when I was leading the Canadian wings my Spitfire's, of course, being "JE-J". To see one's initials painted on a Spitfire's fuselage was a very great thing, the epitome of a fighter pilot's career, really.'

On 7 December 1940, Air Vice-Marshal Leigh-Mallory had drawn up a short-list of potential wing leaders: predictably his favourite, the newsworthy Squadron Leader Douglas Bader, was the first name on it. Early in March 1941, Bader was summoned by Leigh-Mallory who revealed these plans. Fighter Command's two foremost stations were Biggin Hill and Tangmere, the latter situated on the south coast near Chichester. Bader was given the choice of either. Biggin Hill, he thought, was far too close to the social distractions of London. He chose Tangmere; Sailor Malan got Biggin Hill – arguably the RAF's premier fighter station.

And so it was that on 10 March 1941, Wing Commander A.G. Malan DSO DFC handed over 74 Squadron to the equally newly promoted Squadron Leader John Mungo-Park DFC, and became the new Biggin Hill Wing's first Wing Leader, his new command comprising 74, 92 and 609 Squadrons.

At the end of March 1941, the Air Ministry published another list of the top-scoring aces. Ranked first was Pilot Officer James 'Ginger' Lacey, who had flown Hurricanes with distinction during the Battle of France and Britain, with twenty-three victories; sixth was Sailor Malan, accredited with twenty.

Sailor's appointment as Biggin Hill Wing Leader heralded the start of a new and relentless period of offensive operations, for which Sailor would need all his skill and energy – and during which he would redefine that list of aces.

Chapter Thirteen

Biggin Hill: Wing Leader

Air Vice-Marshal Leigh-Mallory considered that, having survived the Luftwaffe onslaught of summer 1940, Fighter Command was now in a position to be 'cocky', dubbing his new policy of 'leaning into France' the 'Non-stop Offensive'. In not too long, the Germans would have another name for it: the 'Non-sense Offensive'. Nonetheless, Sailor Malan was now Wing Leader at Biggin Hill and these were stirring times indeed, considering that only a few months previously Fighter Command had been on the back foot. As Air Chief Marshal Douglas acknowledged, however, the enemy coast was defended by a formidable foe – so yet again the scene was set for derring-do.

From Fighter Command's perspective the object of the exercise was to draw German fighters to battle, and to do so, as the Germans had found during the Battle of Britain, that meant mounting heavily escorted daylight bombing raids which the enemy could not ignore. Certainly there were plenty of targets in north-west France – German airfields, railway marshalling yards and other communications centres, distilleries, factories supporting the German war effort and much-else besides – but nothing that was going to strategically cripple Germany. Consequently the defending German fighters could pick and choose when and where to attack the RAF 'Beehive', that mass of fighters escorting, usually, a few Blenheims – and did so only when the tactical circumstances were favourable. As Sailor had mentioned before, the enemy fighter pilots knew better than to hang around dogfighting; having the height advantage, it was all about ambushing an unsuspecting enemy in a high-speed diving pass – and away – famously dubbed the 'Dirty dart' by 19 Squadron's Sergeant (later Wing Commander) David Cox, who also remembered what an odd sight it was on one occasion to see '200 Spitfires escorting ONE Stirling!'.

Importantly, by late 1940 the Spitfire Mk II equipped all front-line Fighter Command squadrons. The Mk IIA remained machine-gun-armed, but by early 1941 Mk IIBs were appearing, enjoying the benefit, at last, of four machine guns and two 20mm cannon. There was, however, some difference of opinion over whether the cannon was as advantageous as believed. Certainly the destructive power of a 20mm round compared to the comparatively puny rifle-calibre bullet of a machine gun was indisputable, but the debate revolved around the accuracy required to score hits. Eight machine guns harmonized at 250 yards produced a shotgun type effect, spraying the sky with so many bullets that some at least were likely to find their mark. The cannon's slower rate of fire required greater accuracy – and not all fighter pilots were as gifted a shot as the likes of Sailor Malan. Wing Commander Douglas Bader at Tangmere favoured machine guns for that reason, and because he argued that the cannon's greater power would encourage pilots to open fire from too far away. Typically the headstrong Bader never changed his mind. Sailor and the others persevered with the cannon, the worth of which was proven. The cannon did add more weight to the aircraft, the Mk IIA and B being powered by the same engine, so there was a slight reduction in the latter's performance – and so development continued, relentlessly, to keep Spitfire performance abreast, if not ahead, of the Me 109. The issue of range remained a problem. Just as the German single-engined fighters had suffered from a lack of range in 1940, so too would this handicap Fighter Command in 1941, as the Spitfire, like the Me 109, a short-range interceptor, was pressed into a long-range offensive role for which it was unsuited. As Sergeant (later Flight Lieutenant) Ron Rayner of 41 Squadron remembered, 'Crossing the water with one engine was always a concern, and of course we monitored our fuel gauges very carefully.'

From the German perspective, the coastline had to be defended from the Netherlands to the Bay of Biscay, and the *Kanalfront Jagdfliegerführer*, General Theo Osterkamp, an ace in both world wars, clearly had to inflict maximum losses on the enemy while preserving his own limited forces – as had Air Vice-Marshal Park the previous summer. Osterkamp's *Kanaljäger* now upgraded from the angular Me 109E of summer 1940 to the curvaceous and superior Me 109F. This new German fighter had a top speed of 390 mph at 22,000 feet, a service ceiling of 37,000 feet and range of 440 miles; an ingenious nitrous oxide pack, known as 'Ha ha', was added to the F-2, providing exceptional boost. While the F-1 retained the two nose-mounted machine guns firing through the propeller arc, the wing-mounted cannon was replaced by an engine-mounted 20mm cannon. The F-2's engine-mounted weapon was the 15mm Mauser MG 151 – firing a combination of high-explosive, armour-piercing and incendiary ammunition at a rate of

700 rounds per minute. Suffice it to say that the 109F was the zenith of the entire *Ein-hundert-Neun* series of fighters – but across the Channel, in May 1941, Fighter Command was replacing its Spitfire Mk IIs with the improved Mk V. This new Spitfire was powered by the Rolls-Royce Merlin 45, the performance of which compensated for the cannons' extra weight. The Mk V's top speed was 359 mph at 25,000 feet, an altitude it could attain in just over eight minutes – seven minutes later it could be higher still, at 35,000 feet. Even so, the Me 109F still had the edge. Nonetheless, much to the delight of Wing Commander Malan, the Biggin Hill Wing would be the first squadrons to receive the new Mk V.

Needless to say, Sailor lost no time in flying operations with the Spitfire Mk V, making his first combat claim in the new type and as Wing Leader at 1250 hrs on 17 May 1941:

'I was leading a high patrol of six Mk V Spitfires from Dungeness – North Foreland at 32,000 feet. Reduced height to 23,000 feet over Dover, on information received from base, and sighted six Me 109s at 20,000 feet, approaching on dive from Canterbury. We half-rolled after them and chased them into Channel but never got closer than 800 yards. Four pulled up into climb and two dived towards France. I pulled over the starboard flank but got out-positioned by two Me 109s and had to withdraw towards sun. On return to scene I surprised four Me 109s flying in two pairs 2,000 feet apart at 18,000 feet and 20,000 feet.

'I attacked lower pair on steep turn to starboard and gave one of them several bursts. The last burst with half deflection hit him around cockpit and engine, and hood or some part of cowling came off, and most of E/A obscured by black smoke. I had to break off in dive as top pair opened fire on me.

'The last I saw of E/A they were circling around the one I had hit, which was emitting heavy black smoke and was on its side.

'My engine had been vibrating very badly and I landed at Hawkinge and returned to Biggin Hill by Magister.'

The Me 109 was recorded as probably destroyed.

Sailor's next combat was on 21 May 1941 – exactly a year since having made his first kills over Dunkirk:

'I was leading 609 Squadron with fourteen aircraft acting as cover for Kenley escort Wing returning from Gravelines at 12,000 feet. We patrolled in three sections separated ten miles North of Deal at 14,000 feet.

'At 1800 hrs… two Me 109s appeared on port bow below and two E/A starboard bow, turning to starboard… I dived to attack the 109 on port bow. My No 2 attacked right-hand E/A… the three Belgian officers unfortunately followed him and lost him. I continued and gave three bursts with slight deflection from 300 yards and one 2 second burst, from dead astern, in dive at 200 yards, and E/A emitted heavy smoke.

'Three E/A on right turned towards me and I turned to starboard and evaded them. I then saw I was by myself and attempted to rejoin three Spitfires two miles to the West, but was attacked by four 109s and evaded them by spiralling and pulling up into sun. Four Me 109s chased me in straight dive and were overhauling me rapidly at 9,000 feet in my Mk II Spitfire and I had to turn and spiral away.'

This 109 was credited as damaged. The combat report is interesting. Note Sailor's use of nautical terms ('bow'), indicating his maritime past. Also Sailor was flying with 609, and not 74 Squadron, which it might be assumed he would naturally favour – raising an interesting matter concerning leadership.

Down at Tangmere, Wing Commander Bader had chosen to fly exclusively at the head of 616 Squadron, basing himself with Squadron Leader Billy Burton's unit at the Westhampnett (Goodwood) satellite. This was because Bader was familiar with 616 Squadron from Duxford Wing and 12 Group days, and quite possibly Burton being a fellow Cranwellian could well have had something to do with it. The Tangmere Wing was dispersed with 610 and 616 Squadrons at Westhampnett, and firstly 145, then 41, at nearby Merston. Flight Lieutenant Frank Twitchett was a sergeant-pilot on 145 Squadron at Merston, and recalled that Bader:

'did create problems through persistently basing himself at Westhampnett and flying solely with 616 Squadron. We very rarely saw him at all. In fact having been with 145 for its entire tour at Tangmere in 1941, I can only recall having seen him twice.'

Flight Lieutenant Ron Rayner, a sergeant-pilot on 41 Squadron, added, 'At Merston we rarely saw Wing Commander Bader… He would definitely have created more team spirit if he had not led solely with 616,' but 'For us, the most important thing was the Squadron, and our own Squadron CO, not the Wing or its leader. In fact you might even say that your own particular Flight and Flight Commander was more important.'

Air Vice-Marshal Johnnie Johnson was a pilot officer in 616 Squadron with Wing Commander Bader at Westhampnett: 'Because Douglas always flew at the head of 616 Squadron, our CO, Billy Burton, was unhappy as he never got the chance to lead his own Squadron. I do not think it necessary for Douglas to do this.'

Air Marshal Sir Denis Crowley-Milling, a pilot officer in 1941 with 610 Squadron of the Tangmere Wing, was more supportive of 'Dogsbody': 'Douglas always led with 616 Squadron and always wanted "Cocky" Dundas and Johnnie Johnson with him. I can see both sides. Bader wanted pilots with him in combat with whom he was thoroughly familiar, and they with him.'

Air Vice-Marshal Johnson commented further and significantly on this subject: 'Later in the war, when I was a Wing Leader myself, I flew with all of my squadrons by rotation, although I liked to keep the same No 2 in each one.'

According to Wing Commander Roger Boulding, of 74 Squadron, 'Malan did not always lead with the "Tigers" but usually did. I do not recall that being seen as unusual, given his close association with 74 Squadron, and it certainly didn't cause any resentment with the other squadrons. It was just accepted, was never a problem.'

Flight Lieutenant Bob Poulton, also of 74 Squadron: 'We were based at Manston and then Gravesend during Malan's time as Wing Leader. He often led with us but there was never a problem like that you have told me about at Tangmere.'

On 17 June 1941, eighteen 2 Group Blenheims were detailed to bomb a chemical factory at Chocques, near Béthune – Circus 13. The North Weald Wing was on the Form 'D' (operational order) as Close Escort, while the Biggin Hill Wing was to provide Top Cover. The Hornchurch Wing was to sweep ahead, while the Kenley Wing brought up the rear. The Tangmere Wing flew an offensive free-ranging fighter sweep, and further support was provided by several other 11 Group squadrons in addition to the 12 and 10 Group wings. Amongst Air Vice-Marshal Leigh-Mallory's fighters was 308 'City of Krakow' Squadron of the Northolt Polish Fighter Wing. Pilot Officer (later Flight Lieutenant) Kazek Budzik flew with 308, and explained just how complex an operation a Circus was:

'When we were to fly an operation, the Squadron would be on stand-by: one hour, half an hour, and so on, until we would have a briefing with all of the pilots who would be taking part in the operation. This would include pilots from the whole Wing, not just our Squadron. We would first be told what kind of sortie we were to fly, whether it was to be a fighter sweep, a Circus, or whatever.

'On the wall of the Briefing Room was a big map. This would show the formation's route to and from the target and indicate rendezvous times. The Wing Commander (Operations) would then give a briefing on the tactics to be used, identify the air leaders, and your individual position in the Wing formation.

'After the briefing we would go out to our Spitfires, start the cockpit checks and sign the Form 700 to say that we accepted responsibility for the aircraft. When complete we would pause for a few moments and then start our engines, taxying forward into position for take-off. All the pilots would be watching the leader. When he moved we all followed him and took off, not always together, sometimes in twos and threes, but always straight after each other and roughly in the formation in which we had been ordered to fly. Once airborne we would do one circuit of the airfield, to ensure that everyone was together, and slot into our allotted positions. Afterwards we would head for our rendezvous with the bombers.

'Sometimes the German fighters would harass the formation even before we had crossed the English coast. At that stage there would only be a couple of them and they would be very high up, diving as if to attack but pulling up at the last minute, just being a nuisance and trying to distract our pilots. It would be later, over France, that we would encounter the large formations of Me 109s. I also remember that we used to think the ones with yellow noses were particularly aggressive, possibly from an elite unit [author's note: this was a widely believed misconception; the yellow markings simply identified a particular *Gruppe* or *Staffel* within a *Geschwader*].

'Our targets were often Le Havre, Brest, Boulogne, Calais, Amiens and Lille. All of the targets were heavily defended by anti-aircraft guns. As the formation approached the target you could see black puff-balls of smoke from exploding flak shells, getting bigger and bigger and closer all the time. It also got thicker as more guns opened fire. From a distance the flak bursts looked like harmless smoke, but as you got closer you could see a fire burst inside the smoke ball. The flak didn't really bother Spitfire pilots at the time, as we could fly fast and as we were so manoeuvrable we could fly above or around concentrations of flak. The reason I describe the flak is because the bomber crews could not fly above or around it. The main concentration of flak was over the target when the bombers commenced their run. They therefore had to fly straight and level through a murderous hail of fire. I cannot emphasize enough my respect for the bomber crews: they were extremely brave men, all of them. They could not deviate from their bombing run to save themselves – I want to make that point very clear.

'Over the target, after the bombers had dropped their bombs, there was a little confusion as the formation tried to stay together and get out as quickly as possible. The flak would still be banging away as the bombers turned after their bombing runs. The Close Escort Spitfire squadron now had to remain with the bombers and protect them on the return journey across the Channel. Now the Me 109s would start repeatedly attacking the formation all the way back to England. The Top and Medium Cover squadrons would mix it with the Me 109s and soon a huge air battle would develop as the "Bee Hive" withdrew. As a result, these squadrons would soon be scattered, the pilots often coming home in ones or twos. Only the Close Cover squadrons would remain with the bombers, come what may.

'Close Cover Escort would leave the bombers when safely over the English coast and near to their base. We would then return to Northolt and be de-briefed by the Intelligence Officer. That is when we would complete and file any combat claims or report any observations of interest.'

On Circus 13, Wing Commander Malan positioned his Top Cover Wing with 74 and 609 Squadron above and on either side of the bombers, while Squadron Leader Jamie Rankin's 92 Squadron flew higher still, guarding against a potential high-flying ambush. The eagle-eyed Biggin Hill Wing Leader spotted a *schwarm* of Me 109Fs and led two sections of 74 Squadron to intercept, but the 109s broke away. A pursuit ensued and Sailor hurried to assist a Spitfire under attack from a 109, in turn being assailed by two more himself. Turning with one of his assailants, Sailor used cannon to blow that 109's port wing off. After another skirmish the Wing Leader was unable to reach and assist another Spitfire pilot, who baled out. This was Flying Officer Roger Boulding, flying a Spitfire Mk IIA that day:

'I was leading a section of four 74 Squadron Spitfires. Sailor Malan led the Wing, 74 Squadron in the van, and we were flying top cover. Having dived onto some Me 109s, and in accordance with the standard drill of that time, we didn't follow them all the way down but attempted to re-form, climbing towards the sun and weaving. I was following Sailor, and another Spitfire was following me. After a while Sailor came on the radio telling someone to "Look out behind!" I quickly did so and saw the chap still behind me, and screwed my head around some more, still looking for the trouble. Then I saw

Sailor below me, violently rocking his wings. Suddenly there was an almighty bang on the armour plating behind my seat and it became rather obvious that the chap behind me had been replaced by someone rather less friendly! With controls gone I had to jump out and floated down from 12 - 15,000 feet in broad daylight. Naturally I found a substantial reception committee waiting. And that was that, as the Germans kept on saying, "For you ze var is over!".'

74 Squadron also lost Pilot Officer H.F. Parkes, who was likewise captured. In this action, elements of JG26 had scrambled at 1915 hrs and climbed hard, above the Beehive, and pounced on the Biggin Hill Wing near Calais. Oberleutnant Westphal of 8/JG26 recorded his tenth victory in the subsequent combat, and 1/JG26's Leutnant E. Neumann scored his first; which enemy pilot shot down which 'Tiger', however, it is impossible to say. In total, JG26 claimed sixteen RAF fighters destroyed; the actual cost to Fighter Command was eleven, with five pilots killed, five captured and another wounded. In response, the Spitfire pilots claimed fifteen Me 109s destroyed, seven probables and eleven damaged – confusion always abounding when mass formations were engaged, and the escorting wings numbered some 250 aircraft. So far as is known, for reasons soon evident, only JG26 was involved in this engagement – losing a single Me 109E-7, 2/JG26's Feldwebel Bernhard Adam being killed near Boulogne. Although Sailor claimed a 109F and not an 'E' destroyed over Boulogne (and there was no mistaking that his victim really was destroyed) it is likely, nonetheless, that this was Adam – and the first in a long line of combat successes during the 1941 'season'.

21 June 1941 saw the greatest RAF effort to date. During the morning, Circus 16 saw seventeen 11 Group squadrons escorting six Blenheims attacking the enemy airfield at St Omer-Wizernes. That afternoon, Circus 17 was flown, a raid by six 110 Squadron Blenheims on the German airfield at Desvres. The Biggin Hill Spitfires were detailed as the Target Support Wing, taking off at 1555 hrs. *Jafü* 2 scrambled I/JG26 and elements of JG2 to intercept, but no contact was made until after the target was bombed. At 1620 hrs III/JG26 was scrambled from Ligescourt and hurried to join the fray. West of Boulogne, the Biggin Hill Wing was engaged by III/JG26. Wing Commander Malan:

'I saw an Me 109F flying towards Boulogne at 15,000 feet and closed to fifty yards and gave two short bursts with cannon and machine gun. E/A burst into flames and I was covered in oil. No pilot could have got out and my No 2 saw it go down on fire just inland of Boulogne.

'I then went up with six Me 109Fs at 12,000 feet, just off Le Touquet. Four dived towards land and two remained. I attacked right-hand E/A in turn to starboard and gave one short deflection burst but missed. E/A then straightened up and I delivered short burst from dead astern, at fifty yards. E/A jerked violently forwards and went vertically into sea at mouth of river off Le Touquet. No pilot got out. Both of these were seen by my No 2, Pilot Officer Sandeman, who was just behind me. I then returned and met up with bombers and escorts at Dungeness, and returned to Biggin Hill.'

It is likely that the latter 109F was Unteroffizier Heinz Carmienke of 8/JG26, who was killed.

In total that day, Fighter Command claimed twenty-six Me 109s destroyed, although in reality, so hectic and confused was the fighting, only nine were lost. Similarly, the Germans claimed twenty-four Spitfires destroyed, whereas the actual figure was six. The following day, Fighter Command's claims bore little resemblance to reality: twenty-nine German fighters were claimed as destroyed but JG26 lost but one machine, while JG2 suffered just three casualties. This was surely *déjà vu*: as the wildly exaggerated claims of the Big Wing had been accepted during the Battle of Britain, so was the case now – providing a completely false impression of the Non-Stop Offensive's actual success. The pilots themselves, of course, made their claims in good faith, so had no idea that in reality Fighter Command was losing this daylight battle by a ratio in excess of 2:1. Indeed, that summer Flight Lieutenant (later Air Commodore Sir) Archie Winskill of the Tangmere Wing's 41 Squadron was shot down over Calais and evaded with assistance from the French Resistance; when asked by Sidney Bowen, a visiting British agent from an escape organization based in Marseilles, why more Spitfires were crashing in France than Me 109s, the Spitfire pilot 'had no answer for him'. Nonetheless, owing to a particularly significant event occurring on 22 June 1941, the Non-Stop Offensive suddenly became a necessity – and eminently political.

During May 1941, the nocturnal Blitz on British cities had reached a terrible crescendo on the nights of 10 and 11 May 1941, with terrible raids on London. Although the Bristol Beaufighter night-fighter was now in service, Spitfires were still being sent up on 'Fighter Nights' – 74 Squadron's Pilot Officer Roger Boulding shooting down an He 111 near Ashford on one such occasion at this time. Thereafter the pressure eased – but the reason was cleverly concealed by the enemy. From the middle of May 1941, the large-scale transfer of Luftwaffe units on the western front actively engaged in air operations against Britain were transferred east. By the end of May, the whole of Luftflotte 2 had left France. From now on, the Channel coast would just be defended by two fighter groups, JGs 2 and 26. This massive movement of 2,500 aircraft, personnel and equipment took place behind a veil of spoof radio messages and signals, providing an impression of business as usual.

On 22 June 1941 the world was shocked when Hitler invaded Soviet Russia, Operation *Barbarossa* achieving complete surprise. In doing so, Hitler contravened the Nazi-Soviet Non-Aggression Pact and turned the focus of his territorial ambition eastwards. This was always Hitler's plan, unlike the proposed seaborne invasion of Britain, the potential opportunity for which arose unexpectedly. The war in Russia would be a fight to the death of unprecedented ferocity and barbarity between two completely opposed ideologies. Naturally Hitler was expecting to repeat his success against the West, a lightning-quick campaign against an inferior enemy. The Soviet dictator, Stalin, called upon the western Allies for help, but as with Poland, geographically any military intervention by Britain was impossible, even had Britain been in a position to provide such support. Stalin, though, was unappeasable and demanded that a Second Front should be opened by Britain, which was clearly impossible. The air war by night and day over north-west Europe was the only realistic means of indirectly assisting the Soviets, by attempting to tie down units that would otherwise be sent east. It became most important to prove to Stalin that every effort was being made to provide support, and so the Non-Stop Offensive assumed an even greater importance. Demonstrating success was vital, hence why combat claims were so readily accepted.

That same day Hitler's forces poured eastwards, Circus 18 was flown during the afternoon, an attack by six Blenheims on Hazebrouck. Again, Sailor led the Wing with 74 Squadron, destroying another Me 109 near Dunkirk. The pressure was relentless. On the evening of 23 June 1941 came Circus 20. At 1947 hrs, Sailor led the Biggin Hill Wing, comprising 74, 92 and 609 Squadrons, each with ten Spitfires, to support six Blenheims attacking the enemy airfield at Mardyck. The Wing crossed the French coast at 2020 hrs, climbing from 25,000 to 27,000 feet:

'On crossing the coast I saw a number of red AA puffs about 4,000 feet below. These were obviously pointers. A minute later while the Wing was on its course to St Omer (a feint movement) I spotted about 15 – 20 aircraft flying at 20,000 feet in a large vic and in pairs from Boulogne towards Hardelot to investigate red puffs.

'Calling on 92 and 74 Squadrons to follow, I approached E/A which I saw to be Me 109Fs. 74 did not receive my call and only 92 Squadron followed me. Singling out an E/A on the right-hand side of the formation, I closed to 50 yards and gave him a short burst of cannon and machine gun with slight deflection. The E/A blew up in flames and I found myself flying into a shower of pieces. Some of these damaged my port wing and starboard wing root. When I landed I found that one piece was still wrapped around the pitot tube.

'Seeing another climbing to the right, up-sun, I followed, and closing to 50 yards opened fire with cannon and machine gun with a two second burst. I hit him and he half-rolled into a dive inland emitting heavy smoke. I carried on after him using up the rest of my ammunition down to 8,000 feet. I broke off at this height when the air speed indicator was nearing 450 mph. I saw the E/A completely disintegrate at about 5,000 feet; the wings broke off and the fuselage crashed to the ground approximately 10 miles SW of Boulogne. I had now used up all my ammunition so I returned home.

'It was most unfortunate that my R/T was not functioning properly – for had I been able to get orders to the Wing, the bag would have been very much greater. The two E/A I shot down are confirmed by pilots of 92 Squadron. Pilot Officer Dougall saw the tail come off the second E/A with first burst. This I did not see as it was behind the nose of my aircraft.

In this engagement, neither 74 or 609 Squadrons made any claims, while 92 Squadron, which followed the Wing Leader into action, claimed one Me 109 destroyed, a probable and another damaged. That evening, the Blenheims had arrived too early at the rendezvous and consequently set course before all of the escorting wings had assembled – resulting in five bombers being shot down. Pilots from JG2 claimed six Blenheims destroyed, while Hauptmann Gerhard Schöpfel, Kommandeur of III/JG26, claimed another. JGs 2 and 26 also claimed twelve Spitfires (although only four were actually lost), but only one of these was reported in the St Omer area, this being by a 4/JG26 pilot. JG26 lost no fighters and what, if any, losses JG2 suffered is unknown.

Circus 21 came the following evening, a raid on the power station at Comines:

'I took off with the Biggin Hill Wing at 1950 hrs and climbed as cover through the clouds to North Foreland, where I met the Tangmere Wing at 2015 hrs and proceeded on course 136 magnetic for target area. Visibility over France was exceedingly poor with traces of haze up to 18,000 feet.

'We arrived in the vicinity of the target area at approximately 2035 hrs and did a circuit there with 92 Squadron as lower squadron at 20,000 feet. I then followed what I could see of the Tangmere Wing back to the coast, which we hit at Dunkirk, and had not at any stage seen the bombers or escorts. We circled between Dunkirk and Gravelines for some time and encountered several formations of about six Me 109Fs which were above us at about 25,000 feet.

'As we were split up into fours I did not know what took place with the Wing as a whole. I went into a series of climbing turns with one formation of six Me 109Fs over Dunkirk but no engagement followed as I could not reach this height and they would not attack. I then broke off and proceeded towards another six Me 109Fs five miles NW of Dunkirk and a similarly inconclusive engagement followed and I lost the rest of my section in turns. I then saw the main formation crossing out over the coast at Gravelines and I broadcast to the Wing that I was joining up with them. I was about 4,000 yards behind the top rearmost Spitfire squadron of the Escort Wing at about 19,000 feet when three 109Fs did a dive from about 5,000 feet from the port flank and one of them attacked one of four Spitfires. I saw him firing but did not observe results. They turned to starboard and I followed suit by climbing right-hand turns and delivered a two-second burst from fifty yards at the leading E/A, which had fired at the Spitfire. I hit him underneath his fuselage and two large pieces drifted away from him but as I was practically on my back and in the turn of a spin, I only had time to see him emitting heavy black smoke and doing two turns of a spin, towards Gravelines, inland.

'I straightened up in a dive as another 109 fired at me from the beam and passed across my nose, having missed me. I pulled out at 15,000 feet and proceeded on a zig-zag course towards the English coast and landed at Biggin Hill.'

All that was required to destroy this Me 109 was a two-second burst at fifty yards – further evidence of the excellence of Malan's flying and shooting. It is possible that the Me 109 involved was 9/JG26 flown by Leutnant Erdmann Neumann who was killed, over Gravelines at 2040 hrs. Wing Commander Malan's combat was timed between 2035 – 2045 hrs, minutes earlier than the other combat claims made by RAF pilots that evening.

The pressure of operational flying was intense. At this time, Sailor did not reside in the Biggin Hill officers' mess, but lived out with his family. Polish Spitfire pilot Kazek Budzik, who was flying with the Northolt Wing, once commented, 'I don't think people realise how stressful it was. Being pilots and officers we had good living conditions and food, and being stationed on the outskirts of London had a good social life off the station. For an hour or so each day, sometimes twice or more a day, you could suddenly be whipped out of that comfortable and safe environment and find yourself fighting for your life over France. Then, a few minutes later, you would thankfully be safely back at base, resuming normality. This was an absolute contrast, and psychologically difficult, over time. I know that the "Poor Bloody Infantry" are in the muck and bullets constantly, but at least then you have a focused mindset. It was very different for us. A bit odd, really, and I definitely don't think people have considered this aspect of our lives at that time.'

At lunchtime on 25 June 1941, Sailor led the Biggin Hill Wing on Circus 22, a raid on the Hazebrouck marshalling yards; the Wing Leader's subsequent report regarding what was a comparatively protracted engagement, taking place between 1230 – 1245 hrs, makes exciting reading:

'When at 28,000 feet between St Omer and Gravelines I saw two Me 109Fs at 25,000 feet. I led my section down to attack and saw one of my pilots attack from close range. I closed to attack the other but saw two other Me 109Fs closing, so I broke away and attacked them. I attacked from astern with slight deflection from 300/250 yards, and fired all my cannon shells. The shooting was inaccurate as my reflector sight was not working properly. The E/A repeatedly put its nose downwards and this made my engine cut. Eventually my sight came on again and I closed to 50 yards, fired my machine-guns and saw E/A smoke heavily. The second E/A, which was flying in line abreast, broke away at 5,000 feet to the beam, so I broke away and met it head-on. I broke off after second E/A with 450 mph indicated air speed and met it on opposite course. I then saw large explosion and fire on port quarter, about one mile away, which seemed quite obviously to be the E/A I had shot.'

This combat concluded at 5,000 feet, Sailor's Me 109 being 'confirmed'. On this occasion the Biggin Hill Wing had engaged elements of JG2, which lost two Me 109Fs. In this engagement, the only other Biggin Hill Wing pilot to file a combat claim was Flight Lieutenant Alan Wright of 92 Squadron, who destroyed the other JG2 Me 109F over 'St Omer-Gravelines', while Pilot Officer Neville Duke of the same unit shot down and killed Feldwebel Bartholomaeus Eierstock of 9/JG26 over Dunkirk. Sailor's victory on 25 June 1941 was the last of seven claims for destroyed Me 109s made on five consecutive days – an incredible achievement. Neville Duke, who often flew as Sailor's No 2 when the great man led with 92 Squadron, learned much from his Wing Leader, later becoming an ace himself and ultimately an enormously accomplished pilot, in both war and peace; he recalled Sailor as a gifted tactician who would never fall for a feint, always picking the right moment to attack; a brilliant pilot, an exceptional shot who always held his fire until within range – and preferably the closer the better – summed up in one word: 'formidable'. Beyond doubt, those early years on the farm provided an opportunity for Sailor to develop his natural talent for defection shooting – now honed to perfection. In his book *Tiger Squadron*, Wing Commander Ira Jones recounted how on a visit to Biggin Hill he had driven Sailor's car across the airfield with the Wing Leader toting a loaded shotgun and looking to bag a hare:

'Suddenly a hare got up near the centre of the drome and about forty yards ahead of us. I put my foot on the accelerator and went flat out after it. When we closed up with the hare it began to zig-zag. I followed, keeping formation with it. When I got to within twenty-five yards of the target I was doing between fifty and sixty mph and the car was jolting a good deal. Sailor lifted the gun to his shoulder. There was a bang – and in front of us was a dead hare. Having picked it up, Sailor said: "Taffy, I think there is another one over there." He pointed in the direction I was to drive and, sure enough, up got another hare, and I did some more dirt-track driving. Again Sailor waited until we got to within thirty yards before firing. And once more we picked up a dead hare.'

During the return journey to the Officers' Mess, Sailor also shot a couple of plovers out of a covey flying overhead. Jones was astonished at the afternoon's proceedings and knew that he had discovered 'one of Sailor's secrets as an air fighter: a steady aim and good deflection shooting'.

On 26 June 1941, Circus 24, an attack on the Comines Power Station, went ahead, Sailor claiming a 'probable' Me 109F. The following day, however, would be a sad day for 74 Squadron and Sailor personally. The Biggin Hill Wing Leader took off at 2045 hrs, leading his three squadrons as 'extra high cover' to twenty-four Blenheims raiding 'steel and engineering works' at Lille. Crossing out over North Foreland, the Spitfires described a 'large turn at 18,000 feet', during which Sailor received notification that the bombers and escort were three minutes early. On crossing the French coast at 20,000 feet, 74 Squadron, providing 'middle cover', was attacked by Me 109Es from I/JG26. Owing to radio interference, despite repeated transmissions, Sailor was unable to contact Squadron Leader Mungo-Park, leading 74 Squadron, and ascertain whether assistance was required to beat off the enemy attack. There was a thick haze up to 16,000 feet, making it difficult to see what was happening, so, receiving no reply, Sailor proceeded with the main formation. Meanwhile, Flight Lieutenant Saunders of 74 Squadron fired at one of the Tigers' assailants as it flashed past, the 109 immediately streaming a plume of white glycol vapour. Then, the bombers having successfully attacked their target, 609 Squadron was attacked on the way home, just south of Dunkirk, Flight Lieutenant Richey damaging an Me 109F, but the 'West Riding' Squadron suffered no casualties. Elsewhere, 19 Squadron lost two Spitfires, their pilots captured, as did 266 Squadron, one pilot also becoming a prisoner while the other was killed. The highest-ranking RAF casualty of the day was Wing Commander Piotr Laguna, leading the Northolt Polish Wing, who was hit by flak and killed during a low-level attack on the airfield at Coquelles, near Calais. At 2330 hrs 74 Squadron landed at Gravesend – but three pilots were missing: Squadron Leader Mungo-Park, Pilot Officer Sandeman and Sergeant Hilken.

While Sandeman and Hilken were both later duly confirmed as prisoners, John Mungo-Park, a 23-year old ace decorated with the DFC (and soon a Bar), was dead. According to 74 Squadron historian Doug Tidy, the Tigers 'had lost the gayest and one of the most gallant of all Commanding Officers'. Mungo-Park's Spitfire crashed at Adinkerke, just inland of and equidistant between Bray Dunes and De Panne, where the gallant 'Tiger' was buried – possibly shot down by Unteroffizier Albrecht Held of 2/JG26, who chalked up his first victory that day.

This loss of a highly popular commander was also a personal blow to Sailor: the pair were firm friends. Earlier that year, Paddy Treacy, another friend of the Malans, had been promoted to command 242 Squadron but was killed on 20 April 1941 when his Hurricane collided with two others over the Channel. Treacy was to have been godfather to Sailor's son, Jonathan, and Mungo-Park had been selected by Sailor and Lynda as an appropriate replacement – sadly, not to be. The war, nonetheless, went on, whatever the personal cost.

At 0750 hrs on 28 June 1941, Sailor led the Biggin Hill Wing off at the head of 609 Squadron. This was Circus 26, yet another raid on Comines Power Station. The Wing was to provide cover to withdrawing bombers over the target area with Wing Commander Bader's Tangmere Wing. On this occasion the Wing was flying in sections of three and four, with

609 Squadron leading, crossing the French coast at 20,000 feet, while 92 Squadron was at 23,000 feet, and 74 Squadron providing 'top rear cover' at 30,000 feet. Reaching the target on cue, the fighters orbited in a wide turn and shepherded the bombers back to the coast after their attack. On the return journey, a series of skirmishes with enemy fighters developed. As the 11 Group report to Fighter Command HQ recorded:

'Following one E/A, however, the Wing Commander, from 400 yards behind, saw it open fire on some Spitfires. The Wing Commander's windscreen frosted during the dive, and when it cleared he found himself mixed up with a number of Spitfires and two Me 109s diving away. He then followed a Me 109E in a dive towards Calais, and while doing so avoided two others who approached from port beam. The Wing Commander eventually came within striking distance of a Me 109E when, at 8,000 feet, on a course between Gravelines and Calais, he saw one E/A diving to attack a Spitfire in the rear. Overtaking, the Wing Commander opened fire from astern at 200 yards with machine-guns only. Closing to 150 yards he fired with cannon and machine-guns a three-second burst. E/A then rolled slowly to starboard. Clouds of black smoke and flame emerged from the engine and the 109 slowly rolled again with nose down. Wing Commander Malan reports that he was convinced that the pilot of this aircraft was either killed or badly wounded. Turning, he lost sight of the E/A, and seeing more 109s diving from Calais area he flew home at 5,000 feet.'

The enemy aircraft was confirmed destroyed. The only one of Sailor's pilots to open fire was 609 Squadron's Flight Lieutenant Paul Richey DFC, who was forced to break off his attack on a 109 when other German fighters appeared, forcing him to break away. 92 Squadron, however, had been unable to bring Me 109s to battle near Gravelines, and 74 Squadron encountered no 'bandits' throughout the operation, during which the power station had been so badly damaged that it was inoperable for three months.

There was no action the following day, doubtless a welcome respite, and at 1300 hrs the BBC broadcast over the radio an interview previously recorded with Sailor:

'I have been in Fighter Command squadrons for some years now and I know the British fighter pilot well. During the early months of this year, when things were quiet, the fighter pilot was almost unhappy, but now he is more walking around with a grin on his face. He is happy because he is making the Hun pipe to our tune. I have been fighting the Hun quite a lot now and my personal experience is that, generally speaking, he is a magnificent bully but a poor fighter. For instance, last year, over Dunkirk and England, when our pilots were badly outnumbered, they never failed to sail in and mix it. But the German will very seldom engage in a fight unless he has tactical advantage and numerical superiority, and, even then, he will rely on a quick dive and a squirt, and never stay around to mix it. Another thing, the German aircraft were equipped with cannons at the outbreak of the war – now we have cannons, and they don't like it.

'You have heard of enemy fighters being blown up in the air by cannon fire, this is no exaggeration and I have experienced three similar incidents myself. Only the other day I was crossing the French coast just south of Boulogne, when the ground defences fired a series of red Ack-Ack puffs in our direction. This we knew to be a signal to their fighters, so I continued on course for St Omer for one minute, then did a quick turn with one of my squadrons towards Boulogne. We sighted about twenty Me 109s of the new 'F' type, flying in a large "V" formation, in pairs. We dived in behind them and I singled out the right-hand flank man and closed to fifty yards before I opened up with my cannon. His machine literally exploded in the air, and large pieces from him damaged both my wings as I narrowly missed his main fuselage, which was turning over and over. One piece wrapped itself round my pitot tube, which is fixed beneath the port wing, and when I landed it was still attached. Fortunately the Spitfire is an exceptionally strong machine and the aeroplane suffered little more than superficial damage. All of this naturally only took a few seconds. With my overtaking speed I closed in on another Me 109, which was doing a right-hand climb into the sun. During my turn I saw two more Messerschmitts spinning down in flames and knew that the rest of the boys were doing their stuff. I closed in to within about fifty yards of the second machine and gave him a short burst of cannon fire. Again, I was lucky, for his tail came off. In fact, the No 3 in my formation said afterwards that the fin with the swastika on narrowly missed his cockpit as it went hurtling through the air. I saw the wings tear away from the fuselage, which plunged into the earth with a terrific explosion.

'I know that we have got old Jerry rattled on quite a lot of these offensive operations. Every time he pops his nose up in the area in which our bombers are operating, there is a whoop of delight, as Spitfires shoulder each other out of the way to hit him on the head. After about thirty seconds the scene is transformed, with Messerschmitts streaming down towards the ground with Spitfires on their tails, pumping lead into them, with the usual circle of disappointed pilots circling the area where the Hun had been, and cursing their luck at not being in the right place at the right time.

'A few days ago we saw three formations of Messerschmitts approaching us. They were in widely spread "V" formation and looked almost formidable as they made tiny silhouettes against the white top of the clouds. Someone called out over his radio, "Tally Ho! Ten o'clock. Surely they must be friendly?"

'Then, someone else said, "I have them, they're Huns. Now come on and cut yourself a slice of cake!" Our pilots don't just escort bombers, they go looking for trouble as well. One squadron leader, a Scot from Edinburgh, has shot down eight Me 109s since Fighter Command assumed its latest offensive.

'One sunny afternoon recently I saw a big formation of fighters slightly to the right and below us, so I ordered the squadron leader to investigate to see if they really were enemy aircraft and if so to deal with them. He led his boys down with shrieks of delight. He got two himself. The first one, which he got with his cannon, just blew up in front of him. He remarked afterwards "There's a lot to be said for seeing them blow up in the air." That Squadron got four down altogether in that little party. During this flight, a rather amusing thing happened to a sergeant-pilot, who darted down on a 109. He didn't have to press his gun button at all, he was diving down on the Hun when the pilot tried to escape by making a steep turn, but made a complete mess of it. He made what we call a "ham-fisted turn". Before our sergeant-pilot could open fire, the German was spinning into the ground; he must have been terrified at the sight of a Spitfire coming down on him like that.

'Then I'd like to tell you of another sergeant-pilot who shot down three in one sortie. He was over France when he saw two 109s and with his second burst at close range he saw the enemy aircraft go straight down in flames. He got separated from his Section and saw seven 109s above him. Two of them peeled off to attack, so he closed his throttle and one of the Huns overshot. The second was about to overshoot when the Sergeant turned and opened his throttle again. Closing to short range he opened fire with his cannon and machine-guns, and the Hun simply disintegrated and a lot of little pieces spun out of the sky where he had been. Then he had a swarm of Messerschmitts around him, but he took evasive action while they were firing at him from all angles. His Spitfire was hit several times and he found himself flying upside down with the top of his head pressed hard against the cockpit hood. However, he righted himself, carried on towards England, and near the French coast overtook a 109 which he shot down just short of the Dunkirk beaches. It must have been very satisfying to see the Hun crash in flames on that old battleground of last year.'

The broadcast is a unique record of air-fighting and an insight into Sailor Malan (see YouTube link in Bibliography). Surprisingly, he comes across as softly-spoken and, considering his South African and Afrikaner background, virtually accent-less. Clear is the high-morale of Fighter Command. The RAF pilots were on the offensive, as opposed to defending their homeland from the very real threat of invasion. Although we know now that Fighter Command's losses exceeded those of the enemy, this was unknown at the time. There is a big difference between an actual combat loss and a claim. The RAF pilots believed that their combat successes significantly exceeded their losses, and were unaware of the actual balance sheet. This kind of broadcast was inspirational to the public and essential to maintain the people's morale.

On 30 June 1941, the power station at Pont-à-Vendin was the target for Circus 27. The Biggin Hill Wing took off at 1735 hrs with orders to rendezvous with twenty-four Blenheims and the Northolt Wing, the close escort, thence to partner with the Hornchurch Wing and provide Target Support. After crossing the coast and heading towards Lens, St Omer onwards, and on the return flight, various small formations of Me 109s, mainly 'Es', were seen, but neither 74 or 92 Squadrons were close enough to engage. 609 Squadron, however, did contact the German fighters, claiming three Me 109Es destroyed, a probable and another damaged. Wing Commander Malan reported:

'I was approaching target at Lens with Wing when I spotted a vic of eight or ten Me 109Es doing a gentle right-hand turn at 12,000 feet, 5,000 feet below me. I gave the order to attack and dived with two sections of 74 Squadron towards E/A. E/A straightened up into a fast dive with the exception of two on right-hand flank. I closed in on one of these and delivered continuous fire from about 350 – 100 yards with cannon and machine-gun. As I broke off, E/A was completely obscured by black smoke from his engine, which was on fire. This was confirmed by my No 2, Sergeant Lockhart.'

This Me 109E was credited as destroyed. It is likely that elements of JG2 were involved, although their only loss was an Me 109F-2, which crash-landed back at base as the result of combat damage. JG26 suffered no losses this day.

On this day, the Air Ministry issued another list of the top-scoring aces. The fighting to date of spring and early summer 1941 had already revised the previous list, published in March. 'Ginger' Lacey, the previous top scorer, had not increased his tally and was now third in line. Top of the list was Wing Commander Malan – now a household name – with twenty-nine aerial victories. Sailor was now officially the RAF's top-scoring ace.

On 2 July 1941, Sailor began another run of kills, on Circus 29, to Lille:

'The Biggin Hill Wing left Biggin Hill at 155 hrs and climbed to North Foreland with 74 Squadron in the lead, 92 Squadron in the middle and 609 Squadron on top. The Wing was scheduled to leave North Foreland at 1215 hrs and left at 1214, on a course of 120°.

'About two minutes after leaving North Foreland with the leading squadron at 19,000 feet, Controller passed the message: "Your friends are five minutes early." I immediately opened my throttle but unfortunately Garrick (92 Squadron) and Beauty (609 Squadron) Leaders misunderstood the message to read "You are five minutes early," and consequently drew behind. As I was approaching Dunkirk, another message was passed: "Your friends are seven minutes early, proceed with all possible speed." As I crossed the French coast I attempted to communicate with Garrick and Beauty Leaders but I could not establish sensible communication between myself and Garrick Leader.

'I made contact with the main formation about five miles inland. About five miles from the target some Me 109s in small groups of twos and fours at about 25, 000 feet, which were flying on the port beam, attempted to deliver their attacks with the usual dive and levelling out from behind.

'It was at this stage I saw Garrick Squadron above, coming in on a converging course.

'The attacks appeared to be delivered with the intention of attacking 74 Squadron. A general melee ensued but by turning the Section towards each attack a certain amount of success was gained. I fired at one from beam as he went past but missed and followed another down through some of the Spitfires of the escort wing. For some time visual touch was still maintained with the main formation and the fighting continued till well past the target area. At one stage two 109s dived through the formation and pulled up in a climb. I followed with my Section and just as the leader was near stalling point I hit him with a burst of cannon from about 150 yards. A large explosion in the fuselage was observed and his nose went vertically down and I followed him for about 8,000 feet when he was emitting streams of petrol.

'My No 2, Sergeant Lockhart, was apparently firing from my starboard beam at the same time, and continued firing after I stopped. We therefore claim half each. Squadron Leader Meares [Squadron Leader S.T. 'Charlie' Meares, who had succeeded the late Mungo-Park in command of 74 Squadron] saw my strikes mainly in front of the cockpit and confirms the engagement.

'The bombers must have turned off the target as at about this stage I lost visual contact. I collected about five of 74 Squadron and several of the Tangmere Wing. As I had done several aileron turns my compass was behaving in a distorting manner, and as the sun was practically vertically above and the wind had drifted me southwards, I shaped the best course I could for the coast. Two 109s shadowed us from the port beam at about 4,000 feet above for a while, and several smaller formations were following us behind. Eventually I turned towards the two on flank to prevent them from reporting our position by making them dive away. I could not afford to give chase because of my lack of petrol.

'I eventually hit the coast near Boulogne and went out at Étaples, landing at Hawkinge with about five gallons of fuel.'

The foregoing report emphasises how critical the Spitfire's lack of range could be when pressed into such a long-range offensive role. Again, it is likely that the Biggin Hill Wing engaged fighters of JG2, which lost three Me 109s, but no pilots killed. JG26's only loss was to friendly flak. Fighter Command, however, claimed twenty-four 109s destroyed, four probables and seven damaged. Offset against this, eight RAF fighter pilots were lost and two Blenheims with their crews.

3 July 1941 saw Circus 30, an attack on St Omer. Again, the Biggin Hill Wing provided Target Support:

'The Wing broke up into fours over St Omer – Hazebrouck area. Several Me 109s, mainly Fs, were encountered in small groups but attempted to avoid engagement and in some cases tried to lead our units towards a concentration which they obviously had south of St Omer. I fired at one of a pair from about 300 yards and Squadron Leader Meares reports that he saw this E/A emitting heavy smoke and diving gently away to the left. I turned northwards with four aircraft and met several pairs of 109Fs at about 23,000 feet which were menacing a group of Spitfires 2,000 feet below them. A series of dogfights ensued and I was struck by their extreme manoeuvrability which, however, appeared to be not quite good enough for the Spitfires. My four split up into two pairs and at one stage I did one turn of a spin with my No 2, Group Captain Barwell. The E/A at about

100 yards range flopped onto his side and as he was almost stationary I gave him a short burst with full deflection. I must have hit him with cannon and machine gun. As he straightened up in a fast dive, I saw his undercarriage. The starboard wheel was apparently fully down and the port wheel was waving about loosely. I closed in on the dive and used up all my cannon ammunition at about 150 yards, and closed in until I nearly collided with him, firing my machine guns continuously. I broke off to avoid collision and saw the port oleo leg tear away. I blacked out at this stage and saw no more of E/A as I straightened up in a climb.

'As I saw no smoke I claim a damaged.'

Sailor's No 2 was the Biggin Hill Station Commander, Group Captain Dickie Barwell DFC, at 34 one of the youngest group captains in the service at that time. According to his son, John Barwell, writing in 2009, Group Captain Barwell believed that to properly play his part as a commander in the Non-Stop Offensive he 'had to share in the fighting experience and frequently flew on operations, usually as No 2 to a wing or squadron leader.' On 1 July 1942, the day before his 35th birthday, the Group Captain was killed in a tragic friendly fire incident on one such sortie.

The German reaction to Circus 30 saw I and II/JG26 together with pilots from JG2 contact the RAF formation over St Omer. I/JG26 lost 40-year-old Hauptmann Bieber, apparently an ardent Nazi, and the Kommodore of JG2, Hauptmann Wilhelm Balthasar, went down in flames. The RAF pilots claimed seven Me 109s destroyed, there being no doubt that Squadron Leader Michael Lister-Robinson DFC, CO of 609 Squadron, was responsible for Balthasar's death, whose wing was blown off by his cannon fire.

The Choques chemical works near Béthune was Circus 32's target on 4 July 1941; Sailor was in action between 1500 and 1600 hrs in the vicinity of Choques–St Omer–Gravelines:

'I was leading the Biggin Hill Wing acting as Top Cover for the Close Escort. After crossing Gravelines at 18,000 feet, cloud conditions were encountered and developed to 10/10ths.

'Somewhere in the vicinity of the target area, just as the bombers were starting to turn, 109Es, which had been following above and behind, commenced a series of attacks by diving underneath the fighter cover and approaching the bombers from dead astern. I saw the first one coming and found that I could catch him up before he reached the bombers. I delivered a short burst with machine guns as he was approaching the rear vic of

Blenheims. I pulled away to avoid flying into the bombers and believe that I hit the 109.

'I then re-climbed to my formation on the port flank and saw two 109Es which had lost most of their diving speed and were attempting to climb away from the port flank. I attacked one of these from about 200 yards with cannon and machine gun and he poured out heavy black smoke. Sergeant Pietrasiak (Polish, 92 Squadron) also attacked this E/A, which he saw destroyed. He claims a half destroyed and I claim half.

'Another 109 then appeared travelling slowly in the same direction under my port wing. I put my nose down and delivered about two seconds cannon and machine-gun fire at 100 yards range. He practically blew up and he went down on his side belching smoke and flames.

'My No 2, Group Captain Barwell, also claims a probable at this stage and I believe I saw his 109 sinking to the right. He rejoined me and we did a steep turn to try and re-form with the main formation which, owing to the fact that we had been on a reciprocal course for about one minute, had drawn some way ahead. I gave chase but found myself flying underneath twenty or thirty 109s which were flying the same way as the main formation but they were not attempting to attack. A series of attacks by 109s on us then ensued. They were a mixture of Es and Fs. We parried these attacks by turning sharply towards each one and continuing the circuit, then straightening up as the attacks got heavier and more and more 109s joined in. It became impossible for us to stay together and at the first opportunity we dived away in aileron turns to try and make cloud cover. I eventually made the clouds at 5,000 feet and dodged several 109s by popping out at the top and bottom alternately, and altering course as best I could.

'Eventually I emerged from the top of the cloud over St Omer, just as a 109E was doing the same on a course at right angles to mine. I pulled over onto him and gave a burst of about two seconds at about 200 yards range. I saw some cannon strikes but nothing more as he immediately went into the cloud on his back. This I claim as damaged.

'I came into clear air by St Omer and made for Gravelines after I had climbed to 10,000 feet. As I was crossing Gravelines at 5,000 feet with my nose down, an Me 109F appeared astern of me with fast overtaking speed, partly due to a dive. I again waited until he was 500 yards away and turned towards him and completed my circuit as he pulled up and drew away. I then returned to base.'

Sailor claimed one Me 109 destroyed and another shared with Sergeant Pietrasiak, who also destroyed one more personally, and one Me 109 damaged. Squadron Leader Meares of 74 Squadron also claimed a 109 destroyed, while Squadron Leader Lister-Robinson and Flight Lieutenant Paul Richey of 609 Squadron both damaged 109s. In total, Fighter Command claimed seventeen Me 109s destroyed, five probables and fourteen damaged. Unfortunately, yet again, these claims bore no resemblance to actual German losses on this day, although the RAF pilots did come out on top: JG26 lost two Me 109s, JG2 three, offset against three Spitfires lost – two of which were from the Biggin Hill Wing, Sergeant Henderson of 74 Squadron who was killed, and 609's Flying Officer Ogilvie captured; in addition, Group Captain Harry Broadhurst, leader of the Hornchurch Wing, was wounded. Since 14 June 1941, JGs 2 and JG26 had been the only German fighter groups defending north-west France, and had collectively lost forty-eight aircraft and thirty-two pilots between that date and this. Conversely, Fighter Command had lost sixty-two pilots and eighty aircraft – representing comparative statistics of virtually 2:1 in the Luftwaffe's favour. Significantly, during the same period, Fighter Command had claimed the destruction of 214 enemy fighters, plus 84 probables and 95 damaged. In terms of the RAF's claims for aircraft destroyed, this represents an over-claiming ratio of 4.45:1. Hence the Non-Stop Offensive appeared over four times more effective and successful than it actually was. The RAF High Command, however, must have known the reality of the situation due to German signal traffic being intercepted by ULTRA – but for morale and propaganda purposes the claims stood. Politically, it was not just important to evidence support for the Soviets, it was equally vital to emphasise to America, which remained neutral, that Britain was still very much in the game and worth backing. And so, the intensive operations over France continued unabated.

On 5 July 1941, Circus 33 targeted steel works at Lille, the Biggin Hill Wing tasked with Target Support. At this time, the Short Stirling, the first RAF four-engined heavy bomber, was entering service and on this occasion three of these huge aircraft replaced the usual raiding force of multiple twin-engined Blenheim medium bombers, making the new type's first appearance on daylight operations. A lone Stirling, surrounded by RAF fighters, also bombed the Abbeville motor pool. The escorting RAF fighters did a good job, as the enemy failed to penetrate the fighter screen to attack the new bombers. Sailor reported:

'I was leading the Biggin Hill Wing, flying with 74 Squadron, and arrived at Lille ahead of the bombers. As the bombers arrived over the target area, small groups of Me 109s were observed diving from the flanks. I dived onto two of these and opening fire at 300 yards saw strikes from cannon and machine-gun enter one of these E/A. This I claim as damaged.

'On the way home I saw twenty-seven "R" boats about five miles off the French coast between Gravelines and Dunkirk, travelling NE. I dived down and attacked the rearmost boat. Squadron Leader Meares of 74 Squadron also attacked this boat from 1,000 feet.'

During this operation, Fighter Command claimed four Me 109s destroyed, two probables and three damaged. No German losses, however, are recorded for this date. Three Spitfires were lost, one pilot baling out over and rescued from the Channel, wounded, while another was captured and one killed.

The afternoon of 6 July 1941 saw Circus 35, another raid on Lille, this time by six of the new Stirlings. Again, Sailor's report relates events:

'I was on the port flank of the Close Escort with four aircraft at 20,000 feet between Lille and St Omer when several 109Fs were seen overtaking us from behind. The rear pair, led by Squadron Leader Meares, turned to the left slightly before I did and a series of dogfights ensued. The two pairs became separated and eventually we all four became separated. At the first opportunity I dived away in a series of half-rolls and aileron turns until about 400 mph was indicated. I pulled out at 5,000 feet where I straightened up for Gravelines. I was about one mile from Gravelines with my nose down when I saw a shadow across my own shadow flying in a down-coast direction. I immediately spotted a 109F and as I had a good speed I turned onto his tail, overtaking him rapidly. He was flying at 500 feet and I closed to 400 yards and gave a four second burst with cannon and machine-gun, closing in to about 50 yards. He was enveloped in smoke and did about four quick spins and went straight in.

'I then heard bullets whistling past my aircraft and did a steep turn to my left, receiving three strikes of bullets which grazed my helmet and ricocheted off the bullet-proof windscreen into my instrument panel.'

This was a lucky escape indeed! Rarely had the enemy damaged Sailor's Spitfire, much less come close to taking his head off. Was this just the luck of the draw – or was it a sign that the master was tiring? It must be remembered that Wing Commander Malan had been flying with a front-line fighter squadron since 1936, and when war broke out in September 1939 was a flight commander with responsibility. The following year had seen the desperate fighting over Dunkirk and during the Battle of Britain, when he became CO of 74 Squadron, and we have seen the intensity of the air-fighting in 1941, in which Sailor had a greater role as Biggin Hill Wing Leader. The current operations were also over enemy territory, on a daily basis, sometimes twice a day, and crossing the sea, twice, with a single-engine and limited range was stressful in itself. On top of this, Sailor had seen friends come and go, some killed or missing, plus he had the added pressure of being in the public eye. Clearly Sailor Malan was a very tough character – but not inhuman. Everyone has limits. Later Sailor acknowledged that he had 'made a mistake – a mistake I wouldn't have made if I had been fresh. You don't get the chance to make mistakes like that more than once.'

The day's subsequent events may have underlined that to the South African:

'During my turn, I saw about six 109Fs which gave chase. I went down to fifty feet and crossed just east of Gravelines in a series of jinks and received a lot of attention from every conceivable type of light flak and from what looked like coastal batteries. I found it fairly easy to avoid by watching the streams of tracer and stuff hitting the water.

   'I levelled out and steered a course for the English coast in the haze, but was repeatedly attacked from behind by Me 109Es which forced me to turn towards them each time and making them pull up. They appeared to be very bad shots for on several occasions I was surprised but, fortunately, I could see their bullets striking the water under one wing or the other, thus giving me warning. I shook them off about mid-Channel by a series of jinks, but just about the North Goodwins I was attacked by another one. I nearly got onto his tail but he used superior speed and climbed into the sun.'

Back at Biggin Hill, there was bad news: 74 Squadron had three pilots missing. According to the 11 Group Intelligence Report: 'Wing Commander Malan succeeded in destroying one of these [attacking Me 109s] and then he and several others were chased as far as Manston. During this chase, several of our aircraft were shot up.' Sergeant W.G. Lockhart, who had previously flown as Sailor's No 2, was shot down and crashed at Herly, between the coast at Le Touquet and Aire-sur-la-Lys; fortunately Lockhart evaded capture and made a 'Home Run'. Sergeant L.R. Carter, however, was shot down over the sea, and remains missing. A keenly felt loss was the third missing 'Tiger', Pilot Officer Bill Skinner DFM, 74 Squadron's longest-serving member, one of the Few with over a dozen victories to his credit. Crashing at Wormhoudt, Skinner had actually survived being shot down by Hauptmann Walter Adolph, Gruppenkommandeur of II/JG26, and was in due course reported to be a prisoner. 92 Squadron had also lost a pilot, Sergeant C.G. Todd, who was shot down and killed over France. Three other Spitfires were lost by other squadrons, while Fighter Command claimed ten Me 109s destroyed. JG26 reported damage to two Me 109s but no losses, and no evidence can be found confirming any loss to JG2.

The following day, 74 Squadron flew its final operation, an uneventful one, with the Biggin Hill Wing, before flying north on 8 July 1941 to rest and refit at Acklington. It was the end of a long and testing period of operational flying – and the end of an era for Sailor. Taking the 'Tigers' place in the Wing was 72 Squadron, commanded by 66 Squadron Battle of Britain ace Squadron Leader Bobby 'Oxo' Oxspring DFC, another fine fighter pilot and squadron commander to join Squadron Leaders Jamie Rankin DFC of 92 and Michael Lister-Robinson DFC of 609.

By this time, Sailor was streets ahead of the competition in the list of top-scoring aces. By the end of that first week in July 1941 he had claimed the destruction of some thirty-five enemy aircraft. This score was widely publicized. According to certain previous commentators, it has been said that neither Sailor nor the RAF's most famous wartime pilot Wing Commander Douglas Bader, were concerned with their personal scores. The evidence, however, suggests otherwise. Bader, the Tangmere Wing Leader, had also been flying operations since before Dunkirk and was also tired. Repeatedly asked to take a breather, Wing Commander Bader steadfastly refused, continuing to increase his personal tally, which at this time was twenty destroyed. Likewise, the signs of strain had been recognised in Biggin Hill's exalted Wing Leader, but the 31-year-old Sailor likewise refused to take a break from operations, even though, according to Walker, 'the demands by senior officers that Sailor take an extended rest were becoming more insistent.' Sailor said:

'It wasn't an order, they just came up and said how did I feel about it? I thought I was all right, and I refused. The feeling is hard to explain. Since I'd first been approached I had more than doubled my score. I kept thinking "Just a few more before I go".'

The score was the confirmation of a pilot's ability and prowess, and in Sailor's case there was a public expectation for him to continue knocking down German aircraft. Air Chief Marshal Dowding, however, emphasized that the personal score, while important, was not the primary driver:

'I probably knew Sailor better than I knew most officers serving in squadrons during that time of stress known as the Battle of Britain. I looked on him as one of the great assets of the Command – a fighter pilot who was not solely or mainly concerned with his own "score", but as one whose first thoughts were for the efficiency of his Squadron, and the personal safety of his junior pilots who fought under his command. I know that he was regarded as a heroic figure by the small fry over whom he spread his influence, and I personally shared their opinion.'

When the prospect of rest was suggested, Sailor was understandably reluctant to leave the Wing he had formed and led since its inception. But the signs of strain had been recognised, and the time fast approaching when the matter would be taken out of his hands. Responsibly, from this point on, the Biggin Hill Wing was increasingly led in the air by 609 Squadron's CO, Squadron Leader Michael Lister-Robinson, another highly experienced Battle of Britain veteran and decorated ace. Robinson was a natural and worthy successor to the great Malan, and these were opportunities for him to gain experience of leading the Wing before formally taking over.

On 22 July 1941, a Bar to Wing Commander Malan's DSO was gazetted. The citation read:

'This officer has displayed the greatest courage and disdain for the enemy while leading his Wing on numerous recent operations over Northern France. His cool judgement, exceptional determination and ability have enabled him to increase his confirmed victories over enemy aircraft from nineteen to twenty-eight. In addition, a further twenty damaged and probably destroyed. His record and behaviour have earned for him the greatest admiration and devotion of his comrades in the Wing. During the past fortnight the Wing has scored heavily against the enemy with forty-two hostile aircraft destroyed, a further fifteen probably destroyed and eleven damaged.'

This made Wing Commander Adolph Gysbert 'Sailor' Malan the first RAF officer to receive a double DSO and DFC. On the same day, both Sailor and Michael Lister-Robinson were awarded the Belgian Croix de Guerre in recognition of the support provided to 609 Squadron's Belgian pilots.

After a three-week break from operations, spent at a picturesque Kent cottage with his family, Sailor was back leading the Wing on 23 July 1941, Circus 60, an evening attack on Mazingarbe's oil refinery:

'Leading 72 and 609 Squadrons across the Channel I encountered a shelf of cloud stretching down the Strait between 26 and 30,000 feet and tried to fly round it. But I found this would take me north to Dunkirk, so I made for Calais, where I crossed at 28,000 feet.

'Soon after I saw sixteen Me 109s in St Omer area and dived to attack. E/A dived away so I pulled up again. Several more formations were then encountered and a general melee ensued. Fighting was continued all the way to the target and back to the coast.

'During these series of dogfights I noticed that several 109Fs got inside our formations and the E/A could not turn inside our aircraft tight enough to open fire.

'Seeing one Me 109 below, I dived and attacked with cannon and machine-gun and saw strikes on port wing and fuselage. I saw this E/A roll over and dive. I was forced to break away and pull up as my Section was being jumped on. I therefore claim this as a "damaged".'

According to one secondary source, Sailor led the Wing again the next day, on 24 July 1941, claiming a 109 as damaged during Circus 61 to Hazebrouck. No primary confirmation of this supposed combat claim can be found however, and so it must be assumed that the claim on 23, not 24, July 1941, as it turned out, represented the great air-fighting legend's final combat claim.

At the beginning of August 1941, Fighter Command lost its second highest top-scoring fighter pilot: Flight Lieutenant Eric Lock DSO DFC. Known as 'Sawn-off' on account of his short stature, Lock shared in common with Sailor being a farmer's son, from Bomere, Shropshire, who had grown up with a shotgun in hand, shooting game on the wing and being a natural deflection shot. On 3 August 1941, Lock's tally stood at twenty-six destroyed and eight probables, when he was shot down off Calais by Oberleutnant Johann Schmid of Stab/JG26 – Lock, doubtless destined to lead a wing himself, remains missing. At that time, Sailor was, at last, rested. His recent three-week break in the country had made him realise 'how really clapped-out I was'. He also acknowledged that his reflexes had become dull through fatigue, which was potentially dangerous for those he led. Without doubt Sailor was rested just in time. Down at

Tangmere, Wing Commander Bader had likewise repeatedly refused to leave his beloved Wing and take a break from operations. On 9 August 1941, Bader was lost; Air Vice-Marshal Johnnie Johnson, who was flying in Wing Commander Bader's Section on that fateful flight, commented:

'When Douglas was shot down it really was his own fault. He was tired, ready for a rest. Leigh-Mallory had asked him to come off Ops. Sailor Malan, leader of the Biggin Hill Wing, had already done so, recognizing in himself the signs of strain. Douglas wouldn't go, of course, and so the AOC agreed to let him stay on until the end of what we called the "season", the end of September when the weather started failing. Peter MacDonald, our Adjutant, a former MP who had served with Douglas in 1940, also recognised the signs of strain and had insisted that Douglas, Thelma, and he go off on a week's golfing to St Andrew's – they were, in fact, booked to go on 11 August. Douglas was tired and irritable, he couldn't see things quickly enough in the air. On the day in question, when Ken Holden sighted the 109s and Bader was unable to see them, he should have let Ken come down and attack as he had suggested. In not allowing this, he lost us six, maybe seven, seconds, by which time the high 109s were down on us. But, of course, Douglas was a bit greedy and would not, therefore, allow this. When I was a Wing Leader later in the war, such a situation often arose and it made sense for me, if I couldn't see the enemy, to stay put and cover those who could while they attacked. This is what should have happened that day over St Omer when we lost Douglas.'

Men like Wing Commander Bader and Flight Lieutenant Lock were irreplaceable, as were the likes of Wing Commanders Brendon 'Paddy' Finucane and Bob Stanford Tuck, both of whom went the same way the following year. Fortunately Wing Commander Sailor Malan would not. For him it was the end of an incredible intensive and accomplished period of operational flying, both defensive and offensive, with victories by day and even night, his personal score raising the bar and setting a new benchmark – which would take three years for just one pilot to exceed.

The Non-Stop Offensive continued. Michael Lister-Robinson was promoted and succeeded Sailor, as planned, as Biggin Hill's Wing Leader, scoring his first kill in his new role on 7 August 1941. The daylight operations over France went on, and on, until seventeen Spitfires were lost on Circus 110, 8 November 1941, bringing the season to a close. If the aim of Fighter Command's 'reaching out' was to draw German units away from Russia, it failed: JGs 2 and 26 were not reinforced and more than just held their own.

For Wing Commander Sailor Malan, officially the RAF's top-scoring and most decorated fighter pilot, the fighting was over.

Chapter Fourteen

A '...League of Nations of miniature'

On the same day that Wing Commander Bader found himself descending over St Omer by parachute, 9 August 1941, Sailor made his second BBC radio broadcast, in which he paid tribute to the spirit of RAF air and groundcrews:

'A large proportion of these pilots came from the Dominions, especially in Fighter Command, not to mention the Free French, Belgians, Dutch, Poles, Czechs, and other nationalities who have joined in this great struggle for freedom and the rights of mankind. I have met a few South African pilots, and without exception they make good flyers and fighters. My ambition is to get together a group of South Africans and form a South African squadron, which I hope to have the honour of incorporating in the Wing that I lead.'

This is interesting on several levels. There were Polish, Czech, Belgian, French, Australian, Canadian and all-American squadrons, but there was never a dedicated South African squadron. South Africa had its own air force, which would serve with distinction in the Western Desert, during which campaign its eleven squadrons flew 33,991 sorties and claimed the destruction of 342 enemy aircraft, but South Africans serving in the RAF, like Sailor himself, were embedded in RAF squadrons. Sailor's aspiration of forming and including a South African RAF squadron in his Wing, however, never came to pass. The multi-nationality of the RAF at this time provided opportunities for men and women of different races and cultures to serve alongside each other in a unique formation. Indeed, the largest non-British presence in the wartime RAF were volunteers from the Commonwealth, making up no less than 46 per cent of aircrew. These men, however, were from the white, not indigenous, populations of the countries they hailed from, including South Africa. The composition of the RAF was, argued Martin Francis (see Bibliography), a 'decidedly imperial affair'. To Sailor, the RAF was by now 'a sort of League of Nations in miniature'.

There was a paradox between a war to defend, in Sailor's words, 'the rights of mankind', and waging a war against the evils of racism, when there was a colour bar on service in the RAF. The Air Force (Constitution) Act of 1917, which restricted recruits to white men of European descent, and was backed up by recruiting regulations in 1923, was officially lifted in October 1939. Britain remained an Imperial power at the head of a great Empire, consistently refusing its colonies self-determination. The Second World War, though, dictated a reshaping of Britain's relationship with its colonial populations. This did not change the prevalent beliefs regarding racial differences and a colour-based hierarchy, but it did mean, so as not to undermine the loyalties of non-white British subjects, that such men had to be included and seen in the fight against fascism. Consequently, according to the Air Ministry, by early 1945 there were some 442 'coloured' aircrew and 3,900 non-white personnel serving in the RAF as groundcrew. Like white South Africans, these men were not formed into single-nationality squadrons, but interspersed throughout the service.

The RAF is a technical service, and a much smaller one than, say, the British Army, in which over half-a-million Africans served during the Second World War as both combatants and non-combatants. This, perhaps, and a generally higher standard of education amongst the 'rank and file', made the RAF a more forward-thinking entity than the Army, entrenched as it was in centuries of tradition. Indeed, an Air Ministry order dated June 1944 emphasized that 'All ranks should clearly understand that there is no colour bar in the RAF... any instance of discrimination on grounds of colour by white officers or airmen or any attitude of hostility towards personnel of non-European descent should be immediately and severely checked.' Owing to this great diversity of nationalities serving side-by-side within its ranks, which the RAF embraced, the service soon became more enlightened than both the other services and civilian employers. Air Vice-Marshal Johnnie Johnson always maintained that the RAF was much more of a meritocracy: where a man was from or what he had materially was not important; what mattered was how well he did his job and whether he was 'reliable'.

War accelerates the progress of many things, including social change. For Sailor Malan, his wartime service in the RAF provided an opportunity to experience serving alongside and mixing with men of other nationalities – including those of colour. This experience undoubtedly underpinned much of his later life, as we will see, but now we must return to 1941.

On 10 August 1941, Sailor and Lynda Malan's son was christened Jonathan Winston Fraser Malan, at Holy Trinity Church, Church Crookham,

Kent. The young Malan's godfather was Winston Churchill, whom Sailor had asked during a visit by the great man to Biggin Hill after the death of Sailor's friend Squadron Leader John Mungo-Park. The Prime Minister himself was unable to attend the ceremony on account of being en route to a meeting with President Roosevelt, so his brother, Major John Churchill stood proxy. The happy occasion even made a few seconds on the *British Movietone News*, played to the British public at cinemas nationwide. The film headlined that Sailor was the RAF's leading ace and first pilot to win a bar to both the DSO and DFC. That Churchill had accepted the invitation to become Jonathan's godfather also emphasizes the esteem in which Wing Commander Malan was held in the highest of places.

Now came a new opportunity for Sailor to use his immense ability and experience: to train new fighter pilots. His next posting was as Chief Flying Instructor at 58 OTU, based at Grangemouth in Scotland. Now he was able to start passing on his wisdom to a whole new generation of fighter pilots.

He would only be at Grangemouth a few weeks however: along with other leading RAF pilots, he was chosen to travel to America on a mission to impress and inspire Britain's still neutral transatlantic cousins, to evaluate lend-lease aircraft, and lecture American air force pilots on tactics. The RAF party included two other fighter pilots, the most senior of which was Group Captain Harry Broadhurst, formerly Hornchurch Wing Leader, and Wing Commander Bob Stanford Tuck, previously commanding the Duxford Wing. Three bomber pilots made up the numbers, Wing Commanders J.N.H. Whitworth, the Australian Hugh Edwards VC, and Group Captain J.N. Boothman, a Schneider Trophy racer. Arriving in Halifax, Nova Scotia, on 25 October 1941, the airmen flew to Washington, meeting senior officers of the American Army Air Corps. Three days later it was off to New York for a press day, thence to talk to test pilots and inspect new aircraft at various air bases. Comparison flights took place: Broadhurst flew an American P-38 Lightning while Tuck flew the familiar Spitfire. Lecturing American aircrew and discussions with test pilots followed, concluding with a presentation about the war at Wall Street's famous Stock Exchange. Tuck would later recall that the trip was 'pleasant... if very busy.... We had great fun in America, were feted and entertained.'

There was a bit too much 'fun' for Sailor at times however, who was frustrated at having no flying at the first half a dozen or so air bases visited. Sailor thought these were wasted opportunities. Although neutral, there was every hope that America would enter the war on the side of the western Allies, as 'Uncle Sam' had done in the First World War. That being so, the

American pilots would need all the advice they could get before taking on the Luftwaffe – and yet here was a wasted opportunity to learn from the best. Exasperated, Sailor made representation to the AOC, leaving him in no doubt as to the consequences of offering him another cocktail instead of a flight. It was a point well made. Sailor was provided a Bell P-39 Airacobra and took off to 'intercept' an American formation. In less than five minutes he was back, his cine-gun evidencing the fact that he had 'shot down' all twelve aircraft. For Sailor this was no victory, it was depressing: the Americans were using exactly the same outdated tactics that the RAF had entered the war with. Sailor impressed upon the American airmen four primary qualities essential to success as a fighter pilot: the ability to shoot; reasonable flying accuracy; quickness in reacting to any situation; and good eyesight.

'Not everyone is gifted in these ways,' Sailor acknowledged to his American audiences, 'but a reasonable pilot by diligent practice can make himself a good marksman. Having learnt to fly accurately it's your business – if you are in the RAF – to make yourself proficient in applied flying. To a fighter pilot this means chiefly the ability to handle your aircraft like a gun platform. Whenever you go up you should take every opportunity of practising forms of attack, curves of pursuit, and aiming your machine at targets, both moving and stationary. Practice throwing your machine into quick turns onto clouds or any moving target within reason. You will also find that by constantly whipping your machine into turns at high speed and half-rolling and pulling out, you will increase your black-out threshold.

'Good eyesight is also a gift. But eyes can be trained. The chief training for a fighter pilot's eyes is practising to focus them on distant objects. Whenever you've a spare moment at dispersal point, instead of gazing vacantly into space, or reading a book, spend as much time as possible looking at distant objects and spotting details.'

The RAF's greatest ace then went on to provide valuable insights from his experience of air fighting, and leadership:

'Now for a few basic rules. Superior height always gives you the initiative. So always strive for it. Many pilots who admit this have deluded themselves in combat that other factors are just as important. One fallacy, for instance, is that if the aircraft is designed to give its best performance at a certain height, a pilot feels this is the best height to fly. He is thus throwing aside the important fact that an enemy aircraft with perhaps 50 mph less in speed can obtain extra speed as well as initiative, by starting a fight from a few thousand feet higher with a diving attack.

'Always cruise at high speed, and train members of your formation to cope with a leader who is giving them the minimum amount of extra boost and revs to play with. It is better to cut down your radius of action and increase your performance. If the strategy demands that you operate at low cruising speeds and weak mixture in order to gain your objective, the strategy is faulty.

'A lot has been said about fighter formations. In my opinion a fighter formation is only effective if it combines manoeuvrability, flexibility, and simplicity. A fighter formation must never, I repeat that, *never*, dive to the attack without leaving at least one-third of its strength above as a top guard. This is a rule never to be departed from.

'Strict air discipline is essential for successful combat. It is good for teamwork and therefore morale. Team rules should be few and simple, but rigidly enforced. After each engagement a post mortem should be held. One definite rule I would stress is that the unit should fight in pairs. No 2 must always remain with his leader, not as an attacker, but as a rearguard while the leader attacks. A junior officer acting as No 2 can thus gain experience for the time when he is a leader.

'A few points about lines of attack: nearly all attacks develop along a curved path of pursuit in the initial stages. This may not sound important, but it is vital. If the attacker is seen, it is generally important to avoid a stern chase, for obvious reasons. With a certain amount of practice a fighter pilot can soon learn what stage to commence his turn into a target. In order to prevent a stern chase it will immediately be found that the curve-in must be commenced from well before the beam if the target is doing a reasonable speed, i.e. if he is not a glider or a slow biplane. It will also be found that an attack can be delivered on a much faster aircraft provided the turn-in is commenced in plenty of time.

'Once having closed the range, it can be decided whether to attack with deflection or to swing round to the dead astern position. Of the two main types of target, i.e. fighter and bomber, the problems are not at all similar. The bomber is most vulnerable from a head-on attack, and has its armour and armament astern and on both sides. The fighter, on the other hand, has its armour forward and aft and its armament generally forward. With the bomber, surprise is difficult, whereas with the fighter it is comparatively simple. It is safe to state that with the next phase of the war it will be found unprofitable to attack bombers from anywhere except from ahead and the flanks, particularly when they are flying in formation, which is naturally their chief form of protection.

'When attacking bomber formations, the best plan is to deliver the initial attack from ahead, provided strategy permits. After that the next line to adopt should be to attempt to break up the formation if this has not already been achieved by the head-on attack. Whereas against the bomber the attack should either be from ahead or developing in a curve from the flanks, with the fighter the head-on attack should at all costs be avoided and, if surprise can be achieved, attack with overtaking speed from below and dead astern, fire being withheld until extremely close range. Resist the impulse to fire at any range except harmonized or closer ranges. Range estimation, although it is one of the fighter pilot's chief enemies, is the cause of most of the "probables" and "damaged", and is a very simple matter to overcome. And always aim at the top edge of the target.'

The American fighter pilots were surely aware that their speaker was the living embodiment of a samurai sword-master, the *sensei*, the all-knowing expert – the teacher of all. He was a man who had been there and done it – the RAF's top-scoring ace, who knew exactly what he was talking about in every respect. The lecture and delivery of it also confirms a passion for passing on hard-won experience.

Eventually the tour was over and the RAF mission looked forward to returning home and getting on with the war. While Sailor and colleagues were homeward bound, on 7 December 1941 Japanese aircraft attacked the American Pacific fleet at anchor in its Pearl Harbor base in an undeclared act of war. At last the United States was brought into the Second World War on the Allies' side, immediately declaring war against Japan. Four days later, Germany and Italy, astonishingly, also declared war on the Americans, meaning that Hitler was now fighting a superpower on both western and eastern fronts. It was the end of what had been a long hard road for Britain since the Fall of France. Had Britain not remained in the war during 1940, thus maintaining an essential base in north-west Europe from which the liberation of enemy-occupied Europe could one day be launched, the outcome of the Second World War would have been very different. And it was Sailor Malan and Fighter Command who were at the sharp end of achieving that during those dark days which, thanks to Churchill rhetoric, have passed into history as Britain's 'Finest Hour'. Now America's long-awaited intervention heralded the beginning of the end for the Axis powers – and not a moment too soon.

Back in 'Blighty', in December 1941, Wing Commander Malan was posted to command the Central Gunnery School at Sutton Bridge, on Lincolnshire's East coast. There is no doubt that Sailor had a natural leaning towards ensuring that new pilots were provided the best possible instruction and advice – and shooting accuracy was obviously a crucial skill. When the CGS was formed in November 1939, it was purely for the aerial gunners of Bomber Command. Surprisingly, there was no provision for a dedicated gunnery school for fighter pilots. Before and during the very early war period, operational training for new pilots and conversion to front-line fighters took place on squadrons. In January 1940 however, Fighter Command decided that an adequate operational training system needed establishing, so that pilots were already converted, and had some idea of operational flying, on arrival at their first posting. Initially there were two Operational Training Units for fighter pilots, but Air Chief Marshal Dowding objected to the creation of a third until the aircraft supply requirements of his squadrons were met; indeed, some even saw, owing to the rate of accidents, OTUs as an ill-afforded luxury. The course was usually around a fortnight's duration, although cut to varying degrees during the time of crisis. Student pilots would first fly the two-seater Harvard trainer, then solo on the Spitfire, typically accumulating ten to fifteen hours practising local flying, cross-country map-reading, aerobatics and dogfighting practice. If they were lucky, the opportunity might arise to fire their guns for a few seconds at a ground target, or if luckier still, in the air at a towed drogue. And that was it. Considering the crucial importance of deflection shooting, this is somewhat surprising – but the truth was, the need for replacements for casualties suffered during the Fall of France and Battle of Britain meant there was no time for this instruction. These essential skills had to be learned on operations, in the face of the enemy – hardly satisfactory. Anyone wishing to consider just how complicated aerial gunnery and deflection shooting can be needs only to study the 'Bag the Hun' section of the *Forget-Me-Nots For Fighters* published by 13 Group in 1943. Sailor recognised this and argued the case to the Air Ministry that a dedicated fighter gunnery school should be created – and now got his wish. Of shooting, Sailor wrote:

'A fighter pilot should approach the problem of teaching himself how to shoot and fly in exactly the same way as he would learn to use a shot-gun. First your shot-gun instructor would show you a shot-gun, the various parts of it, its trigger action and safety gadgets, so your instructor shows you your aeroplane and explains the flying controls and knobs in the cockpit. Then you handle the shot-gun and get used to the feel of it and forget how the barrel appears when you want it in a flash of time. So you learn to fly and how to handle your aeroplane so that you can get your sights in the right place in the quickest possible time.

'When you can handle the gun instinctively your instructor will tell you the ways and wiles of ducks, and how you can find them and approach them. So you will learn the tactics of fighter operations and how to fight. Your Spitfire is nothing but a gun with a couple of wings and an engine to keep it in the air. Your job is to use it as a gun and fly it as part of you with your attention outside of it, until you have something in your sights when your whole concentration is along the sight and on the target. Taking my own experience as standard, if every fighter pilot had an adequate shooting training, as I had not, our scores of enemy aircraft destroyed would be exactly four times what they are.

'Unless you take a tremendous grip of yourself on operations you're certain to fire at twice the range you ought to. It feels easier to shoot when the range is great; the contrast between the size of the enemy aircraft from the speck it was when you first saw it, and the size of it when you feel close enough to shoot makes it look as if it is two hundred yards away when it is six hundred. It is only by kicking yourself that you won't shoot out of range.

'Sheer determination alone will make you hold your fire. There are two ways of judging range. One is to learn by means of the range bars, or by knowing how much of the ring the target should fill at, say, three hundred yards – and never shooting when it is smaller. The other is to notice at a particular range how much detail of the aircraft you can see – the crosses, oil streaks, the pilot's canopy – and never shoot when you can see less.

'Whatever kind of attack you're making, always bring your sight up to the target from behind it, and carry it through the target along its line of flight until you reach the correct deflection; then fire. Don't hold the sight ahead and wait for the target to meet it. Unless you do this, it is impossible to hold a steady aim without skidding and making the shooting phenomenally difficult for yourself. This is infinitely more true with an aeroplane than it is with a shot-gun because an aeroplane is slower to handle and you are firing a continuous burst, and even with a shot-gun you must always swing through from behind.'

It was not just gunnery that Sailor Malan preached. During 74 Squadron's rest period at Kirton the previous year, Sailor had produced his 'Ten Rules for Air Fighting', which, according to Wing Commander Ira Jones, assumed the status of 'Biblical quotations for the "Tiger" pilots'. These rules had been published and shared widely throughout Fighter Command, and were commonly found displayed throughout RAF stations and training schools. Now that he was officially working in a training role, Sailor had a real opportunity to impress this essential advice upon the inexperienced pilots he clearly cared so much about. Of the ten rules, Wing Commander Malan wrote:

'Generally speaking, tactics in air fighting are largely a matter of quick action and ordinary common-sense flying. The easiest way to sum it up in a few words is to state that, apart from keeping your eyes wide open and remaining fully awake it is very largely governed by the compatibilities of your own aircraft in comparison with that flown by your opponent. For example, in the case of the Spitfire versus the Me 109F, the former has superior manoeuvrability, whereas the latter has a faster rate of climb. The result is that the Spitfire can afford to "mix it" when attacking, whereas the Me 109F, although it tends to retain the initiative because it can remain on top, cannot afford to press the attack home for long if the Spitfire goes into a turn. Obviously, there are a lot of factors involved which must govern your action in combat – such as the height at which you are flying, the type of operation on which you are engaged, the size of formation etc.

'There are, however, certain golden rules which should always be observed. Some are quite obvious whereas others require amplification. Here they are: -

1. Wait until you see the whites of his eyes before opening fire. Fire short bursts of one to two seconds, and only when your sights are definitely 'on'.
2. While shooting, think of nothing else. Brace the whole body with feet firmly on the rudder pedals and have both hands on the stick. Concentrate on your ring sight.
3. Always keep a sharp look out even when manoeuvring for and executing an attack and in particular immediately after a breakaway. Many pilots are shot down during these three phases as a result of becoming too absorbed in their attack. Don't watch your "flamer" go down except out of the corner of your eye – "Keep your finger out!"
4. Height always gives *you* the initiative.
5. Always turn and face the attack. If attacked from a superior height wait until your opponent is well committed to his dive and within about 1,500 yards of you. Then turn suddenly towards him.
6. Make your decisions promptly. It is better to act quickly, even though your tactics are not of the best.
7. Never fly straight and level for more than thirty seconds in the combat area.

8. When diving to attack, always leave a proportion of your formation above to act as to guard.
9. Initiative, aggression, air discipline and teamwork are words that *mean* something in air fighting.
10. Go in quickly. Punch hard. Get out!'

In truth, these ten rules were little different to those worked out by fighter aces during the First World War. Indeed, Ira Jones had given almost identical advice to 74 Squadron pilots at that time – indicating that apart from increased aircraft performance, little had changed. The important thing was that these rules were now published in a succinct format and shared – widely. Moreover, everyone knew that these were not maxims written by some tactician tucked away at the Air Ministry writing only from the standpoint of theory and doctrine, they were written by the revered Malan. No, this was sound, practical, advice, from experience hard-earned in combat – by the RAF's leading fighter ace with a double DSO and DFC. The 'Ten Commandments', as they came to be known, could carry no greater gravitas.

In the *Forget-Me-Nots For Fighters*, Sailor continued his sermon, covering other crucial aspects of air fighting and providing us today with a unique insight into the RAF tactics used in 1940/41:

'Formation Flying: When adopting a type of formation, certain points must be borne in mind. The main point is whether you are on defensive operations, or on the offensive over enemy territory. For defensive work, formations should be manoeuvrable and compact. When flying on an offensive operation the formation should be stepped up and back from the given patrol height and should be divided into attacking and defensive units.

'Fighter formations must maintain extreme manoeuvrability, while guarding the dreaded "blind spot" behind. You'll soon find out that if you try to find the answer to the blind spot by simply spreading your machines over a broad front, you'll have lost the first essential, i.e. manoeuvrability. If you choose line astern, which is very manoeuvrable, you'll be blind behind.

'At a very early stage of the war I discovered that the only satisfactory answer was to fly in line astern and have the leader change the course of the whole formation at regular intervals.

'Squadron Tactics: At this point it would be a good thing to take you on three main types of operation.

'First we'll put you into a squadron at "readiness" on a station in SE England, with bomber raids coming over. If fighters are expected it is always advisable to climb for your height outside the combat area. Your raids are reported at 20,000 feet, therefore enemy fighters may be stepped up to at least 25,000 feet. If you have no other squadrons supporting you, you should aim to intercept, if possible, from the sun, from about 23,000 feet, unless you have time to get higher. You intercept and, if there are not fighters present, you must first destroy the bombers' main method of defence, i.e. formation flying. A good manoeuvre would be to attack with a section of four, with the object of breaking up the formation – obviously the most effective method of achieving this is to attack from ahead. But this is generally difficult. The next thing is for the remaining eight machines to work in pairs and attack – two to one bomber. We found that formation attacks did not work in practice, for many reasons which I will not discuss here. Deflection shooting on the whole is a difficult operation, and the most effective form of attack is a diving attack approaching originally from the flank and developing into a curve which brings the attacker, with about 100 mph overtaking speed, 2,000 yards behind and below. At this stage, throttle back and, at about 8,000 yards, come up to the level position and give a short burst to put the rear defence off as you are closing in; at about 250 yards, open fire, first at the fuselage and then concentrate on each engine in turn. This was found very effective with eight machine guns – the result with cannon would be quite devastating.

'Should the bomber formation have fighter escort, about one-third of your formation should be detailed to engage the attention of the fighters without actually going into combat, while the remainder go in two waves, with the same object as before. In the case of the squadron, one section of four would maintain height and fly on the flank in such manner as to menace any enemy fighters who attempt to engage the attackers.

1. Operating from the same station during raids by bomb-carrying fighters at 23,000 feet with escort.

'If the Hun approaches from the Dover area it is best to climb well towards the flank in a southerly direction, in three sections of four in line astern on a narrow front, climbing on a zig-zag course, keeping in a look-out, until a height of 27,000 or 28,000 feet has been reached. Having attained your height out of harm's way, the course from now on is shaped according to the raid information. If there is any possibility of intercepting before the enemy reaches his objective, every attempt should be made to meet him from the sun and with superior height of 2,000 to 4,000 feet. If, on the other hand, it is not possible to meet him on the way in, it is best to curl round and attempt to meet him head-on on his way out. It is well to remember that the enemy must come home sometime and usually he has not sufficient petrol to play around. Therefore it is best to get between him and his home with superior height because, if he dives away, as is usually the case, you can start your half-roll and dive in sufficient time to prevent the fight developing into a long stern chase. The basic rule applies here as elsewhere, i.e. one section of four will remain up and guard against surprise attacks on the attacking eight.

'(NOTE: Had it been possible to gain height in time to await the enemy on his inward journey, a good method would be to patrol about two miles up sun from his predicted course in line astern and with the sun on either one beam or the other. A useful hint when patrolling in the rarefied atmosphere at height, and when attempting to search in the direction of the sun, is to raise a wing-tip until it covers the sun. It will be found that the area both sides of the wing will be quite free from glare).

2. An offensive sweep over enemy territory.

'When deciding upon a formation for offensive work the aim should be to spread the units loosely, and stepped up or back, or up and to the flanks, having the major proportion on the lower level, and smaller and looser units acting as a top guard. Owing to the clean lines and high speed of the modern fighter an engagement usually develops from an empty sky in a matter of seconds. If the enemy sights and decides to engage, the tendency will be for him to spot your lower and more obvious formations, and miss seeing your light top screen in the heat of the moment.

'In most cases the patrol height is decided upon before departure. One of the important points in patrolling the other side is conservation of fuel, so climb and cruise at an economical speed with a weak mixture. If the patrol height decided upon were 27,000 feet, I would climb the formation to about 31,000 feet, and with the units stepped behind and down until crossing the lines. From then on, I would proceed on a very gentle dive to 27,000 feet and leave my rear units above and stepped up as arranged, when the lower units would be primarily for attack, whereas the upper screen would always remain up, and act purely as a defensive screen.

'Rigid air discipline is essential, and idle chatter of the R/T should be a courts-martial offence. It is impossible to lay down rigid rules. The two main rules, however, are that each unit must know the role it has to play – and that a unit should never go down to attack: always leave a top guard. If you dive, pull up again after you attack. Don't give away height.'

Sailor also gives a view on German fighter tactics:

'Characteristics of the Hun: In his training the Hun fighter pilot appears to pay a great deal of attention to tactics. This is a good fault but, unfortunately for Hitler, the German fighter seems to lack initiative and "guts". His fighting is very stereotyped, and he is easily bluffed. Another factor is that his fighter aircraft in this war have been less maneuverable than ours. There are certain things which it is well to remember when fighting him.

'His tactics, as I have stated before, although basically sound, are generally executed without a great deal of imagination, and he repeats the same old tricks with monotonous regularity. There was a saying in the last war: "Beware the Hun in the sun". In this war it seems to be truer than ever for three reasons:

(a) The Hun seldom attacks from any direction but from the sun.
(b) The modern machine, with its clean lines and good camouflage, is more difficult than ever to spot against the sun.
(c) With the fast speed achieved by the modern fighter little warning will be given before he gets within range and, furthermore, it is a well-known fact that the man who knocks you down in aerial combat is usually the one you do not see.

'For some reason or other, the Hun prefers to resort to what he considers a clever trick to catch the unwary, rather than make full use of his initial advantage and go in with a solid punch. For instance, a common trick is to detach a pair of decoys, who will dive past and in front of the British formation, hoping that someone will be fool enough to follow them, when the rest will immediately do a surprise attack from above. I am sorry to admit that some British pilots have been caught out by this tactical manoeuvre. The obvious, and most effective, action in this case would be for the Hun to make full use of his initial advantage in height and surprise by immediately attacking the formation below him.'

In the same training publication, Sailor added the following in the 'Notes' section, entitled 'DON'T LOOK NOW! ... But I think you're being followed.'

How many times have we been asked the same question: "Please sir, what do I do to get a 109 off my tail?" As if we knew. The answer really is: "Why did you let it get there anyway?"

'ATTACK: the essence of dogfighting is always to be the attacker. If you find yourself on the receiving end, we hardly like to say so, but you weren't really looking hard enough, were you? Or if you and a Hun have met suddenly, your reactions were a bit slow, perhaps. Anyhow, you're up the creek.

'DODGE: For example, a 109 dives on you – he's got superior speed, so you can't hope to fly away from him. Try foxing him then by closing the throttle and tightening up the turn. He's going too fast to out-turn you, so he overshoots. Give him a moment to get by you, then, stick forwards a bit, get behind him and shoot him down. That trick has worked many times.

'FACE THE MUSIC: Next, if you are about to be attacked, always turn and face your attacker once he is committed to his attack, even if you haven't any ammunition left. Look aggressive, that'll immediately cut down his self-confidence by half. As he comes up, turn in behind him. Whether you have any rounds left or not, it'll make him worried. If you have, why, go in and shoot him down. If not (say when you are coming back from a sweep), choose a moment when you're pointing the right way, go straight down in a bit of a spiral, pull out, and streak for home. It'll take him probably ten seconds to realise you're no longer on his tail – then he has to turn and spot you – by which time you're well on your way. If he comes at you again, try the same trick or pull another out of the hat…

'FEINT (DON'T FAINT): Such as doing a head-on attack and going down in a vertical spiral directly you pass him. He's fairly sure to lose you. That doesn't mean you don't have to weave though! Keep weaving till you are home – and remember: a good look out in time is worth any amount of evasive action.'

On 15 September 1942, Wing Commander Malan made a radio broadcast to South Africa, emphasizing that these famous war heroes were a real asset to the propaganda machine; the first part of Sailor's broadcast concerned, surprisingly, the bombing offensive, which by then was gathering ferocious intensity, by day and night:

'Our Bomber Command has been increasingly active by day, and often out of range of fighter escort. I need only mention the epic flight to Augsburg led by the South African Squadron Leader Nettleton, for which he got a well-earned VC. We have already carried out heavy day bombing attacks on

Northern France. Has it occurred to you that we might carry our daylight offensive even further afield? In my opinion there is only one limiting factor to our offensive, and that is the weather.

'Our progress has been the very reverse of the Germans. They began with daylight bombing attacks, and have through these two years been forced onto the defensive. Against that, our offensive has continually expanded in both scope and weight. Hitler knows that no part of German air territory he has overrun is safe from the Allied air offensive.

'This is a long-term assault which is gathering momentum all the time. German civilians never expected their invincible armada to be wrecked by so few opponents. And certainly they never expected retaliation of such duration and on such a scale. That's the difference. Our offensive is concerned with maiming the German war machine and its transport, and our ideal is to leave the German armed forces without the means to fight. That is our ideal and we are steadily forging towards it.'

As Air Marshal Sir Arthur Harris had famously predicted that same year, the Germans had 'sowed the wind, and now they are going to reap the whirlwind'.

Sailor then paid tribute to his fellow fighter pilots:

'Not all my fellow pilots in 1940-1 have lived to see us gain supremacy in the air. As I grieve their loss I consider the legacy they have left the entire Allied air force. It is for us to remember that those who died two years ago made possible the ascendancy we now have and will hold. Because of them I have been able to speak to you in South Africa from Britain and wish you "Alles van die beste" – all the best.'

The Union of South Africa was divided regarding support for the war. Under the 1931 Statute of Westminster, the country had become a 'co-equal Dominion', its head of state being the ruling British monarch. The South African Prime Minister upon outbreak of war, J.B.M. Herzog, was leader of the anti-English and pro-Nazi Afrikaner Nationalist Party and desired South Africa to remain neutral. This was constitutionally impossible, as legally South Africa was obliged to support Britain. The National Party, however, did not hold sway, as since 1934 it had ruled jointly as the United Party, partnered with the pro-British South African Party led by war hero General Jan Smuts. The day after Britain and France declared war on Hitler's Germany, the United Party refused to accept Herzog's neutral stance and replaced him with Smuts. Two days later, South Africa's new Prime Minister declared war on the Axis, so there was no question of the nation not fighting for Britain. Taking aside issues concerning racism, South Africa was, therefore, a deeply divided country over allegiance to Britain and supporting the war against Germany. For Sailor, this was further complicated by his Afrikaner origins, with many Afrikaners seeing him not as a war hero but as a traitor to that community's anti-English leanings – and complicated further still by the fact that certain Afrikaner quarters had never wholly accepted him on account of being half English. Nonetheless, such a broadcast by Sailor Malan, the RAF's greatest ace, remained of great value to maintaining public morale and support at home and abroad.

That same day in 1942, the first Battle of Britain reunion dinner took place, at London's Savoy Hotel, hosted by the American Generals Eisenhower, Carl Spaatz and Jimmy Doolittle, now in-country and overseeing the American air effort against Germany. Sailor was amongst the Few in attendance, as was their revered former chief, the bowler-hatted Lord Dowding, as he had become. It was a far cry from the desperate and violent events of two years before, and in his radio broadcast Sailor had paid tribute to what the Few had achieved.

Having made a unique and immense contribution to the training of new fighter pilots, on 1 January 1943 Sailor was promoted to Acting Group Captain and posted to command RAF Station Biggin Hill.

There could not have been a better to start to the New Year.

Chapter Fifteen

Biggin Hill: Station Commander

According to the *Daily Sketch*, in 1943 Biggin Hill was 'Britain's leading Fighter Command station' – and the press lost no time in trumpeting the appointment of the newly promoted Group Captain Malan as Station Commander. At 32, Sailor was now amongst the youngest officers of that rank, and acknowledged in the papers as combining 'masterly tactics with superlative leadership in aerial combats and will maintain the great tradition of Britain's Fighter Station No 1.' Group Captain Malan became the subject of an iconic photograph taken for the *Sunday Graphic*, 'in the cockpit of his new super-Spitfire'. It was not, however, the Station Commander's job to lead his Station's units in the air – that responsibility fell to the Wing Commander (Flying). Various station commanders had flown with their base's wings though, to keep their hand in – not always with happy endings. The fearless Irish commander of RAF Kenley, for example, Group Captain Victor Beamish, was reported missing on 13 February 1942 while flying with the Kenley Wing, and Group Captain Dickie Barwell, Biggin Hill's Station Commander while Sailor was Wing Leader, had been tragically killed in a friendly fire incident over the Channel on 1 July 1942. It was highly unlikely that Sailor was not going to fly on certain operations, especially with his 'super Spitfire'. Perhaps fortunately however, Sailor had missed the whole of 1942 from an operational perspective, during which there had been various developments leading to a much-changed scene since his days leading the Biggin Hill Wing – and owing to the presence of a new German fighter, which outclassed the Spitfire Mk V in every respect, a 'super Spitfire' had been desperately required.

The new menace in the sky was the Focke-Wulf 190, appropriately known by the Germans as the 'Butcher Bird'. The 190 had first appeared in small numbers during September 1941, its radial engine initially generating confusion amongst RAF pilots. The possibility of a superior new German fighter was at first dismissed by RAF intelligence, which stated it more likely to be a Curtis Hawk (some airworthy examples of which had been captured by the Germans in 1940). In October 1941, however, cine-gun film confirmed that this was no obsolete Hawk but a potent new enemy fighter.

The FW 190 was powered by a 1,700 hp BMW 801D-2 fourteen-cylinder radial engine. This provided a maximum speed of 312 mph at 19,500 feet; with a one-minute override boost it could accelerate to over 400 mph. The 190's operating ceiling was 35,000 feet, and it could climb to 26,000 feet in twelve minutes. By comparison, the Spitfire Mk VB, with which Fighter Command's squadrons were most commonly equipped at that time, could reach 371 mph at 20,000 feet, but could not operate much above 25,000 feet (359 mph), and took some twenty-five minutes to reach that height. The Spitfire Mk V was essentially a Mk II airframe coupled with a more powerful Rolls-Royce Merlin 45 engine, and a stop-gap measure, quickly providing a fighter with a better high-altitude performance than the Mk II. By October 1941, over 100 FW 190s had been delivered and began engaging on an increasing basis. Initially, the first pilots to fly the new fighter, II/JG 26, were forbidden from operating further than the French coast for fear of being brought down over or close enough to England for a 190 to be captured and examined by the British. The German pilots were impressed with the 190's rate of roll and acceleration, but, significantly, although it was extremely manoeuvrable it was unable to out-turn a Spitfire Mk V. Air Vice-Marshal Johnnie Johnson remembered: 'The 190 caused real problems. We could out-turn it, but you couldn't turn all day. As the number of 190s increased, so the depth of our penetrations over France decreased. They drove us back to the coast, really.'

22 June 1942 saw a significant event when Oberleutnant Armin Faber of Stab III/JG 2 landed by mistake at Pembrey in South Wales – presenting the RAF with an intact 'Butcher Bird'. Rapidly evaluated at Farnborough, the essential data discovered was immediately fed into the Spitfire development programme. Fighter Command's need to get the Spitfire back on top was urgent, and the engineers responded to the call. That month the first Mk IXs began reaching the squadrons, this new type being essentially an improved Merlin fitted with a two-stage supercharger combined with a Mk VC airframe. But production increased slowly, and so for some time most RAF fighter squadrons had to sally forth with the obsolete Mk V. Sailor's 'super Spitfire' was a Mk IX, which by January 1943 was the RAF's front-line fighter, eventually becoming the most numerous marque of Spitfire produced. The 'Nine' could achieve 404 mph at 21,000 feet, climbed at 4,745 feet per minute and had a service ceiling of 42,500 feet. The Mk IX dealt with the

190 menace, and as Squadron Leader Danforth Browne said, 'When that two-stage blower cut in, the sky belonged to us,' Johnnie Johnson adding that the RAF pilots 'hacked them down wherever we could find them.'

Sailor missed the 'big show': Operation *Jubilee*, on 19 August 1942, which had seen the heaviest air-fighting since the Battle of Britain. By this time the Wehrmacht was rolling ever onwards to the Russian Caucasus, having annihilated 300,000 Soviet troops at Kharkov and Kiev; the Japanese were overrunning the Far East and even threatening to link up with advancing German forces in Russia; in North Africa, things were also bleak, the British Eighth Army in headlong retreat. In spite of demands made by Stalin for the Allies to invade France, such an enormous undertaking was clearly impossible at this time. Yielding to pressure from the Soviets, and because ultimately the Allies intended to liberate enemy-occupied Europe, it was agreed to probe the enemy's coastal defences. Operation *Jubilee*, an amphibious landing at Dieppe, represented the largest combined service operation of the war so far.

Dieppe, a thriving French coastal town, was protected by high cliffs, on which were situated heavy coastal batteries. Overlooking the town, it was necessary for commandos to destroy these guns prior to a seaborne assault by two brigades of the Canadian 2nd Army and a Canadian Tank Regiment. Of the 6,000 men involved, 5,000 were Canadian. The operation's intention was to ascertain whether the harbour town could be seized and held for a day. While on French soil, Allied troops would also destroy installations and any naval vessels moored in the harbour. The operation ended in disaster for the Allies. The Germans reacted swiftly and some 1,096 Allied soldiers were killed, 1,943 captured, and 397 were missing. None of the intended objectives were achieved. But valuable lessons were learned. When the liberation of Europe was eventually mounted, no attempt was made to seize a French port; to avoid another Dieppe, the Allies towed a prefabricated harbour in sections across the Channel.

From an aerial perspective, 11 Group believed that it had achieved considerable success. Nearly 100 enemy aircraft were claimed destroyed, and 170 probably destroyed or damaged. Actual German losses were forty-eight destroyed and twenty-four damaged. Unpalatable though the thought may be, RAF losses of ninety-seven aircraft to enemy action and three more to flying accidents, with sixty-six others damaged, made Dieppe a victory for the *Jagdfliegern* and German flak gunners. To further confirm the point, the RAF lost forty-seven fighter pilots, against the Luftwaffe's thirteen. In total, the RAF had flown nearly 3,000 sorties, the enemy 945. It was the last time that air fighting on such a scale would be seen on the Channel coast.

The other big change in the air war over north-west Europe was American intervention. In February 1942 the Americans had sent staff officers, under the command of Brigadier General Ira Eaker, to England where they prepared for the arrival of US combat units. These men and machines of the Eighth Air Force were to be based in England for participation in operations against Hitler's *Festung Europa*. Eaker believed in the concept of strategic bombardment as a war winning use of air power, and had already spent two years in England studying RAF operations. Although the Eighth Air Force and the RAF were to work alongside each other, there would be a major difference in their respective operations: while RAF Bomber Command continued to pound the Third Reich by night, the Americans intended to do so by day, thus creating 'round-the-clock' bombing. Having already suffered heavy losses very early on in the war during daylight bombing operations, the RAF was sceptical of the Americans' intention to attack without the protective cloak of darkness.

Regardless of RAF concerns, at the Casablanca Conference on 21 January 1943, the Combined Chiefs of Staff agreed that a combined RAF Bomber Command/Eighth Air Force strategic bomber offensive should be mounted, beginning in 1943, immediately the weather sufficiently improved. The 'Combined Bomber Offensive Directive' (CBOD) was intended to be a strategic preparation for Operation *Overlord*, as the proposed invasion of enemy-occupied France was codenamed. The Directive to Allied air force chiefs was clear: 'Your primary objective will be the progressive destruction and dislocation of the German military, industrial and economic system and the undermining of the morale of the German people to a point where their capacity for armed resistance is fatally weakened.' Targets were listed in order of priority: U-boat construction yards, the German aircraft industry, enemy transportation networks, oil installations and 'other targets' connected with the German war industry. On 17 April 1942, General Eaker had flown in the lead aircraft of the second wave of B-17 Flying Fortresses attacking the railway marshalling yards at Rouen-Sotteville. Visibility was excellent, and from 23,000 feet Eaker's bombardiers dropped 36,900 pounds of general-purpose bombs. The bombing was reportedly 'reasonably accurate', with half of the bombs falling within the target area. The mission's success confirmed the Eighth Air Force's unshakeable faith in high level precision daylight bombing, and, arguably, from that day, the Third Reich's fate was sealed. American losses were initially heavy, as penetrations into enemy territory increased, owing to the existing Allied fighters' inability to escort the bombers all the way to their targets and back, even with auxiliary fuel tanks. Nonetheless, the Americans literally stuck to their guns, in spite of wavering public opinion over mounting casualties, and, with the arrival of long-range, dedicated, escort fighters like the P-51 Mustang, P-47 Thunderbolt and P-38 Lightning, ultimately prevailed. Until then it had fallen to the Spitfire pilots to provide whatever protection they could, and such sorties had heavily occupied the Biggin Hill Wing in Sailor's absence.

By this time, Air Marshal Leigh-Mallory, as he had become, was head of Fighter Command, although multiple squadrons were no longer how fighter wings were composed; instead, squadrons operated in pairs, providing more tactical flexibility, as should always have been the case. At the 'Bump', Group Captain Malan found the incoming new Wing Leader to be the Scottish Wing Commander R.M. 'Dickie' Milne DFC. One of the Few, Milne had flown Hurricanes during both the Fall of France and the Battle of Britain with 151 Squadron, scoring a number of victories for which he received his first DFC. After rest as an instructor, Milne became a flight commander at Biggin Hill on 92 Squadron before taking command of 222 at North Weald. Further victories followed, and a Bar to his DFC. Promoted to wing commander, he took over from Wing Commander Eric 'Tommy' Thomas DFC, another successful Battle of Britain pilot, and became Biggin Hill's fifth Wing Leader. The pair of fighter squadrons comprising the Milne's command, emphasising the international identity of Fighter Command, so important to Sailor, were the Australian Squadron Leader Hugo Armstrong DFC's 611 Squadron, and the Free French 340 'Ile de France' Squadron led by Commandant Jacques-Henri Schloesing. Both squadrons were operating the Spitfire Mk IX. Morale was mildly depressed on account of winter weather curtailing action, so the arrival of the great Sailor Malan generated a new buzz around this premier station, and action was never far away.

Unbeknown to Biggin Hill's personnel, *Luftflotte* 3 was planning the greatest daylight attack on England since the Battle of Britain – as a reprisal for Bomber Command's raids on Berlin on two consecutive nights, which had taken place several days before this *Vergeltungsangriff* (Vengeance Attack) was scheduled to take place on 20 January 1943. This was not to be a repetition of bombers escorted by fighters though, but one *staffel* of single-engined fighter-bombers from both JG2 and 26, escorted by fighters, attacking in three waves. The first wave was to cross the Channel at zero feet and attack London's docks. The second wave was to follow ten minutes behind, and hit London at medium level. The third wave comprised just fighters, patrolling the south-east British coastline and covering their comrades' withdrawal. The operation was to involve ninety aircraft and on the day, shortly after noon, the first wave, comprising fighter-bombers and fighters from the *Stab* and I/JG26, was detected by British defences incoming over the coast between Beachy Head and Rye. Inland, the raiding force separated, one section making a diversionary attack on Maidstone while the main formation raced towards London. Tragically it was a primary school at Sandhurst Road in Catford, London, which bore the brunt of the attack, thirty-eight children and six teachers losing their lives, along with other civilians nearby. The raiders actually passed over the northern end of Biggin Hill aerodrome, bound for London.

Squadron Leader Armstrong's combat report describes his part in the ensuing combat:

'At 1230 hrs we were scrambled from the lunch table and took off in pairs as pilots arrived.

'With my No 2 (F/Lt Colloredo) I climbed to 10,000 feet over London and was then told of bandits between Kenley and Beachy at zero feet, so dived down, heading South. When halfway to Beachy we saw five aircraft about three miles in front, also at zero feet. I followed these aircraft, three of which turned port and then starboard and crossed the coast at Pevensey Bay. Light AA opened up from the coast and the E/A started weaving, enabling me to catch up fairly quickly. I fired two bursts from very close range at the starboard aircraft, the first hitting the wing tip and the second hitting the cockpit. The whole aircraft blew up and went into the sea about one mile off the coast and two to three miles in front of three minesweepers. Several pilots also saw the oil patch where the aircraft went in.

'I carried on after the two remaining Me 109s and at about 800 yards, fired a burst over them which struck the sea and made them weave. I fired again from about 300 yards and hit the port radiator. The third Me 109 had then turned and started to fire at me. I turned with him and saw three Spitfires behind me and told them to attack. I did not see the Me 109 again, but saw the trail of glycol left by it. F/Lt Colloredo was with me and saw the aircraft hit the sea. My R/T was u/s so I returned to base. I claim two Me 109Fs destroyed.'

Off Dungeness, Wing Commander Milne shot down the FW 190A-4 of 2/JG26's Oberfeldwebel Paul Kerstein, who was killed, and claimed a 109 destroyed South of Pevensey Bay.

340 Squadron was also engaged:

'At 1230 hrs, amidst great excitement all available aircraft were scrambled to intercept raiders who had crossed the coast at 0 feet and were heading for the aerodrome. Before the Wing was airborne fifteen aircraft passed to the north-east of the drome, apparently having missed it. They dropped bombs in the SE suburbs of London, and then turned back. The Wing was ordered to intercept Me 109s and FW 190s. Individual combats took place over the Channel, as a result of which the Squadron claimed one Me 109 damaged (Lt Roos), and two FW 190s destroyed and one FW 190 probably destroyed (S/Lt Gouby). The latter pilot met a formation of nine FW 190s and his aircraft was hit in the ensuing combat, but he returned safely to base.'

Sous-lieutenant Gouby had killed 5/JG26's Feldwebel Alfred Barthel, whose FW 190 crashed into the sea.

On this infamous day, JG26 lost eight aircraft and pilots, JG2 lost one pilot killed and another wounded. As opposed to 1940, by now the attackers were too weak, the defenders stronger – flying 214 sorties against the ninety raiders. Never again would German fighter-bombers venture over England in strength by day. Some published accounts claim that Group Captain Malan scrambled with the Biggin Hill Wing, but no primary confirmation can be found confirming this. Nonetheless, it is highly likely that he would have done – and either way Sailor's arrival at the 'Bump' had certainly gone off with a bang.

Interestingly, in January 1943, there was a black Jamaican pilot, Flight Sergeant Vincent Bunting, serving at Biggin Hill with 611 Squadron. Although the prohibition on non-white recruits had been officially removed on 19 October 1939, black volunteers continued to be turned away during the first half of 1940. This had led to protests by black British members of organisations including the League of Coloured Peoples. Such pressure led to a token easing of the colour bar, and by 1945 it is believed that some 500 black aircrew had or were serving in all RAF commands except Transport, on account of those aircraft travelling to countries 'sensitive' about coloured troops. Most of these aircrew volunteers were from the Jamaican countries, of which some 30 per cent lost their lives either in action or as the result of training accidents. The first black aircrew volunteers were selected to train as fighter pilots – not bomber pilots, because in the RAF the pilot is the aircraft captain and it was feared that white crews would not accept a black skipper. Having trained in 1941, Sergeant Bunting, of Kingston,

Jamaica, was posted to fly Spitfires with 611 Squadron at Biggin Hill in December 1942, remaining with the unit until October 1944. Shortly after Group Captain Malan became Station Commander, the RAF's greatest ace was officially photographed in conversation with Bunting and other 611 Squadron pilots at dispersal. This was surely confirmation to Sailor of the truly multi-national force the RAF was fast becoming, with no less than twelve nationalities serving at Biggin Hill during the Second World War. The photographs were well circulated and doubtless reassured young black men from the colonies that they would be valued and respected by the RAF, inspiring more volunteers to answer the call. Today, the best source for historians of first-hand interviews and writings by Sailor originate in Oliver Walker's 1953 biography, *Sailor Malan*; while the photographs of Sailor and Sergeant Bunting do not appear in that book, presumably Walker was aware of them. Although Walker covers Sailor's post-war story, he makes no mention of his subject's attitude towards black servicemen, and how he felt about having a black pilot at Biggin Hill – which was truly a huge stride forward for diversity. Considering that Walker so extensively interviewed Sailor, it is frustrating that no mention is made of either 'Barking Creek' or of Sailor's impressions of serving alongside black airmen – why the latter is such a vexing omission will become evident in due course.

Returning to RAF Biggin Hill under Sailor's command, the fighting continued, relentlessly – and February 1943 transpired to be a bad month for this premier fighter station. Following a morning attack on Hailsham by JG26 FW 190 fighter-bombers on 5 February, one of the raiders was destroyed by a Typhoon, the pilot baling out into the Channel. II/JG26 then took off to search for the missing pilot and cover ASR vessels – provoking a reaction from 11 Group, which scrambled Spitfires, including 340 Squadron, to intercept. Squadron Leader Armstrong of 611 Squadron was already airborne, engaged on a routine training flight, and hastened to join the fray. Very low over the sea, Armstrong and his No 2 pursued a 190 which climbed into cloud – the German pilot, Unteroffizier Heinz Gomann, dropping out in due course to find himself directly behind the two Spitfires. Gomann opened fire, the leading RAF machine crashing into the water – killing Squadron Leader Armstrong. Then, on 13 February 1943, Commandant Jacques-Henri Schloesing, 340 Squadron's boss, was shot down near Hardelot by Hauptmann Wilhelm-Ferdinand Galland, younger brother of the famous Adolf and II/JG26's *Kommandeur*. The Free Frenchman was more fortunate than Hugo Armstrong, as he successfully evaded and returned safely to England.

Worse followed on 14 March, during a Rodeo operation (188). Hauptmann Galland's 190s had been scrambled in good time to position themselves at height, and on sighting the Spitfires below, two sections of German fighters were sent down as bait. The Biggin Hill Wing Leader attacked – and in turn was bounced by Galland's superior force. Wing Commander Milne was shot down and captured, and the replacement COs of both 340 and 611 Squadrons and a sergeant-pilot were also missing. These losses indicate that the skies over northern France remained a dangerous airspace.

The loss of Wing Commander Milne meant that a new Wing Leader had to be appointed at Biggin Hill – and there were at least two potential candidates: Squadron Leaders Al Deere, who had been promoted to command 403 (Canadian) Squadron in April 1942, and Johnnie Johnson, who took over 610 Squadron three months later. Deere, having flown with distinction over Dunkirk and during the Battle of Britain, was the more experienced and senior man. Johnson had missed the 'hot' Battle of Britain owing to a shoulder injury, coming to prominence the following year with Bader's Tangmere Wing. Both men were highly capable fighter pilots and leaders, decorated with double DFCs. Deere's tenure of 403 Squadron had concluded in August 1942 when he joined the staff of 13 Group. Early in 1943, the action-hungry New Zealander argued that a staff officer must maintain operational awareness and achieved his AOC's consent to temporarily fly with 611 Squadron at Biggin Hill as a supernumerary squadron leader. An uneventful fortnight later and his time up, with 'Sailor's connivance' Deere managed to stay on for a few more days, desperate to fire his guns in anger – eventually bagging a FW 190 on 16 February 1943. Two days later, Deere's return to 13 Group HQ was ordered, tempered by Sailor's invitation to 'come here at any time you like and fly with the Wing'. Deere had known Sailor for some years, on account of both 54 and 74 Squadrons having shared Hornchurch in previous years. Back at HQ, Deere was promoted to wing commander and appointed to lead the Canadian Wing at Kenley. News was then received of Milne's loss, and Group Captain Malan was straight on the 'blower' requesting that Deere's posting was changed to Biggin Hill. This made perfect sense: Deere and Malan knew and respected each other well, had flown together, and the former's recent stint on operations meant that he was already acquainted with the way things were done on the 'Bump'. Consequently, Deere was switched to Biggin Hill, while Johnson went to command the Kenley Wing – which, as it happened, proved a huge success.

With news of his posting to join Sailor at Biggin Hill, and lead the famous Wing, the newly promoted Wing Commander Deere felt that he was 'on the crest of a wave again'. Also a tactician, Biggin Hill's new Wing Leader intended to introduce 'a number of changes'. Deere wrote, 'In Sailor Malan as Station Commander I had to my way of thinking the best fighter tactician and leader produced by the RAF in the Second World War.' When putting his ideas forward in the Station Commander's office, his new boss said, 'You're the Wing Leader and the tactics you adopt are entirely a matter for you to decide. Naturally, I'm interested but have no intention of interfering, unless things go wrong.' Deere then explained that he intended to provide section leaders 'complete freedom of action… squadrons in the Wing formation should be independent, yet inter-dependent, and that the same should apply to sections.' Sensibly, Deere's intention as Wing Leader was to maintain responsibility for routes and timings, far-sightedly allowing 'squadron and section leaders being free to act on their own initiative to engage enemy aircraft on sighting… I was keen to get away from mass-controlled attack and to rely on mutual support between the squadrons and sections within the Wing as the tactical basis of a more flexible and profitable form of attack.' All of this was far-removed from Leigh-Mallory's 'Big Wing' balderdash and the shambles leading to Wing Commander Bader's loss over France on 9 August 1941. It was men like Malan, Deere, and indeed Johnson, who truly understood fighter tactics and were at the forefront of driving innovative and effective change. Deere also proposed other changes, the benefits of which Group Captain Malan immediately recognised, adding that to make them work, the new Wing Leader would need support from his two squadron commanders, now being Squadron Leader Charlton 'Wag' Haw of 611, and the French Commandant René Mouchotte leading 341 Squadron, which had recently relieved 340. This was real leadership, involving and respecting subordinates, achieving 'buy-in' and ownership. Unsurprisingly, both squadron commanders readily agreed to implement the required changes. Exciting times lay ahead – and the Malan/Deere combination would prove a match every bit as perfect as Johnnie Johnson and Kenley's tough Canadians.

On 1 April 1943, a milestone in RAF history was reached on what was the twenty-fifth anniversary of the junior service's founding. In an inspired example of inclusive leadership and man-management, Group Captain Malan addressed *all* personnel of his famous fighter station, focusing on the unsung heroes of his command:

'You are members of the Sector Station which has produced the most outstanding achievements in the Battle of Britain and which, not being content with the standards set in 1940, has continued to lead as the foremost sector in this Command.

'Today, as most of you know, Biggin Hill Sector is very close to approaching its thousandth confirmed victory, not to mention the "probably confirmed" and "unconfirmed".

'I would like to say a few words in recognition of the magnificent support the pilots have always received from ground personnel, whether their duties have been concerned with the direct servicing of aircraft at dispersals, the dirty and arduous work in the workshops, or whether they have been concerned with the supply of equipment for pilots or aircraft, or whether they have been concerned with their payment, their clothing, their cooking, or their living conditions.

'You people who work in the background seldom get either official or public recognition. This is chiefly because your duties are not so glamorous and do not make "front page news". When you leave this parade today I want you to bear in mind that your duties, however boring and non-essential they may appear at times, are absolutely vital to the successful continuation and termination of this grim war. Whenever you feel bored, tired or dispirited I would like you to remember this. I want you to realise that you are honoured by being allowed to serve in a fighting machine that has performed wonders in the past and is playing a major part in the war effort. Every minute of every day you spend at your work you are performing a task which is making history and which will go down to posterity as the most glorious achievement by a magnificent service at a time when its country and Empire needed it most.'

Sailor's reference to the approaching thousandth kill generated a buzz on the Station, which organised a sweepstake: £150 for the winning ticket, and £300 to the successful pilot – the equivalent of £13,500 in buying-power today, so a significant sum. The press soon descended on the Station, the matter being of national pride and interest. As the year progressed and the weather improved further still, the target was approached, albeit slowly…

On 4 April 1943, Sailor flew as Wing Commander Deere's wingman on Ramrod 51. While escorting bombers across the Channel, the Wing Leader was forced to return owing to engine trouble. Group Captain Malan took the lead, completing the sortie, but of the Luftwaffe there was no sign. On 13 April, Deere led the Wing on Circus 281, an attack on Abbeville's marshalling yards, with Sailor again flying No 2 – but still no reaction from the Germans. That evening, Sailor himself led 611 Squadron on a

Ramrod – fighter sweep – over St Omer, but again the enemy remained on the ground. The period of inactivity broke on 18 April, when Squadron Leader Jack Charles blasted a 190 into the sea over the Baie d'Authie. Two days later, Sailor flew as Deere's No 2 on Circus 288, an attack on Boulogne, but no German fighters engaged. The following day, Sailor was once more the Wing Leader's No 2 and had to take the lead when Deere was unable to jettison his auxiliary fuel tank. This time FW 190s were evident but prevented from attacking the Ventura bombers due to skilful parrying by Sailor – but no German fighters were shot down.

For the Malan family, April 1943 bore witness to a personal loss: on the 26th, Flying Officer Francis Malan, Sailor's younger brother, was killed in action. The younger Malan had followed in his esteemed brother's footsteps and travelled to England, joining the RAFVR. After flying training, he was posted to fly Spitfires with 72 Squadron. For a time, in 1942, after Sailor had handed over the Wing and before commanding the Station, 72 Squadron was part of the Biggin Hill Wing. On 15 April 1942, Sergeant Malan, as he then was, participated in Circus 124, damaging a FW 190 over Boulogne. In July 1942, Squadron Leader Bobby Oxspring DFC took command of 72 Squadron and recalled that, like Sailor, Francis had 'exceptional' eyesight, giving the squadron 'the edge over the opposition'. In January 1943, Oxspring took 72 to Tunisia, the unit operating out of Souk el Khemis. 'Oxo' recalled that on a sweep east of Medjez, 72 Squadron intercepted a gaggle of enemy aircraft attacking army positions – which were already subjected to 'a hail of British flak' as his Spitfires engaged. Francis Malan was badly hit by friendly ground fire and badly wounded. Crash-landing, army surgeons were 'shocked at the bitterness with which he cursed all "Pongos".' On the day of his death in action North of Bon Arada, Francis was 'last seen weaving frantically to avoid flak at 1,000 feet', while 72 Squadron was engaging German fighters. Whether he was hit by flak, again, and killed, or shot down by an enemy fighter, nobody knows. Today Flying Officer Malan, who was a married man of 23, lies at Massicault War Cemetery.

Back home in Cape Town, Sailor's family were already known as the 'Fighting Malans'. In addition to Sailor and Francis serving in the RAF, Stanley was an army sergeant, a tanker, while Ralph was an observer in the South African Air Force. Having falsified her age, their mother, Evelyn, served as a pay clerk in the SAAF.

Back at Biggin Hill, unsettled weather was decelerating the Sector achieving that all-important 1,000th victory. The pressure was on, with the press 'continuously on our doorstep', as Al Deere later recalled. On 4 May 1943 the score stood at 994. That evening, Deere led the Wing escorting B-17 Flying Fortresses bombing Antwerp, personally destroying a 190 and increasing the tally to 995.

Ten days later the number was the same. On that day, the Biggin Hill Wing escorted Fortresses bombing Courtrai. En route, according to the 341 Squadron ORB, the Wing was 'busily engaged with several Hun formations', and after the Americans had accurately bombed the target, 341 was heavily attacked and scattered. Attacked by four FW 190s, Capitaine Christian Martell shot one down in flames – this was the squadron's first victory. Over the target, the CO of 611 Squadron, Squadron Leader Jack Charles DFC destroyed another 190, while Sergeant E. Clark of the same unit collided with the 9/JG26 Me 109G of Leutnant Paul Schauder, both pilots baling out. With the score at 998 and the weather set fair, excitement was at fever-pitch.

According to the 341 Squadron ORB, 15 May 1943 dawned 'an exceptionally fine day with good visibility'. Circus 297 was to be flown, six B-25 Mitchells being briefed to attack the JG2 fighter airfield at Caen-Carpiquet, which would then be pounded by Typhoons; Poix airfield was also to be attacked by Boston bombers. Such an aggressive operation would undoubtedly provoke a violent reaction from the German fighters, and so yet again Sailor flew as the Wing Leader's No 2.

341 Squadron reported that 'twelve Spitfire IX led by Commandant Mouchotte took off at 1621 hrs as a free-lance wing with the object of bouncing Huns, which might be aroused by the bombing of the airfield at Caen. The Squadron crossed the French coast at Trouville. When about ten miles SE of Caen, 611 Squadron was mixed up in a general dogfight 2,000 feet below. Commandant Mouchotte led 341 Squadron still on a westerly course ready to bounce any stragglers which may have been split up by 611 Squadron fighting below. He had the good luck to bounce a lone FW 190, which after a long burst dead-astern, slightly above, exploded in mid-air. In the dogfight below, 611 Squadron's boss, Squadron Leader Jack Charles, shot down two FW 190s, bringing Biggin Hill's tally to 999, Commandant Mouchotte's Hun being the 1,000th. As there is some doubt as to the exact moment of destruction of the CO's FW 190, the honour may be shared with 611 Squadron. This is for the Station Commander, Biggin Hill, to decide.'

Over Caen, the Biggin Hill Wing had been attacked by I/JG2, which lost four pilots, including 2/JG2's Oberleutnant Horst Hanning, holder of the Knight's Cross with Oak Leaves, who was one of Squadron Leader Jack Charles' victims. Both of Charles' victories were timed at 1710 hrs, Mouchotte's at 1711 hrs. According to Al Deere, at the debrief René Mouchotte 'chivalrously claimed he had seen Jack Charles' two victims go down before his own – which is borne out by the combat report timings – but Charles, a Canadian, generously refused to accept this and insisted that the honour and prize should be shared. Group Captain Malan agreed. It was a proud moment in the history of all concerned. While Sailor would undoubtedly have dearly loved to have scored the 1,000th victory, there was some solace: he won the £300 sweepstake! The press soon arrived in droves, journalists, cameramen and radio broadcasters all demanding interviews, while letters to the two conquering heroes, requesting signed photographs, arrived in their hundreds.

By coincidence, 341 'Alsace' Squadron had arranged a party that night at the Hyde Park Hotel, celebrating their first victory. The occasion now became an extended affair. Wing Commander Deere requested that the Biggin Hill Wing be stood down from operations the following day, given that the party was likely to be a 'late affair'. Although this proved impossible, Deere was assured that his Wing would only be used as a 'last resort'. The party was a great success, but at 1030 hrs next day Deere was leading his Spitfires to Portreath, from where they escorted Venturas bombing Morlaix airfield. The exhausted pilots returned to Biggin Hill late that evening, fortunately having encountered no enemy opposition – with the official celebration of the 1,000th kill yet to come.

The official party was arranged for Wednesday, 9 June 1943. That day, Simon Wardell reported in the *Daily Express*:

'Some of the brightest stars of Fighter Command will gather in London tonight to celebrate the triumph of the Biggin Hill Sector in shooting down 1,000 German planes.

'They and their womenfolk will assemble in the Great Room of Grosvenor House, Park Lane, W1, and dancing will go on till 3 am.

'At least 1,000 guests are expected on the invitation of Group Captain "Sailor" Malan and the officers of the Sector.

'Squadron Leader Charles and Commandant Rene [Mouchotte's identity was concealed, to protect his family still in occupied France], who shared in the destruction of the 1,000th plane, will be there. So will Charles's squadron commander [incorrect: should be Wing Leader], the great New Zealand fighter Alan Deere, who recently added a DSO to his decorations.

'At the top table will sit Air Marshals Sir Arthur Harris and Sir Trafford Leigh-Mallory, leaders of Bomber and Fighter Commands.

'For days, the preparations have gone on like this:

'At Biggin Hill. In the messes there and at the other airfields of the Sector – their names are still on the secret list – fighter pilots have talked between sorties of the girls they will bring. Batmen have been getting out their officers' smartest uniforms, polishing buttons until they shone like gold.

'At Grosvenor House. A stream of officers and men were hurrying to and fro last night. "It's been more like an air force station than a banqueting office for the last day or two," commented the banqueting manager, Mr A.T. Abbot.

'In front of the gallery along one wall of the ballroom, with its silver-sprayed columns and cream distemper – it used to be a skating rink – eleven of the Biggin Hill ground staff were putting up a full-scale model of a Spitfire in flight, measuring 36 feet 10 inches from wing-tip to wing-tip.

'It had been brought from Woking's "Wings for Victory Week"; on Thursday it will go on to Richmond. Behind it will be draped light blue ensigns of the RAF, and the Spitfire will seem to be banking out of a cloud as the limelight from the gallery opposite plays on it.

'And on the top table will be placed a perfect miniature model of the Spitfire Mark Nine, with its four-bladed airscrew and cannons – just like the plane that destroyed the 1,000th raider.

'Tonight, the snacks will be provided by the officers, for the hotel management said they would find it impossible to cater for such a huge gathering. They will find the drinks, however.

'"I suggested 50 bottles of whisky," said the banqueting manager, "But it appears they want much more than that. The band will be a special RAF band, provided by the officers. The cost of the party will be less than £1 per head."

'The ball is fixed to begin at nine – although they doubt whether it will get into full swing before 10 – to allow pilots who have been out on daylight sorties to get to London in time.

'The cabaret is to be provided by Vivian Van Damm, who says he is keeping something up his sleeve. And to round off the evening a showpiece measuring sixteen feet across and painted by a Biggin Hill squadron leader will be unveiled.

'"The paint is still wet, so you can't see it," the artist told me. "It embodies the names of all our squadrons, and of the wing commanders of Biggin Hill – Jamie Rankin, Dickie Milne and other great pilots. A 'V'-sign and the RAF badge are included in the design. And grouped on either side of the main piece will be four plaques symbolic of the four other sector stations."

'But the night-fighters will miss the party. The thousand kills the RAF are celebrating include many shot down by night-fighter squadrons, and their pilots cannot, of course, attend the ball.

'Perhaps, as the daylight aces dance below, they will be winging over the Home Counties after the raiders and intruders that sneak across the coast under cover of darkness.'

As Basil Cardew reported in the following morning's *Daily Express*, Malan's 'Wizard war-time party' was actually 'a double celebration':

'Only a few hours before, his tall, dark-haired wife, Lynda, had a baby daughter in a county hospital in Kent. She is the second Malan child, for Jonathan, their son, is now three years old.

'I found Malan celebrating with Hughie "Taffy" Edwards, lanky VC bomber pilot, in a secluded room away from the dancing crowd. "Lynda wanted a girl to complete the family," said Malan. "Both are doing well. So this is the greatest night of my life."

'Two RAF bands played throughout the six-hour celebration, and there was a cabaret.

'There was an exuberant Wing Commander Al Deere, the cauliflower-eared New Zealand boxer who now leads the Wing at Biggin Hill; broken-nosed Jamie Rankin, who started the station's sweeps against the enemy in 1941; Barkley [author's note: this is incorrect but refers to Tony Bartley] and Sheen, two grand Battle of Britain leaders, and scores of other men who battled against the Luftwaffe.

'Squadron Leader Jack Childs [this is also incorrect and actually refers to Jack Charles] sent a message of good cheer from his bed, where he is recovering from bronchitis. But the French pilot, Commandant Rene, the other victor, had brought along a dozen more Fighting French fliers in their blue uniforms and gold braid. Rene's family live in German-dominated Brest, so his other name must be suppressed.

'Sergeant-pilots as well as officers had been invited. Many of the fliers who brought their womenfolk had scarcely had time to shed their flying kit and tumble into Sunday uniforms. Several pilots I talked with had been out on patrol in the afternoon, skirmishing with the Luftwaffe.

'They held the dance and party in the Great Room of Grosvenor House, Park Lane, W1, and one of the bands that played swing music and languid tunes in sudden contrast had played to the men during the Battle of Britain.

'I have heard and seen them playing at the Biggin Hill Mess at lunchtime, while pilots scrambled a quick meal, in those days of 1940 when Hitler was sending 1,000 planes against us.

'At almost every table these young fighter pilots of Britain re-lived again their battles in the sky...'

On the same day, the *Daily Sketch* also covered the story under the headline 'Air Aces Hold "1,000-V" Party,' although this report somewhat conflicted with the *Daily Express* stating that Jack Charles was not present:

'Biggin Hill, Britain's leading Fighter Command station, last night celebrated the shooting down of their 1,000th plane with the biggest wartime party London has seen for four years.

'Group Captain "Sailor" Malan DSO DFC, Commanding Officer at Biggin Hill, sent out 1,000 invitations but far more than 1,000 people came. The smartest air force uniforms of the Allies and most glamorous evening frocks in Mayfair stormed the sturdy RAF guard of 20 strong, and all got past.

'Sailor Malan went through the evening with a broad grin on his face. "I have a new daughter," he told me. "She was born today at 1 o'clock. That makes the thing perfect. I already have a boy, aged 3, called Jonathan Winston, Mr Churchill is his godfather."

'With him were Squadron Leader Charles and Commandant "Rene", who shared in the destruction of the 1,000th plane.

'And while the day pilot aces danced the night away, the night-fighter squadrons of Great Britain kept their faithful vigil in the skies.'

On conclusion, the London cabbies of the Beaufort Club insisted on getting the pilots and their guests home for no charge. Later, Sailor returned the favour by inviting fifty cabbies to a 'gloriously alcoholic evening' at Biggin Hill, at which the taxi drivers sang a special ditty, composed by cabbie Barney Dowling:

Here's to the lads of Biggin Hill,
Who gave us many a thrill,
When things looked glum.
Now we've got them on the run,
When they fly from Biggin Hill,
Led by Sailor Malan and
His merry band...

Certainly, the tide of war had changed significantly since the dark days of 1940. In North Africa, Rommel, and Germany's Italian ally, had been defeated by British and American forces, leading to the invasion of Sicily and Italy, and collapse of the Mussolini regime in July 1943. On the *Ostfront*, Stalin's massive counter-offensive, launched in November 1942, turned the tide in Russia, culminating in the Sixth Army's virtual annihilation at Stalingrad in January 1943. In the Far East, Singapore had fallen on 15 February 1942 – a decisive victory for the Japanese and described by Churchill as the 'worst disaster' in British military history. By mid-1943, however, the Americans, having achieved a turning point in the Pacific war at Midway in June 1942, were aggressively prosecuting the war against Japan with a series of amphibious assaults on key Japanese-held islands in the Pacific. Germany was being bombed around the clock by Britain and America, draining Luftwaffe resources, although in most respects the air war over northern France continued as it had before. Ultimately, the aim of the western Allies remained to land in France and liberate enemy-occupied Europe, driving into the heart of Germany. Learning from the failure at Dieppe, in July 1943 plans were submitted for such a landing, although detailed preparations for the invasion – Operation *Overlord* – would not begin until after the Tehran Conference on 28 November 1943, at which the 'Big Three' – Roosevelt, Stalin and Churchill – agreed that it should be the primary war aim in the west.

During the summer of 1943, the Biggin Hill Wing continued flying offensive operations almost on a daily basis. Sailor still flying on operations, sometimes leading 611 Squadron or as the Wing Leader's No 2. At the beginning of July, 611 Squadron was rested and replaced in the line by 485 (New Zealand) Squadron, led by the Kiwi ace Squadron Leader Johnny Checketts. The French 341 Squadron were determined to remain in action as long as possible, although Commandant Mouchotte was tiring, as evidenced by this entry in his diary: 'And the sweeps go on at a terrible pace… I am at the record figure of 140. I feel a pitiless weariness from them. It is useless for me to go to bed at 9.30 each night; I feel my nerves wearing out, my temper deteriorating. The smallest effort gets me out of breath; I have a crying need for rest, were it even for forty-eight hours.' Sailor, himself no stranger to the exhausting effect of protracted operational flying, sensed that Mouchotte was tiring, but the fanatical French fighter refused leave when offered by his Station Commander. This was a fatal mistake.

By this time, Germany was advancing its *Vergeltungswaffen* – Vengeance or 'V' weapons – and intelligence received from occupied Europe enabled the Allies to strike at certain sites suspected of being associated with this worrying development. On 27 August 1943, 224 Flying Fortresses were briefed to attack such a suspected target at Watten, in the Pas-de-Calais. The Biggin Hill Wing was flying as close escort to the American 351st Bomb Group, but Wing Commander Deere's engine had failed on take off, so his place in the van was taken by Commandant Mouchotte. The raid provoked a violent reaction from the Germans, with both JG2 and 26 responding. II/JG26 tore through the Biggin Hill Wing, Oberleutnant Walter Matoni, an ace, shooting down one of the hated *Viermotor* – four-engined heavy bombers. The Spitfires engaged the FW 190s in a running battle between St Omer and Calais, 5/JG26 losing Flight Sergeant Magrot, who was killed. 341 Squadron was in trouble with 6/JG26, Feldwebel Wilhelm Mayer shooting down a Spitfire near Merville, while Commandant Mouchotte – isolated and alone – was hacked down off the French coast by Leutnant Radener. Back at Biggin Hill, Group Captain Malan, 'Spy' de la Torre, the Station Intelligence Officer, and Al Deere, awaited their friend's return in vain: the brave Frenchman's body was washed up on the enemy coastline a few days later, his epitaph provided by Sailor: 'He was a leader, a fighter and a gentleman. We shall all miss him.' In his diary, Mouchotte, whose loss stunned his compatriots, had written, 'If I am not to survive this war, let me at least have the satisfaction of falling to the enemy's fire.' The brave Frenchman got his wish.

Then, a few days later, on 6 September 1943, the Wing was covering Marauders bombing marshalling yards at Serqueux, when 485 Squadron was bounced by twenty FW 190s. After shooting down a German fighter, the unit's CO, Squadron Leader Johnny Checketts DFC, was hit and wounded; force-landing near Abbeville, he was hidden by French patriots and, with assistance from the Resistance, eventually returned home safely. But, at the time it was not known whether he was dead or alive, so for Biggin Hill to lose two fine pilots and squadron commanders in such short order was unlucky indeed, when the Allies were in the ascendant and casualties light.

By now, Wing Commander Deere had flown 120 operations as Wing Leader, and was also reaching the end of the line. By 15 September 1943, Al had taken to his bed, suffering from dysentery. Sailor immediately summoned the Station Medical Officer, who in turn sent for a specialist; it was just in time: the New Zealand ace was suffering from acute enteritis, which if left untreated any longer would have been very serious. While the Wing Leader was rushed to hospital, Sailor conferred with the 11 Group AOC, Air Vice-Marshal 'Dingbat' Saunders, who agreed that Wing

Commander Deere should be rested immediately – and had flown his last operational tour.

The question of casualties, and appropriately commemorating those who died, was very much on the mind of Squadron Leader Cecil King, Biggin Hill's padre, who suggested that the names of all who had died flying from Biggin Hill should be recorded and remembered in a memorial chapel. It was felt especially important to commemorate victory in the Battle of Britain, and those of the Few who had made the ultimate sacrifice. This was duly agreed and the St George's Chapel of Remembrance was created on the Station out of three prefabricated huts. The names were written in gold on the reredos and in the hallowed Book of Remembrance. Appropriately, the Chapel was opened by Group Captain Malan on 19 September 1943 – Battle of Britain Sunday. Of the ghosts of Biggin Hill, Churchill wrote:

'My personal association with Biggin Hill during the Battle of Britain lives in my mind. As a nation we have short memories and it is well that Memorials such as this should bring to our remembrance the cost of victory in the days when one of our fighter pilots had to be worth ten. They died without seeing the reward of their efforts; we live to hold their reward inviolate and unfading.'

Reading the opening address at St George's would be Sailor's final significant duty. He too was exhausted, and fell ill at home on 16 October 1943. Sent on sick leave, Group Captain Malan was posted away, effective from 1 November 1943: his long and distinguished association with this most famous of fighter stations was now over.

A new and decisive stage of the war was about to begin...

Chapter Sixteen

19 (Fighter) Sector

On 17 January 1944, The *Daily Mirror* headlined 'Secret Job For Malan of "The Few".' The short report announced that newly promoted Group Captain Hugh Lockhard-Maxwell DSO was taking over at Biggin Hill, while emphasising that 'No specific details can be given' of Sailor's 'new job'. So, what was the 'Secret Job'?

The whole Allied effort in the west, following success at last in the desert, was now gearing up to the liberation of Europe. The question was not 'if' but 'when' would the invasion take place? The tactical necessity for aerial supremacy over the battlefield meant that Allied fighters would become fighter-bombers, attacking enemy ground targets and harrying troop and vehicle movement whenever and wherever possible. In anticipation of this, Fighter Command had been reorganised into Air Defence Great Britain (ADGB), responsible for home defence, and a separate tactical air force which would support the invasion troops. The idea was to create a composite, tactical, force of fighters, bombers, fighter-bombers and army cooperation aircraft, independent of existing Commands. This new tactical air force would exist exclusively for deployment in support of the Allied Expeditionary Force, which was being formed to undertake the proposed invasion. On 1 June 1943 this new aerial entity officially became the 2nd Tactical Air Force (TAF), comprising largely of units formerly from No 2 Group Bomber Command (the RAF's light bomber force) and various squadrons from Fighter Command.

The 2nd TAF's first AOC was Air Marshal Sir John d'Albiac, who on 21 January 1944 was succeeded by Air Marshal Sir Arthur 'Maori' Coningham, who had previously been the Western Desert Air Force's first chief. When he arrived in North Africa in 1941, there was little coordination between the air force and army in combined operations. Coningham therefore pioneered tactical air power, understanding the army's requirements for reconnaissance and air support. Proof of Coningham's success was provided by Rommel himself, who wrote of the second, decisive, Battle of El Alamein: 'British air superiority threw to the winds all our tactical rules... the strength of the Anglo-American Air Force was the deciding factor.' Clearly 2nd TAF would have a crucial role to play in the proposed liberation of enemy occupied Europe.

The plan was that the fighters and fighter-bombers of 2nd TAF would provide tactical support to the advancing British and Canadian armies (the American Ninth Air Force would similarly support American troops), exploiting the experience gained by Coningham in North Africa, Sicily and Italy. Using the 'Cab Rank' system, RAF officers embedded in army units would be able to summon air support from orbiting fighters and fighter-bombers, which could soften up enemy strongpoints. The Allied fighters would also have to ensure aerial supremacy over the battlefield, and become mobile units, living in tented accommodation and able to move quickly, keeping up with rapidly advancing armies. To prepare for this nomadic existence, RAF fighter squadrons and wings were reorganised and were no longer focussed entirely on sector stations. As early as 1942 it had been appreciated that more airfields would be required on the south coast to accommodate the aircraft supporting the invasion, especially in the campaign's early stages, before Allied aircraft could operate from captured bases in France. While some squadrons were dispersed to established stations and satellite airfields, others were accommodated under canvas and in requisitioned properties, operating from new Advanced Landing Ground (ALG) bases with rudimentary facilities, which sprang up all over the south coast – and in this crossover to a mobile tactical air force we find the answer to Group Captain Malan's 'secret job'.

Sailor's posting was to oversee formation of the new 19 (Fighter) Sector, comprising two wings: 132, made up of 66, 331 and 332 Squadrons, both the latter Norwegian, based at the ALG at Bognor, and the Czech 310, 312 and 313 Squadrons of 134 Wing based at Apuldram ALG – both airfields being within the Tangmere Sector, near Chichester in West Sussex. Previous accounts state that in March 1944, Sailor went to command 145 Wing, comprising three French squadrons, with two of which he was well-familiar from Biggin Hill days, 329, 340 and 341, based at Merston, the Tangmere satellite. This is not the case. The initial Wing Leader, Wing Commander Roy Marples, was killed in a collision on 26 April 1944, being replaced by the New Zealander Wing Commander Bill Crawford-Compton, before Sailor's old friend Al Deere took over early in June. The actual fact is that 145 Wing was absorbed into 19 (Fighter) Sector so was one of three wings for which Group Captain Malan had overall responsibility in terms of fighting efficiency, administration and logistics. It was an exciting time, the anticipation palpable as men and materiel built up along the south coast in readiness for the invasion that everyone knew must be soon.

As early as December 1943, General Dwight Eisenhower, known commonly as 'Ike', was appointed by President Roosevelt as Supreme Commander, Allied Expeditionary Force. Eisenhower's appointment was made public in January 1944, as was the identity of the Deputy Supreme Commander at Supreme Headquarters Allied Expeditionary Force (SHAEF): the British Air Chief Marshal Sir Arthur Tedder. The following month, the Combined Chiefs of Staff issued Eisenhower with a clear directive: 'You will enter the Continent of Europe and, in conjunction with the other United Nations, undertake operations aimed at the heart of Germany and the destruction of her armed forces.' Allied land forces were commanded by a Briton, General Sir Bernard Law Montgomery, the Hero of El Alamein whose 'Desert Rats' had defeated Rommel's *Afrika Korps* in the Western Desert. It was Montgomery, in fact, who formulated the plan for the proposed Normandy landings. As the Combined Chiefs of Staff had decreed that *Overlord* should take place in May 1944, from January onwards all Allied efforts were concentrated on training and preparing for D-Day.

Across the Channel the Germans knew that the invasion was coming, but did not know when or where. The Western Front was 600 miles long and, the enemy knew, could not be held with the forces available which, especially after the disaster at Stalingrad, had been drained by the Eastern Front. Oberst Bodo Zimmerman, a staff officer at Western HQ (*Oberbefelshaber West*), later described the German defences in 1943 as 'A mere patchwork. Commanders, troops and equipment were second rate.' To conceal this deficiency Hitler ordered the construction of substantial concrete fortifications along the Channel coast: the so-called *Festung Europa*, the 'Atlantic Wall'. It was also OKW policy to rotate exhausted and depleted units from East to West, so although on paper mighty divisions appeared present in France, the reality was that they were shadows of their former selves. Immediately back to strength, however, these formations were sent back to the Russian meat-grinder. During the late summer of 1943, Hitler, in *Führerweisung* 51 (Führer Directive No 51), decreed that from that point onwards the Channel coast would become the main defence area, to which the bulk of new heavy weapons production and munitions would be sent. Operational instructions were clear: the enemy must not be allowed to maintain a foothold on the coast, but must be thrown back into the sea at once. The coast must be held at all costs and any withdrawal was forbidden. The commander in the West was that old architect of previous victories, Generalfeldmarschall Gerd von Runstedt. He responded, pointing out the reality:

1. Most German soldiers in the West were too old and unfit.
2. Most units were insufficiently mobile and therefore of limited tactical value.
3. There was a severe shortage of heavy weapons, especially tanks.
4. Precious few parachute and Panzer divisions were fit for operations.
5. There was no strategic reserve in the West (for decisive intervention once the invasion had been launched).
6. The Luftwaffe was too weak to contain the Allied air forces.
7. The Kriegsmarine was virtually non-existent and the Channel was too shallow for effective submarine operations.

Although Hitler promised suitable reinforcements, these either arrived in too small numbers or were absorbed by the Eastern Front as one crisis after another overwhelmed the German forces engaged there. Regarding the Luftwaffe, Hitler assured Von Runstedt that immediately the invasion began, all available fighters would be transferred west. Towards the end of 1943, Hitler appointed Generalfeldmarschall Erwin Rommel, Montgomery's famous adversary in North Africa, to inspect the Western coastal defences. Not only did the 'Desert Fox' possess initiative, experience and a sound technical knowledge, but his very personal presence was hoped to be morale-boosting. At a meeting in Paris, Von Runstedt described the situation to Rommel, concluding, 'It all looks very black to me.' Over the Christmas period of 1943, Rommel reported to Hitler his belief that the Allied invasion would be made between Boulogne and the Somme, and either side of Calais. There were sound reasons for this, but Hitler maintained that the landings would be made in Normandy. All along the Atlantic coast in January 1944, the construction of foreshore obstacles commenced. According to Rommel, the object of these underwater obstructions was 'not only to halt the enemy's approach which will be made in hundreds of landing boats and ships, in amphibious vehicles and in waterproof and underwater tanks, all under cover of darkness or artificial fog – but also to destroy his landing equipment and troops.' Within three months, Rommel had immeasurably improved the defences; had he started three months earlier, the success of D-Day would have been in grave doubt. Everyone, both sides of the Channel... waited. And waited.

Having already been postponed due to bad weather in May, the next combination of favourable moon, tide and sunrise necessary for the attack was 5-7 June 1944. Bad weather would again prevent the invasion going ahead on 5 June, but by evening on 4 June it was predicted that the weather would be acceptable on 6 June. A crucial meeting was held at SHAEF in Portsmouth, the decision being Eisenhower's, and his alone. With incredible coolness, Ike said simply, 'OK, Let's go.'

The night sky on 5/6 June 1944 was filled with the roar of Allied aircraft. Over 1,000 Lancasters, Halifaxes and Mosquitoes bombed ten coastal gun batteries in the invasion area, eight of which were covered with cloud and therefore indicated by Oboe sky markers. Five thousand tons of bombs were dropped, the greatest tonnage in one night so far throughout the entire war; just three aircraft were lost. Naturally it was necessary to deceive and confuse the enemy as to where the landings would be made, and so a number of complex operations were flown with this objective. Operation *Taxable* involved sixteen Lancasters of the famous 617 Squadron dropping 'Window' (strips of aluminium to confuse radar), in conjunction with a Royal Navy deception operation, thus simulating an invasion force approaching the French coast near Cap d'Antifer. Operation *Glimmer* saw six Stirlings also dropping 'Window', giving the impression of the Allies approaching Boulogne in the Pas-de-Calais. In Operation *Titanic*, dummy parachutists, together with two SAS teams, were dropped away from the actual invasion area, near the base of the Cotentin Peninsula, East of the River Dives and to the south west of Caen. Over the Somme, Lancasters and B-17s established an 'Air-Borne Cigar' (ABC) ground-to-air radio jamming and 'Window' barrage to distract enemy night fighters away from the transport aircraft inserting Allied airborne troops. Radar Counter Measures (RCM) were also the focus of Stirlings and B-24 Liberators over Littlehampton, which established a Mandrel radar jamming screen between there and Portland Bill, thus hiding the real invasion fleet from German early warning radar. The Mosquito Mk VIs of 21 Squadron, based at Hunsdon, patrolled behind enemy lines that night, attacking trains and transport, and anything else that moved. Finally, shortly before 0630 hours, Allied aircraft dropped leaflets over France, telling French civilians that the long-awaited hour of liberation was now at hand, and urging those who lived near the coast to move inland or seek safety in open countryside.

It was fitting that the naval component of *Overlord*, Operation *Neptune*, was commanded by Admiral Sir Bertram Ramsay, the sailor who had overseen the evacuation of the BEF from Dunkirk in 1940. Four years later, almost to the day, Ramsay was back off the French coast, but this time with the greatest amphibious assault force ever assembled: 6,483 vessels including 9 battleships, 23 cruisers, 104 destroyers and 71 corvettes. No less than 4,000 landing craft of all shapes and sizes would carry the troops and apparel of war ashore. This huge armada was divided into the Eastern Task Force, under Rear Admiral Sir Phillip Vian, and the Western Task Force commanded by the American Rear Admiral Kirk. Vian's fleet left Southampton, Portsmouth, Newhaven, Shoreham, Solent and Spithead, and conveyed British and Canadian troops across the Channel to their destinations – the beaches stretching twenty-four miles westward from Ouistreham to Port-en-Bessin. These scenic stretches of Normandy sand were codenamed Gold, Juno and Sword. Kirk's Western Task Force carried American soldiers to their beaches – Omaha and Utah – West of Port-en-Bessin to Quiselle. The intention was for the Americans, British and Canadians to establish and maintain a bridgehead before linking up; the British 50th Infantry Division was then to push south and capture Bayeux.

Incredibly, given the enormity of the undertaking, Operation *Neptune* achieved complete tactical surprise, the Eastern Task Force anchoring some seven to eight miles off-shore where troops were disgorged into landing craft. At 0515 hours, Bombarding Force 'D', obscured by smoke laid by aircraft, arrived on the eastern flank. Soon the 15-inch guns of HMS *Ramillies* and HMS *Warspite*, each capable of lobbing a shell weighing 1,938 pounds over eighteen miles, would open fire on *Festung Europa*. Before dawn, the bombardment started, the roar of gunfire rolling across the sea, the Normandy coast illuminated by flares and explosions. H-Hour came first for the Americans storming Omaha and Utah beaches. Unfortunately the bombardment of the enemy coastal defences had caused little damage to those in the American sector, which had been covered by cloud. Consequently the Americans were met by a withering hail of machine-gun, artillery and mortar fire. The British and Canadians encountered less resistance, but fighting was still fierce. As H-Hour had been slightly delayed for the Canadians, at Juno the tide was slightly higher than planned, meaning that the mined beach defences took a significant toll of landing craft. The obstacle-clearing parties were under heavy fire from enemy troops just 100 yards away, and the seafront was formidably defended by gun emplacements and determined infantry. Unfortunately conditions at sea had prevented the launching of amphibious tanks, and so the Canadian infantry hit the beach unsupported by armour. In spite of heavy losses to both mines and crossfire, the Canadians somehow not only got up the beach but by nightfall were seven miles inland. At Sword the British faced similar problems to the Canadians, but just enough tanks supported the infantry and made the landing successful. Heavy fighting took place in the built-up area beyond the beach where vicious house-to-house fighting lasted until mid-day. British commandos then linked up as planned with British airborne troops, and by nightfall 3rd Infantry Division was six miles inland. A battalion of infantry, supported by a squadron of Sherman tanks, penetrated two miles short of Caen before dusk, but, lacking appropriate support, was forced back.

From the air, the invasion was undoubtedly a spectacle. A Spitfire pilot, Flight Lieutenant Bob Beardsley DFC, later told the press, 'The sky over the target was absolutely packed with aircraft. Fighters and bombers seemed to fill the air, wingtip to wingtip. From above [we fighter pilots] could see the bombs go down. The whole target area was a mass of flames. It was both an impressive and terrifying sight, and I for one was glad that I was not a German soldier.' A Norwegian Wing Leader graphically added, 'Looking down on the target area was like looking down into hell.' The RAF fighter pilots covering the landings had expected heavy air fighting – but the Luftwaffe's reaction was negligible. As great a spectacle as D-Day was, for the fighter pilots it was an anti-climax in terms of combat. By that time the German fighter force was committed to defending the Reich from round-the-clock bombing, northern France still only defended by JGs 2 and 26.

By nightfall on D-Day, some 175,000 Allied troops had been landed in Normandy, around 10,000 having made the ultimate sacrifice. According to official US statistics, 3,881 were Americans lost on one beach: Omaha. Although the day had been won, and actually at less a cost in human lives than anticipated, not all Allied objectives had been achieved. The Americans at Omaha had yet to link up with the British on Gold, and it was feared that a German armoured thrust, by 21st Panzer Division, might prevent this happening. Neither had it proved possible to take Caen on that first day, as was the plan; indeed that city, contested by the young Nazi fanatics of the 12th SS Hitler Jugend Panzer Division, would take over a month to invest – and at a high price; and the Americans would take three weeks to clear the Contentin and take the port of Cherbourg. Quality German reinforcements, like 2nd SS Panzer Division Das Reich, would eventually reach the battlefield, launching determined counter-attacks with great aggression and verve. The *Bocage* terrain of woods, sunken lanes and high hedgerows, extending fifty miles inland, was unsuited to advancing armour but entirely favourable to small, mobile, anti-tank units. These crucial factors would to some degree negate the Allies' enormous advantages in resources and aerial supremacy, leading to the ferocious Battle for Normandy lasting three long months.

The wings of 19 (Fighter) Sector flew four sorties as part of the aerial umbrella protecting the invasion fleet and landings that day, and it was entirely appropriate that Group Captain Malan also flew over the Normandy beaches, considering his Huguenot origins, with the Free French squadrons of 145 Wing. According to the 340 Squadron ORB, at 2000 hrs, 'Thirty-six aircraft of 329, 340 and 341 Squadrons took off on Ramrod 976. 340 Squadron took off with 329 to escort Albemarles towing Horsas (gliders) to the assault area. Rendezvous was made at Bognor and the operation carried out according to plan. A number of aircraft were seen in the area and one glider was shot down by flak. A ship, believed to be a cruiser, was seen sinking. Paratroops were seen dropping either side of the Orne river. An "R" boat was damaged by 329 Squadron in the Caen Canal.' But there was still no air fighting. On that evening sortie, Group Captain Malan, his Spitfire carrying his initials, 'AGM", had Yellow Section – it must have been like old times, and what a sight to behold below.

There is no record of any other flights during this period, and Sailor's personal flying log books have not survived. According to Walker, however, as the campaign progressed, Sailor and his old friend from Biggin Hill days, Jamie Rankin, also a group captain now, flew across the Channel 'twice a day… to see how things were going, and take on any German planes they could find… He returned to base from one operation carrying a large bouquet. It came as a gift from the villagers of a liberated Normandy village.'

Spitfires had first landed in France after D-Day on 10 June 1944. That morning, Wing Commander Johnnie Johnson's 144 (Canadian) Wing had flown a number of mundane shipping patrols South of Beachy Head before receiving exciting news: a strip, 'B3', had been created at St Croix-sur-Mer, just inland of the British and Canadian beaches and from where 144 Wing could operate. At 0730 hrs Johnnie despatched Squadron Leader Dal Russell and three other 442 Squadron pilots to land at B3 and ensure all was well. So it was that those four Spitfires became the first Allied fighters to land in France for four years, just four days after the invasion had begun. The feedback was that all was well at St Croix, and at 1130 hrs Johnnie briefed his pilots: this time the entire Wing was landing at B3 to refuel and rearm before sweeping further South: 'We took off at 1155 hours and

I was very pleased with this new development. Not only would we have the honour of being the first Spitfires to land in and operate from Normandy, but this would give us the extra range needed to sweep South of the River Loire, where we knew concentrations of enemy aircraft were based. We first made a low pass over St Croix-sur-Mer, familiarising ourselves with the location, and then made a tight circuit to avoid the barrage balloons protecting the beach-head. Bear in mind that this was a strange experience, landing in what had been enemy territory from which we had previously had thrown at us every description of hostile shot and shell. We touched down and left RAF servicing commandos attending to our Spitfires. As we pilots gathered together, the Airfield Commander came over and told us not to stray too far due to minefields and snipers. The airfield control system had been established in an adjacent orchard where we were soon approached by a delegation from St Croix. The villagers brought with them gifts of fruit, flowers and wine. While we and the French rejoiced, dead German soldiers still lay all around.'

Two days after 144 Wing landed at St Croix, the Malan family suffered a second loss: Captain Ralph 'Bull' Malan, an observer on 31 Squadron SAAF, operating B-24 Liberators over Crete and the Aegean, was also killed in action. Like Sailor, Ralph, a married man with a son, is remembered as soft-spoken, slightly reserved – and fearless. Buried at Moascar, Egypt, Ralph was the second and last to die of the four Malan brothers who served during the Second World War.

On 28 June 1944, Wing Commander Johnnie Johnson equalled Sailor's official score of thirty-two enemy aircraft destroyed. The press eagerly followed Johnnie's exploits, awaiting confirmation that Sailor's long-standing record had been beaten. That historic kill came on 30 June 1944. Johnnie:

'I was leading a flight of 441 Squadron on a front-line patrol (1250 hours), when Control informed me that bandits were about, South of Caen. When in the Gace area I saw a general dog-fight well underway at 4,000 – 5,000 feet. There was a thin layer of cloud at 4,000 feet and E/A were avoiding combat by diving in and pulling out well beyond the combat area. I saw a 109 at nine o'clock, some 1,000 feet below and so I turned steeply into attack. I opened fire from 300 yards, angle off 40°. E/A flew through my area of fire and as I broke away I saw him going down, pouring black smoke. E/A crashed in a field and I claim one Me 109 destroyed – confirmed by my Number Two, Flight Lieutenant Draper.'

Johnnie told me that:

'Within an hour or so of me landing the news had spread and a clutch of press and radio correspondents arrived on the scene. Of course they made a big thing of it all and just couldn't seem to grasp why I was so anxious they should emphasise that Malan had fought when the odds were enormously stacked against him. Sailor had fought a defensive battle over southern England when the 109s enjoyed the tactical advantages of height and sun. He had continued the fight until rested in 1941, and his massive experience was then used for the benefit of others. I, on the other hand, had done comparatively little or nothing of this kind of defensive fighting as I had always flown offensively. After 1941 I had a squadron, wing or even two wings behind me. Unlike Sailor, I had, therefore, the opportunity to choose when to strike, stalk and kill our opponents. The only real disadvantage I had to contend with was invariably operating over enemy territory, meaning that a single bullet in a vulnerable part of the Spitfire could mean, at best, a prison camp.'

Johnnie's story and picture was soon splashed across the pages of newspapers throughout the free world – Wing Commander Johnnie Johnson was now the only pilot to officially exceed Sailor's score (ultimately reaching 38½), inheriting the mantle as the RAF's officially top-scoring fighter pilot of the Second World War. Johnnie was absolutely right. His was a different war to Sailor's, and it was to Group Captain Sailor Malan that the credit went for working out a lot of the successful tactics taken forward.

There was, though, another pilot, coincidentally also a South African, possibly more successful that Johnson or Malan: Squadron Leader Marmaduke Thomas St John Pattle, from Butterworth, Cape Province. 'Pat' is believed to have achieved at least forty aerial victories, probably more, over Egypt and Greece, flying Gladiators and Hurricanes, until his career was violently terminated over Piraeus Harbour by an Me 110 on 20 April 1941. The reason Pattle was not the officially top-scoring RAF ace, however, was because so many official documents were destroyed during the Allied retreat from Greece, meaning that his list of victories could not be corroborated through official sources. So Johnnie Johnson is ranked at number one, Sailor Malan number two. Sailor's record had stood for just under four years – indicating the speed at which he accumulated victories during the difficult but target-rich early war years.

By the end of July 1944, the fighting in Normandy was well-advanced, the Allied bridgehead ever-expanding, with more resources continually arriving. The 2nd TAF completely dominated the battlefield and by the end of August it was all over. Although the German army in Normandy was not totally destroyed, certain elements escaping across the Seine to safety, the enemy was soundly beaten in a terrifying demonstration of aerial superiority. From thereon began the 'Long Trek' for the Allied armies and air forces in northern Europe, across France, Belgium and the Netherlands, eventually ending in Germany. Sailor Malan was not to be a part of what Johnnie Johnson dubbed the 'Great Adventure': after what had been another intensive period of service, including a certain amount of operational flying, official and otherwise, in July 1944 Group Captain Malan was posted, coincidentally just as 74 Squadron joined 145 Wing, to command the Advanced Gunnery School at Catfoss. There, fighter aces gathered to evaluate new weapons and theories, and share experiences – under the leadership of the Master.

On the Continent, the war progressed. The battered Germans, however, having reached the refuge of the Netherlands and Germany, regrouped incredibly quickly and defeated the greatest airborne landing of all time, at Arnhem, in September 1944. In this audacious plan, American airborne troops were to capture bridges across the Meuse and Waal, while the British and Polish objective was to seize the bridges over the lower Rhine at Arnhem. Then XXX Corps was to advance sixty miles to Arnhem, relieving the airborne elements along the way. The advance petered out at Nijmegen, eight miles from Arnhem, the furthest bridge proving to be a bridge too far. British and Polish casualties were heavy, and Montgomery's plan to bypass the Siegfried Line and enter Germany via the 'back door', failed. The Rhine would not be crossed until March 1945 – by which time, with the Russians closing in fast from the East, the end of Hitler's Germany was just a question of time. By then, the thoughts of many servicemen, perhaps for the first time, were starting to think of the future – including Sailor – who made the following radio broadcast, providing further confirmation of his care for others:

'When it is all over and the world is free again, what then? I have been in the RAF for some years now, flying and living with these boys. They are an extremely likeable, gallant, and magnanimous crowd. This host of youth, with its terrific potentialities for doing good in the world, must not be thrown away after the war and left derelict on the scrap heap of economic want. The United Nations must fulfil their pledges to the youths who until now fulfil theirs, even to the sacrifice of life and limb.

'Unlike the heavy bomber pilots, there will not be much future for fighter boys in the civil air lines after the war. They were untrained in business, the professions, or any sort of commercial or industrial skill before the war snatched them up. Four years of fighting have done nothing to fit them for commercial careers. It is up to us to see that they do not become a lost generation after this war, as their fathers did after the last. It is a solemn task we have before us and the winning of it may be as hard as the winning of the Battle of Britain and Battle of Germany, which is now on us.'

It was rumoured that Sailor would then be sent to train new pilots in Rhodesia, the *Daily Express* publishing what proved to be a premature report that 'The brilliant battle career of Adolph Gysbert Malan is now at an end... He has fought his last fight.... His accomplishments will never be dimmed.'

On 30 April 1945, with the Russians in Berlin, Adolf Hitler committed suicide. On 8 May 1945 the war in Europe was finally at an end. The war continued in the Far East until the Japanese finally surrendered on 15 August 1945 – by which time the Americans had dropped two atomic bombs on the Japanese cities of Hiroshima and Nagasaki, ushering in a terrifying new age of warfare. On that fateful August day, the Second World War, which had cost some 60 million lives, was all over. Lynda Malan admitted, 'It was only towards the end I began to be really afraid that something might and would happen to John [the name by which Sailor was called by his wife] after all.' Lynda need not have worried: her husband had survived.

But what now?

At first, Sailor attended a six-month staff officers' course at Cranwell, preparing for a career in the post-war service – but nothing was ever likely to stimulate the senses as much as combat flying. Like so many others, Sailor was unable to see himself in the routines of a peacetime service, without that pervasive sense of purpose and excitement of the wartime years. Years before, he had known when to draw a line under a life at sea, and now the time had come to do exactly that with the RAF, after ten years. Sailor was also conscious that throughout the war, Lynda and the children had followed him from camp to camp, living at twenty-nine different addresses. The time had come for the family to enjoy stability, and all the benefits that brought, especially for the children. And home was South Africa.

In 1946, Sailor retired from the RAF, decorated with a double DSO and DFC, in addition to the Belgian Croix de Guerre, the French Légion d'Honneur and Czech Military Cross. Before leaving Britain, he had one last duty to perform: the unveiling of the preserved blackout board from the Biggin Hill fighter pilots' favourite pub: the White Hart at Braxted. Signed in chalk by numerous of the Few and subsequent aces who had flown operationally from the 'Bump', the names included those of many comrades who had failed to return. A number of the Few were present at the ceremony, at which Sailor said:

'My feelings are very mixed. This is a happy occasion in some ways and I am trying to smile. But it would be a strange man who did not have sadder thoughts when he reads some of these names and remembers. We built up a Fighter tradition that will not easily die. I hope you will all come here often to steep yourselves in a bit of tradition.'

Soon the Malans were sailing to South Africa, a country that neither Lynda, Jonathan nor Valerie had yet set foot in, the passage of the country's greatest war hero and his family a gift from the Union Government. During the voyage, Sailor spent much time just sleeping or resting, avoiding other passengers, not wanting to talk about the war. To avoid communal dining, and social contact with other passengers, the Malans were invited to dine in the Captain's private quarters. It suggested an element of what today would be called Post Traumatic Stress Disorder (PTSD).
What lay ahead, nobody could say.

Chapter Seventeen

Going Home: The Man Behind the Medals

While stationed at Biggin Hill, Sailor and Lynda had socialised with a certain Mr H.N. Abrahams, who ran the London-based Diamond Trading Co, brokering sales of the precious stone for, amongst others, De Beers. At the Abrahams' Sundridge home, Sailor had the fortune to meet a giant of a fellow South African, Sir Ernest Oppenheimer, and his son Harry. The connection would have a significant bearing on the course on which Sailor was now set.

Of German-Jewish origin, Sir Ernest first worked in London for a diamond brokerage in London, which sent him to Kimberley, South Africa, as their buyer in 1902. Ten years later, the diamond man was the city's mayor. Five years on, with American and British investment, together with an American friend, Oppenheimer launched the Anglo-American Corporation, which purchased diamond mines in South West Africa, challenging the De Beers monopoly. In 1924, Ernest was elected to the House of Assembly as Kimberley's representative, entering politics on the national stage. In 1927 he took control of De Beers, becoming chairman in 1929, spending the rest of his working life consolidating the company's global monopoly over the diamond industry. It was Harry with whom Sailor really connected.

Born on 28 October 1908, Harry Oppenheimer was two years older than Sailor and heir to a gigantic fortune. He was also intelligent, educated and brave. Having attended Charterhouse School in England, Harry graduated from Christ Church, Oxford, in 1931 with a top degree in Philosophy, Politics and Economics. During the Second World War, Captain Oppenheimer had seen much action in the Western Desert as a 'Rat' with the 7th Armoured Division's 4th (South African) Armoured Car Regiment, a reconnaissance unit which fought throughout the battles of Sidi Rezegh, Gazala, Benghazi, Knightsbridge and the fall of Tobruk. In 1942 the unit was engaged at El Alamein and north of the Qattara Depression, eventually being relieved after three months of contact with the enemy, which included a withdrawal of over 500 miles. The war in the desert won, the 4th ACR ceased to exist, its personnel being welcomed into other armoured units. Like Sailor Malan, Harry Oppenheimer had therefore seen much action. In 1946, Harry was heading home to Johannesburg to become managing director of his father's Anglo-American Corporation. Like Sailor, he also held dear the values of democracy and inclusivity, and in Sailor found a kindred spirit keen to see the qualities which had achieved victory for the Allies transferred to make the United Nations successful and prosperous in peace. The pair became friends and hoped to make their mark on a South Africa that had been worth fighting for.

In 1946, Field Marshal Smuts, who had led the country throughout the Second World War, remained the pro-British Prime Minister in South Africa. The matter of support for the British during the war was a deeply divisive issue for South Africa's white community, especially the Afrikaners; Harry Lawrence was an MP in the Smuts administration, and his son Jeremy commented:

'Sailor Malan was not fully regarded as an Afrikaner because although his father was a Malan of French Huguenot origin, his mother was of English South African stock. And, of course, bad point again, Sailor Malan had fought in the RAF, whereas the National Party was flirting with Hitler and wanted Germany to win, because they wanted this country to become a republic, that was the thinking behind the whole thing.'

Indeed, because of this determination to see an independent and Afrikaner-dominated South Africa, there was a difference between how Malan was perceived in Britain and in his country of birth. Professor Bill Nasson:

'Although Malan was mostly studiously ignored, he was caricatured occasionally in the nationalist press as a deluded flying poodle, a leather and goggles version of a Jan Smuts empire loyalist. A contemptible Malan was squandering his time, helping a British war effort aimed at saving a detested imperialism. At the same time, in overseas Britain… Sailor Malan was, unquestionably, the very finest of its bronzed colonial heroes, lined up with Wing Commander Johnnie Johnson by 1944 as "The Two Greatest Fighter Pilots of the War" (*Tatler*, 6 September 1944).

'Moreover, his public identity was always more than that of one of the RAF's most assured and effective Spitfire pilots. For an Allied Adolph had sprung from a divided white South African society that could not make up its mind squarely over where it ought to stand on the war issue. Instead of humming and hawing, he had had no hesitation in donning the RAF blue and committing himself to the defence of a great British Empire. In that sense, far more than any Canadian, New Zealander or Australian, his life was a parable of true imperial commitment… the truest expression of his patriotic character.'

Jeremy Lawrence:

'Harry Oppenheimer greatly admired Sailor Malan, and Harry had also been fighting… they were roughly the same age… So Harry was always very keen to help people of that sort, which people sometimes forget – the anti-National Party movement. On the side, he played a background role. Clearly, he had all the money to finance opposition groups… Sailor Malan was one of those people who you thought was a good chap and should get every support he could. And that is why Harry made Sailor his PA.'

Nicky Oppenheimer, Harry's son, remembered:

'When Sailor came back here after the war he became my father's Personal Assistant for a bit, which my father said he was completely hopeless at, completely the wrong thing to do.'

Working at Anglo-America's plush offices in Johannesburg, Sailor, however, enjoyed the work:

'It's fascinating work. There's an awful lot to learn and a chap's got to be on his toes. But it's the greatest opportunity I've ever had. I hope I make good,' adding that, alluding to the Cold War now in progress between the western democracies and the Soviets, 'I hope Russia doesn't get too tough. I don't want to lose all this. I prefer the sky just plain blue.'

So Sailor returned to South Africa with a job and highly influential like-minded friends involved with Liberal politics opposed to the right-wing Nationalist Party.

Sailor's son Jonathan:

'During the war, I do remember looking out the window, probably 1943, and calling my mother and saying "Look at these lights!", not knowing that these "lights" were the result of people killing each other in the air. And my mother never told me what was going on, she would say "Yes, aren't they pretty?" and I would watch these explosions, and to me they were just pretty lights. That's the first thing I can remember about the war.

'We lived in twenty-nine different places, I don't know which one to pick. Because as my father was posted, he had to keep his family out of the way. And the other pilots also, had to keep their families out of London. They would find friends, relatives to live with.

'My father was twenty-eight when he got married... his relationship with us kids, I was intimidated by him, if I was naughty, but if I was a good guy, he was a very pleasant to be around. If I was sitting in the back seat of the car, fighting with my sister, he would keep his one hand on the steering wheel, he would turn around and slap me across the head and say "You cut that out!" and I knew what would follow if I didn't do just that. He was intimidating if you upset him.

'I went to St. Johns school in Jo'burg, I was seven years old, and I couldn't understand why I was getting attention. "You're Sailor Malan's son"; I don't think I even knew his name was "Sailor". "Why is your father so famous?" and all I could think of was that he worked at Anglo America for the Oppenheimers, it was a mining company, so I thought maybe he was the strongest guy around so he could move the rocks for the miners, I had to make up something, so my knowledge of him was zero and I began to learn as people told me what my Dad was about. He was known in the family as "John Sailor".... he was shy of all the attention.

'I found life in Kimberley... a great life, I thought it was a wonderfully quiet city, everybody was friendly there. I was told when we stopped at the Halfway House, we parked our car there, like at a roadhouse, you could order a beer, and I was told it was the only place in the world where we can do that. So that's how laid-back Kimberley was in the 50s and 60s.

'Looking back, because my father went to sea at aged thirteen, he was around men from that that time on all the way through, until just before the war. He got married, and shortly after he's married, he's in a war. Again, completely surrounded by men. So I think his family skills were just not present, he did not know how to deal with us kids. We would have some fun and some joking around occasionally, but I always got the impression that he did not know what to do with us, he did not know how to deal with children. But I think that's understandable because of his life experience. I can't hold that against him. It's like being in a boarding school. How do you relate to girls when you've been with boys all your life? You walk around, you feel shy, you don't even know how to date. These things have to be learnt. I think he *learnt* how to deal with us kids, he was a very good father, he always had our best interests at heart. We were his family, and for the rest of my life I will always admire him as a person. Just his nature, his personality, was very admirable. A very nice person. Just don't step on his toes!

'Winston Churchill liked his pilots, he knew he depended on them, and would often visit the fighting stations, trying to encourage the guys there. And he got to know some of the guys, like my Dad, who had senior roles, in planning for the next day. My father asked two of his closest fighting buddies to be my godfather... because I had arrived just a couple of weeks before the Battle of Britain. And both of those very close mates of his were killed shortly after that. And he just went to Winston Churchill one day and said, "Would you be the godfather to my little boy?" and Winston Churchill put his hand on Dad's shoulder and said, "My boy, it will be an honour." So Winston Churchill was a very guy-on-guy type of person. He wasn't always up there. I get the impression that he was a very personable guy.

'My father never, ever, talked about his wartime experiences, he just said it was a terrible time. My parents never went to church.

'He was very inspired by how many men from Jamaica, India, South Africa etc came to join them. I think a swell of pride there. That kept them facing death every day, maybe, I can't explain it. I cannot understand how those guys could have been that brave. It must have been some gift they have. To escape death twice in one day and then get up in the morning and go and do the same thing. And they did that for three or four months almost daily. I cannot understand it, I can't comprehend, I'm at a loss, same as everybody else. I just know they did it. When I was first taken shooting with him at age twelve, I was astounded… he explained to me that Springbok running at 50 mph, you actually have to shoot in front of him. "How do you measure that?" He said, "I don't know"... It's an unexplainable gift I think. To just know where to fire the shot, the brain seems to work that out, and I think that's why he survived the war. He also knew when to turn and run. There is a time when you do not attack. I only found that out recently. But you have to know as a soldier when to run. Otherwise you will die.'

Sailor's daughter, Valerie Crankshaw:

'We moved back to South Africa in 1946… We went to Johannesburg where my Dad had a job as PA to Harry Oppenheimer. In 1948, Harry became MP for Kimberley, so we moved. First of all it was temporary, but in 1948 we moved permanently.

'I went to a primary school in Kimberley as a boarder. When my father decided to go farming in 1952, it was outside Kimberley, so he could not go backwards and forwards, Jonathan, my elder brother, went to CBC as a boarder and I went to Junior Belgrave.

'We lived in West End in Silson road, and just up the road there were kids from the Diamant Veld school who used to cycle into town, and I caught a bus to go to school, this was before I went to the farm. And I was standing on one side of the road ready to cross, and these kids were cycling down into town and they suddenly stopped. One of the girls got off her bicycle, came across the road and slapped me. I did not know what is going on, and it turned out, "This is the Engelse, we are going to get them." Because obviously I was in the uniform of an English-speaking school. I did not know why or what was going on.

'As a child you don't really know them as people, I just remember I would follow my Dad like a shadow around the farm. He loved the farm. I suppose it was too traumatic thinking about the past, the war. I think both of them just wanted to wipe that time out. …I suppose when I was nine or so, somebody at school said to me why does everyone talk about your father, why is he a hero? And I said, "He won the war." That was a child's feeling of it.

'My Mom would talk about funny incidents during the war. But it just was never discussed in our home. I know a lot of war-time people who would get together to talk about the war, chew the fat, but not my dad, never.'

The foregoing interviews by South African independent film maker Desmond Naidoo provide a unique glimpse into the real Sailor Malan, the man behind the medals – and perhaps help us understand the final chapters of his life.

Chapter Eighteen

Torch Commando

As we have seen, by 1945 the RAF had changed almost beyond recognition from the exclusively white, small pre-war service Sailor Malan joined in 1936. The Second World War had dictated a substantial expansion, the enlarged wartime service absorbing personnel from the Commonwealth and Allied lands. The formal prohibition on non-white recruits was lifted, although overall numbers remained comparatively low. Nonetheless, this changing demographic saw the RAF become a multi-national force, in which personnel – including Group Captain Malan – served alongside men and women from many and various countries and cultures. Clearly, this overturned any absurd notion of racial superiority, and, again as previously explored, the RAF, being a relatively new and technical service, became much more of a meritocracy than the two more senior services, in which the 'old school tie', family connections and to some extent colour, became much less important than professional experience and ability. Consequently, Sailor returned to South Africa with an enlightened, inclusive, global, world view – and yet the country of his birth was a place where racism, prejudice and division underpinned the whole of society. Given his father's background, it was perhaps inevitable that Harry Oppenheimer should enter Liberal politics, which he did when elected as Kimberley's United Party MP in 1948. As private and political secretary, Sailor was Oppenheimer's electoral agent during his campaign – setting the scene for everything that followed.

The United Party was born in 1934, a fusion between the South African Party led by Jan Smuts, and J.B.M. Hertzog's National Party, which had been founded in 1915. Hertzog's vision was for a coalition government of Afrikaners, who dominated the National Party, and English-speaking white South Africans of Smuts' party. Both the South African Party and National Party segments of the United Party supported white supremacy in South Africa. However, not all nationalists supported the new party. D.F. Malan's

National Party faction, *Die Gesuiwerde Nationale Party*, better-known as the 'Purified National Party', refused to join and remained a separate entity. Smuts was pro-British, whereas Hertzog, also formerly a Boer War general, and the National Party were determined to see South Africa break all imperialist ties with Britain and become truly independent. This, however, Hertzog was prepared to put aside, at least temporarily, in favour of seeing a strong coalition party created. Unable to accept this, D.F. Malan broke away. In 1939, irreconcilable division arose within the United Party over support for Britain in the Second World War. Hertzog had moved for South Africa to at least remain neutral in the war, but the motion had been defeated at the vote, leading to Hertzog's faction, who were pro-German and Nazi sympathisers, also leaving the party and joining D.F. Malan to form the 'Re-united National Party'. Many of D.F. Malan's supporters and party members supported South Africa actually fighting for Hitler, so this right-wing Re-united Party's brand of fascism exceeded neutrality and crossed over into a partisan relationship with the Axis powers. Most members were Afrikaners. Little wonder, then, that opinion was divided over the war service of the 'Fighting Malans'.

After the war, the white population was uncertain that the liberal United Party would uphold white rule in South Africa. Jeremy Lawrence: 'After the war, Britain rejected Churchill, and in the same way, in 1948, Jan Smuts and the United Party was voted out, and in came D.F. Malan's Re-united National Party.' South African political commentator John Kane-Berman adds: 'It was a great tragedy, and partly it was punishment for Smuts for taking South Africa into the war in September 1939, and it was a very divisive issue in South Africa among the white population, and many whites who were opposed to South Africa's entry into the war voted against Smuts in the 1948 elections. The rest is a terrible story, the steady intensification of the Apartheid system which of course predated 1948, but it was intensified, and plans to liberalise the pass laws [an internal passport system intended to segregate the population, the system only applying to African citizens, restricting their geographic movement], and so on, were shelved by necessity during the war but were also now intensified. It's a dreadful story known around the world.' But is it, really, that well-known today? Certainly the role of Sailor Malan in South African post-war politics remains little-known, even in South Africa, for reasons we will now explore.

After its landmark 1948 victory, the Nationalist government rapidly consolidated control over the state. It became compulsory for white children to attend schools providing an education in their own language, being either English or Afrikaans. Afrikaners soon occupied senior positions in the armed forces, the law, civil service and media, and favouritism was shown to Afrikaner companies when official contracts were awarded. At the 1948 watershed, one Hendrik F. Verwoerd became a senator. He viewed South Africa's population as four distinct racial groups: white, black, 'coloured' and Asian, each with their own individual culture. Verwoerd opined that because whites were the 'civilised' group, they had a natural right to control the state and govern. In Afrikaans, 'apartheid' means 'apartness', and in this context refers to a policy of racial segregation imposed by the ruling white minority over the non-white majority. By separating and segregating the population, Apartheid ensured white supremacy and control. The Prohibition of Mixed Marriages Act of 1949 and the Immorality Act of 1950 legally prevented interracial marriage or sex, the Population Registration Act of the same year classifying every South African citizen by race. Under the Group Areas Act, also passed in 1950, South Africa's population centres were subdivided into segregated residential and business areas. Thousands of non-white peoples found themselves removed from their jobs – which were classified as being white occupations. Other laws ensured that racial segregation permeated every walk of life: public transport – even hearses – leisure, entertainment, sport and access to beaches. Black South Africans were obliged to live on reserves, except when permitted to work on white-owned farms or white towns. D.F. Malan's government also exercised total control over the education of blacks, the Bantu Education Act, 1953, created state-run schools to meet the demand for semi-skilled black labour. The University Education Act, 1959, prevented black students attending university, but created two new colleges for specific non-white groups – staffed by white nationalists. What all of this did, taking aside the violation and removal of basic human rights and dignities, was to create a vast economic gulf between the wealthy, who were almost exclusively white, and the poor, non-white, masses, the majority of whom were black. The non-whites suffered from poverty, malnutrition and disease. It would be the disenfranchising of the black voter, however, that propelled Sailor Malan back into the spotlight.

Being PA to an MP placed Sailor close to these deeply worrying events, which were transforming South Africa and too closely associated with the evils of Nazism which he had fought for years to defeat. It was too painful. In search of peace he decided to become a full-time farmer, attending a course at Oppenheimer's Mauritzfontein farm, near Kimberley, and in 1950 took out a mortgage on the 27,000 acre De Beers farm at Benfontein. With abundant game for shooting, grazing for the 900 sheep he put on the land, and plentiful space for dairy farming, the great fighter ace declared, 'Farming is the life for me.'

TORCH COMMANDO

Valerie Crankshaw:

'Being on the farm, we had lots of animals, dogs, cats, he taught me how to dance, they used to have some really nice parties, they made some good friends here in Kimberley. Just an ordinary life.

'There were shoots. The farm was owned by De Beers, my father leased it from De Beers, and he was allowed in winter to shoot for the pot. Maybe one Springbok a year, and De Beers used to hold shoots on the farm, and there were Springbok and Wildebeest and Ostriches on the farm, but mainly the shooting was Springbok.

'I went out with him once, and when I saw the dead Springbok I said, "That's it. I'm not coming again," I just didn't like it.

'The Oppenheimers had a ranch outside Bulawayo, and my parents used to go there every year. That's where Nicky Oppenheimer learnt to shoot… They used to go bird shooting, and I followed a couple of times, my friends and I ... we were always being told to shut up.'

Nicky Oppenheimer:

'I went with him several times to Benfontein as a little boy, driving around and obviously viewed him as a great hero. I remember only one thing about him, when we were going off to try and shoot a Springbok, him saying to me he'd never shot a Springbok when it was standing still. He thought it was unfair. It was a demonstration of his skill.'

Valerie continues:

'I think it must have been quite a big shock for my mother having grown up in England. We moved to the farmhouse, and there was no electricity. And my Mom said, "I'm not moving in unless there's electricity.' So De Beers set up an electrical connection… They just loved doing it up, they sanded the floors... I think she got used to the life very, very quickly, and loved it.

Jonathan Malan:

'When I was twelve, my father took me hunting for the first time, chasing Springbok. I was astounded, first of all because we were doing 55 mph, I was checking the speedometer, over the Free State veld, chasing down a herd of Springbok, to get close enough for him to shoot a couple of them. We skidded to a stop, he climbed out of his car, put his rifle on the open window

217

and dof, dof, dof, in three or four shots he brought down two Springbok. How the hell did he do that? He said, "That's the only way you can shoot Springbok in the Free State, you will never find one standing still".

'During the winter months we had to cull a thousand Springboks, because three thousand grew into four thousand. And the meat was put in cold storage at De Beers. What De Beers did with it I don't know. One of the agreements was that he would act as their ranger and keep the numbers down. There were also a couple of hundred Wildebeest there.

'We enjoyed just being alive. Can you imagine facing death month after month, and, all of a sudden, you've a family, you're alive and there is peace; it must have been a wonderful feeling for my parents.

'Routine on the farm – he would be up at 5 am, we had thirty-five cows to milk, we had a team of six to eight men who lived on the farm with their families. And he got me to take over that job. And in those years, between 1 and 3 pm, staff were sent home. He and my mother would retire to the bedroom, and that was a no-go zone. Whether they slept, made love, read books, just chilled, it was their private time for two hours each day. And at sunset every evening, they would walk into the sunset, hand in hand, just enjoying a two to three km stroll. And that was every single evening, they just enjoyed each other's company.'

Sadly, this idyllic peace that the thirty-two-victory fighter ace had sought for so long, was not to last.

Between 1908 and 1909, the Convention on the Closer Union of South Africa was held, a constitutional convention leading to Britain passing the South Africa Act and creating the Union of South Africa. This constitution remained the country's underpinning instrument until 1961. A key area of debate during the Convention was the issue of non-white voting rights, a complex area given that the four colonies comprising the country, the Cape, Natal, Transvaal and Orange River, each had their own ways of doing things. It was decided to them leave well alone and allow each colony to continue with its existing franchise for non-white voters. In the Cape, for example, non-white citizens could vote but with certain qualifications of property ownership and literacy. It was agreed to preserve these rights unless, under the new constitution, a majority of at least two-thirds in both houses agreed to remove the non-white vote. In 1936, owing to such majorities, the South African Parliament enacted the Representation of Natives Act, removing black voters from the common voters' roll. Inclusion on the roll meant that both whites and non-whites voted for the same candidates, meaning that the coloured voter had some influence over white politics. Instead, under the new Act, coloured voters were separately listed and permitted to elect three members to the lower House of Assembly. During his election rabble-rousing of 1948, D.F. Malan, campaigning largely on a platform of apartheid, delivered a speech to Parliament in which he claimed that non-white voters were corrupt, immature, and posed a threat to white control. Once in power, D.F. Malan's legislators lost no time in drafting the Separate Representation of Voters Bill, completely removing the right of coloured citizens to vote for members of the House of Assembly. This move was not just motivated by white supremacy though: it also ensured that the coloured vote could not swing constituencies from the National to the United Party.

There was significant opposition. The United Party saw the disenfranchising as a betrayal of assurances previously provided by the National Party, and that it could lead to political alliances between the non-white groups opposing white control. Various opposition groups sprang up – amongst them Major Louis Kane-Berman's 'Rand War Action Committee'. The whole objectionable thing struck a chord with many ex-servicemen – including Sailor Malan – who had fought alongside different races only a few years before to destroy such fascist oppression. John Kane-Berman:

'I think they were horrified, on return from the war, having seen the sacrifice and in particular the voluntary participation of the Cape Coloured soldiers in the western desert at El Alamein in 1942, and in Italy in 1943 and in 1944. They were horrified to find that the National Party government, many of whose supporters were sympathetic one way or another with the German cause, were now planning to throw the coloured voter off the common roll. And they've been on that role since 1853. It was regarded a sacred trust, and here was the National Party violating that trust. And they were doing it in a way that was unconstitutional, because they put through parliament in 1951, the Separate Representation of Voters Act, and didn't follow the prescribed procedure. If you needed to remove voting rights, you needed a two thirds majority, in the joint sitting of the House of Assembly. And they put the legislation through by a simple majority which was of course invalidated by the Appellate Division of the Supreme Court. So it was the insult to the Coloured community, and in particular to the memory of their soldiers, and also an insult that was unconstitutional, and ex-servicemen saw the beginning of an analogy of unconstitutional behaviour, like that of Hitler and Mussolini, and people like my father and Sailor Malan said so very bluntly.'

In 1941, members of the 9th Reconnaissance Battalion of the South African Tank Corps had formed the 'Springbok Legion', an anti-racist and anti-fascist organisation open to all servicemen, regardless of race or gender. Interestingly, a leading figure was a founding member of the South African Air Force, General Kennie van der Spuy, perhaps providing further evidence of progressive, enlightened, thinking in air force circles. However, the Legion's main priority was achieving better pay, and improved prospects after repatriation, and many prominent figures were Communist Party members, including the Legion's chief, Bram Fischer, who was not himself a war veteran or serviceman. Consequently the Legion became a front for the Communist Party – as a result of which its membership dwindled.

By the 1951 constitutional crisis over the coloured vote, the Legion's numbers were waning. Major Kane-Berman organised a torch-lit procession of ex-servicemen peacefully protesting against the disenfranchisement of the coloured vote, marching through the streets of Johannesburg to City Hall for a 'Hands Off Our Constitution' rally. This became the 'Torch Commando', born out of the Springbok Legion, which appealed to a wide range of former servicemen and women. Significantly, it was financed by Harry Oppenheimer.

John Kane-Berman:

'There was a fear that the violation of the constitution, the insult to the coloured voters, was the beginning of a slippery slope into dictatorship. Sailor Malan and my father both talked about the threat of fascism, they knew well that some of the members of the Nationalist Party had been sympathetic to the Germans and the Italians during the war. So they feared this was the beginning of a slide and therefore very important to stop it in its tracks as soon as they possibly could. That was one of the things. The second thing was that the behaviour of the National Party became more and more outrageous. They put the Separate Representation of Voters Act in 1951 in Parliament in an unconstitutional manner, breaking the rules that would serve the power of government. They then announced that they were not prepared to be dictated to by the courts. So they said they were going to introduce legislation that was going to make Parliament the ultimate body of jurisdiction and judicial authority in the country, and in fact they put the High Court of Parliament Act through Parliament. And 100 National Party MPs solemnly gathered in parliament, pretending to be judged and validating the Act that the Appellate Division had declared null and void, invalid and unconstitutional, and of no force and effect. And of course a group of coloured voters were not prepared to take this lying down, so they appealed the High Court of Parliament Act, and that went from the Cape Court, to the Appellate Division of the Supreme Court in Bloemfontein, and that was also thrown out. So National Party behaviour became more and more outrageous. And that of course helped recruit people into the Torch Commando. Within a year of its formal launch in mid-1951, it had 250,000 signed-up paid-up members, which was a huge chunk of the white population.'

Major Kane-Berman invited Sailor to speak at the torch-lit City Hall rally, which he did, rousing the thousands present through his presence alone, wearing his old, iconic, sheepskin flying jacket and medals:

'The strength of this gathering is evidence that the men and women who fought in the war for freedom still cherish what they fought for. We are determined not to be denied the fruits of victory. It is good to see this support in protest against the rape of the Constitution and the attack on our rights and liberties as free men. In Abyssinia, at Alamein and a score of bloody campaigns we won the right to a voice in our country's affairs. And we are determined that our voice shall not only be heard but that it shall also be heeded. This Bill has been foisted upon us in the so-called name of the people – the broad will of the people. We do not like this Bill, and we *are* the people!... depriving us of our freedom, with a fascist arrogance that we have not experienced since Hitler and Mussolini met their fate.'

20,000 ex-servicemen attended the rally, the start of a mass movement of non-violent protest.

Jeremy Lawrence:

'Sailor Malan landed up the head of the Torch Commando, which attracted huge followings, and whether it was Cape Town or Johannesburg or Durban, he was an absolute hero. And our family was delighted when we were asked in July 1953 to spend a holiday in then Rhodesia, now Zimbabwe, on a farm owned by the Oppenheimer family called Shangani Ranch, which was about seventy-five miles north-east of Bulawayo. And Sailor Malan and his wife Lynda and their two children were also in the party of about sixteen or seventeen. That was the only occasion on which

I met Sailor Malan. My memory of him is of a shortish thick set man, very good looking, wide apart eyes, blue eyes, blonde hair, modest, one doesn't remember him talking a lot, a good shot. And that was just two glorious weeks in the middle of nowhere getting to know him and other members of the family.

'It was founded in 1951, and at its height in 52 and 53; because of the nature of things it was almost entirely a white organization, a white anti-government movement of great strength and great power. I thought it might lead to great things. Of course it didn't, because the National Party remained in power for another forty years.

'With great indignation, as always, the National Party tried to belittle it. D.F. Malan made fun of Sailor Malan because British people called him Sailor, and he talked about Group Captain Malan in a sort of derogatory way. The depth to which the government went to denigrate the opposition was quite extraordinary, they stopped at nothing.'

'In spite of the National Party's attempts to ridicule the Torch Commando, the world was taking notice – the British Movietone News broadcast a short film (see Bibliography) concerning the great 'Steel Commando' of jeeps and cars as Torch Commando members converged on Cape Town, where Parliament was in session. By now the movement was attracting many retired senior figures from the services, legal profession and even sport. The following news item, featuring a bemedalled Sailor, was headlined 'Malan v Malan: Torch Commandos Against the Government':

'From many towns and centres around South Africa, ex-servicemen recently assembled for their protest drive to Cape Town. Commandant de la Ray is seen greeting some of them as their leader. He's the man, by the way, who captured Winston Churchill in the Boer War. Group Captain Sailor Malan, Battle of Britain fighter ace, was second-in-command, and the object of Torch Commando, as the demonstration was called, was to protest against the Separate Representation of Voters Bill. The men, a few of whom are seen here on their way South, says the government is breaking its pledges to the Coloured people and is undemocratic. The ex-service vote is 200,000 out of about a million. The object of their torchlight meeting at various towns, and finally in Cape Town, was to achieve either an immediate election or at least throw out Dr Malan's party in 1953. Sailor Malan fights his distant cousin, Premier Malan.'

Without doubt, the Torch Commando had rekindled feelings of camaraderie and a shared endeavour not felt since the war. In Britain, and across the world, Sailor's old wartime comrades and friends must have cheered to see the great fighter ace on great form, positively beaming at the camera.

After the rally, which attracted thousands, violence erupted between the police and young men of colour. The government lost no time in accusing the Torch Commando of inciting the unrest and public disorder, the extent of the mass gatherings, numbering up to 75,000, now being a genuine concern to the Nationalist Party. The main tactic to denigrate the integrity of the Commando leaders were accusations by the right-wing press of being nothing more than puppets of 'Oppenheimer Ltd', it being widely known that the Liberal Harry Oppenheimer was financing the activists. Undeterred, Sailor was elected President of the Torch Commando, while Major Kane-Berman became chairman. The organisation's constitution embraced five primary aims:

1. To uphold the spirit of the solemn compacts entered upon at the time of Union as moral obligations of trust and honour binding upon Parliament and the people.
2. To secure the repeal of any measures enacted in violation of such obligations.
3. To protect the freedom of the individual in worship, language and speech and to ensure his right of free access to the Courts.
4. To eliminate all forms of Totalitarianism, whether Fascist or Communist.
5. To promote racial harmony in the Union.

With a membership of 250,000, the government was rightly concerned about the Torch Commando's popularity – due in no small part to the charismatic involvement of South Africa's greatest war hero, Group Captain Sailor Malan. So concerned was D.F. Malan that a law was passed prohibiting anyone employed in the public service, or serving in the armed forces, from joining. The nationalist-controlled media relentlessly denigrated the Torch Commando and its leaders, accusing Sailor and friends of being traitors on account of having fought for Britain, and unpatriotic given their obstructive stance against apartheid. The National Party also accused the Torch Commando of hypocrisy, because its membership was exclusively white. The Torch's response was that only whites were franchised, and as the objective was the overthrow of D.F. Malan's government at the 1953 election, it was pointless mobilising the disenfranchised. It was a valid point, but while the Torch Commando's membership was exclusively white, its rallies were multi-racial – a fact the nationalist propagandists chose to ignore.

The Torch Commando became a member of the United Front, along with the United Party and Labour Party. At this time, the African National Congress, led by James Moroka, was organising its 'Defiance Campaign Against Unjust Laws', and invited the United Front to join in a coalition against D.F. Malan's government. On the basis that its concern was defending the constitution, the United Front, and Torch Commando, declined to join with the ANC, which launched its programme of mass protest on 26 June 1952. The ANC can take the credit 'for the first multi-racial political mobilisation against apartheid laws under a common leadership'.

Again, in spite of all the opposition and activism, the National Party won the 1953 election. Professor Thula Simpson, Historian at the University of Pretoria, explains why, and what became of the Torch Commando:

'A key moment so far as the United Front is concerned is the 1953 general election. They decided against joining hands with the ANC with the idea that they would potentially be able to topple the National Party in the 1953 election. They succeed but they fail. They succeed in winning the popular vote, as they had done in 1948, but because of the way the constituencies were demarcated on a demographic basis, they lost in terms of seats. The United Party is part of a long-term electoral decline and demise, and the Torch Commando, in terms of its reputation, shares this fate in becoming involved in the mid to late 1950s in increasingly ineffectual politics.'

And so, the Torch eventually flickered and died in the late 1950s. But what a demonstration of solidarity and peaceful agitation against injustice Sailor and friends had whipped up. Sailor Malan, the great air ace, in open opposition to the government. It was an embarrassment, one which the D.F. Malan regime did their utmost to expunge from the historic record; along with the story of the Springbok Legion, the Torch Commando and its leaders were virtually erased by the nationalist narrative.

Jonathan Malan:

'I read a letter after the Torch Commando went home. Reading in between the lines of that letter, resigning as the President, I got the sense, that instinctively, he realized it was leading to another Boer War. And it was not worth it.

'I got the impression it was time for wisdom and not for aggression. The government was becoming very disturbed that most of the people marching in the street were trained soldiers. And they were thinking of bringing the army in, and you know how that can escalate. I think he realized it was time to go home.'

It is perhaps surprising, especially considering the energy and enthusiasm Sailor invested in the Torch Commando, and his work for Harry Oppenheimer, that he did not enter politics. There was certainly no shortage of requests for him to become directly involved in Liberal politics. Initially his excuse was that farming was too time consuming, but the reality went beyond that. He believed in the construction of a better world, and that before white South Africans would consider accepting a universal franchise, other matters needed addressing, such as increasing the minimum wage, better education and health care. Politics at the time was focused on sweeping change, but Sailor did not consider the time was right for this, and that these issues connected with basic human rights required redress first. He did not, then, feel that the current political scene suited him. As Professor Nasson said, 'He's not "Let's transform and change society overnight"... he's a kind of "evolutionary liberal".' So a political career was not for Group Captain Sailor Malan, one-time President of the inspirational Torch Commando.

In any case, by the late 1950s there was a more pressing personal issue: Sailor was terminally ill.

Chapter Nineteen

'In the Shadow of Thy Wings will I rejoice'

Watching the Movietone News film of the Torch Commando in 1951, in which Sailor Malan appears looking hale, hearty and happy, aged 40, it is hard to believe that eight years later this dynamo of a man was suffering from Parkinson's disease – which has sadly claimed other members of the Malan family. It is also possible that in addition to it perhaps having been inherited genetically, the stress of the war years, during which Sailor suffered at least twice from nervous exhaustion, in addition to the physical strain of combat flying, made him susceptible to the disease.

'Parkinsonism' covers several conditions with similar symptoms, including involuntary shaking of parts of the body, slow movement and mobility problems, and rigidity. Most Parkinson's sufferers also experience other physical and psychological symptoms, including depression and anxiety, balance problems, anosmia, insomnia and memory loss. The disease is caused by a loss of nerve cells in the Substantia Nigra part of the brain, leading to a reduction in the chemical Dopamine, which helps regulate the body's movement. Exactly what causes the loss of nerve cells is unknown, although suspected to be connected to a variety of environmental and genetic factors. Parkinson's is thought to affect one in 500 people in the UK, most of whom are fifty plus, although one in twenty experience symptoms under forty. Men are more likely to get Parkinson's than women. As the condition progresses, symptoms usually get worse, some sufferers becoming severely disabled. Parkinson's does not directly cause death, but the condition places the body under great strain, making sufferers susceptible to serious and life-threatening infections. Today, sufferers can expect supportive treatment, such as physio and occupational therapy, medication, and even brain surgery. In the 1950s, however, the disease was even less well understood.

Approaching his fiftieth birthday, Sailor was losing weight and becoming unsteady on his feet. He saw doctors and was hospitalized in South Africa for a short period. In June 1959 he decided to return to England and see a London specialist. Landing at Heathrow, Al Deere and wife Joan were waiting for Sailor and Lynda at arrivals, along with four current 74 Squadron pilots with an invitation to visit the Hawker Hunter jet fighter equipped 'Tigers' at Coltishall.

Valerie Crankshaw

'My father got ill in 1959. I was already in boarding school in Johannesburg. Then after school I went to the UK, and while I was in the UK, he and my Mom came for another second opinion. The doctor had said it's not Parkinson's, when it was very obviously was.'

Jonathan Malan:

'I did not even notice my father's illness at first. I went to join the RAF in 1959, against his advice. He said, "Flying is nothing like you think it is, it's not going to be fun like the Battle of Britain," but I wanted to do it, and I heard that he was becoming ill. I heard that he was in a nursing home in Johannesburg, and eventually my mother wrote to me and said, "Please can you make your way home?" So it was rather rapid, over a period of eighteen months that it became a distinct illness. While I was overseas, he was in London, speaking to a brain specialist, who positively identified Parkinson's disease, because he guessed it was the stress of the war, which puts too much stress on the nervous system.'

In London, Sailor told the press:

'I have Parkinson's Disease. Yes, I am ill and I plan to see Sir Russell Braine, the specialist, while I'm here, but it's not all that serious. I feel all right. And anyway, that's not my main reason for this trip. The other and more important reason is to see a lot of old friends. And I want to "do" London and its shows, theatres and to catch up with old memories.'

Naturally, Sailor and Lynda eagerly visited 74 Squadron, where the special guests were entertained by the Station Commander, Group Captain (later Air Vice-Marshal) Harold Bird-Wilson, another decorated fighter ace, who had flown Hurricanes during the Battle of Britain. Staying with Bird-Wilson for two days of nostalgic visits to places from the past around Norfolk, Sailor

227

was even recognised by locals. While visiting his old squadron, Sailor tried out a Hawker Hunter cockpit, which he signed, and was surprised by a Spitfire flypast arranged specially in his honour. It would be the last time he saw the iconic fighter with which his name is inseparably connected for evermore.

Afterwards, 74 Squadron's CO, Squadron Leader P.W. Carr, received this letter from the greatest of all 'Tigers':

'I am sorry that we had so short a time together at Coltishall. I was so delighted to have seen the Squadron, although it was for such a short time.

'I envy you taking over such a fine Squadron. I joined it straight from FTS, commanded a flight within three months and was a flight commander for three years and squadron commander for about nine months – in fact the only squadron in which I served. The spirit was always absolutely first class both pre-war and during the battle. I think I am correct in saying that when I handed it over to Mungo-Park we had either 156 or 176 confirmed kills with the loss of only twelve pilots. Practically all the kills were enemy fighters. We also destroyed two bombers at night during the first night raid of the war… I shot down both in one sortie.

'Judging by what I saw the other day, the Squadron is just the same as it always was. One can see that the chaps are proud of the fine record in two world wars.

'One doesn't want to have it proved, but if they had to meet the crisis they would acquit themselves as in the past.'

Sailor and Lynda returned home to South Africa, after what would be their final visit to England.

In 1961, Air Commodore Al Deere visited Sailor at Benfontein. Sailor was unable to speak. The tough New Zealander was deeply shocked. It was the last time he would see his old friend alive.

Jonathan Malan:

'I just got back to South Africa. When I arrived at the farm, and went to say "Hello" to my Dad, he could hardly speak. I remember going to my room, one of the few times in my life I just broke down and cried. I could not believe that this vibrant young man was looking like an eighty-year-old. He had no energy and couldn't talk properly.'

Valerie Crankshaw:

'His illness took him very fast. Very, very, fast. It affected his mobility, and his speech. He always maintained his sense of humour, and was a very good patient. But Parkinson's is a terrible disease.

'The Oppenheimers had a horse breeding stud just across the road called Maritzfontein. So whenever they came down, or Harry came down for board meetings, they would get together, Harry and my father. They maintained their friendship. Right until the time he died.

'He was in and out of hospital, he got a lot of pneumonia, his muscles wasted... My mum and I were with him at the end. He was skin and bone, very wasted.'

On the morning of 16 September 1963, Sailor was rushed into Kimberley Hospital when his pneumonia became worse. In the early hours of 17 September, Group Captain Adolph Gysbert 'Sailor' Malan died , aged 52. It was unthinkable that this virile dynamo of a man was dead; as Valerie says, 'It was a very young age to die.'

Jonathan Malan:

'Parkinson's killed him quickly. Within three years. And I think it was a good thing, would you want to live like that for twenty years?'

Three days later, Jonathan's esteemed godfather, Sir Winston Churchill, wrote from Chartwell:

'My dear Jonathan, I was grieved to learn of the death of your father, whose deeds added lustre to the name of the Royal Air Force in the great days of the war. Pray accept my sympathy to you and your family.'

Valerie Crankshaw:

'Everybody felt, the people in Kimberley and other places, felt he should have had a military funeral, but the government would not allow it. So it was a civic funeral. The Mayor of Kimberley was there, thousands of people, Harry and Bridgette Oppenheimer were there. The funeral's all a blur. I just know a lot of people were very, very, unhappy that he was not recognised with a military funeral.'

The National Party denied their hated enemy a military funeral, and even banned uniforms from being worn at the funeral, for fear of the martial spectacle inspiring Afrikaner youth. The service took place at the Cathedral Church of St Cyprian the Martyr in Kimberley. A substantial sum was collected in Sailor's name to set up a fund to further research into Parkinson's at the University of the Witwatersrand in Johannesburg, historically one of South Africa's English-speaking universities.

South Africa's greatest war hero was buried in the city's West End Cemetery.

The epitaph on his headstone reads, 'In the shadow of Thy wings will I rejoice' – from Psalm 63 verse 7.

A month later, Sailor's friends and former comrades-in-arms joined Lord Dowding for a memorial service at the chapel opened by the great man himself at Biggin Hill. In his address, the station padre, Reverend Cecil King, said that Sailor 'had an invincible spirit to win at a time when we needed it'. The Chief of the Air Staff, Air Chief Marshal Sir Charles Elworthy, also paid tribute to the late Group Captain:

'We mourn the passing of a fine officer and gallant comrade who was in the forefront of the Battle of Britain, a man who fought bravely and led fearlessly at a time when courage and leadership in the air was our only safeguard. His name will live on in the history of the Royal Air Force and in the minds and hearts of men of courage everywhere.'

Chapter Twenty

A 'Global South African'

Sailor Malan's air fighting had begun over the beaches of Dunkirk, in support of the evacuation of the BEF from France and Belgium. It was an air operation without precedent and the first time that the Spitfire and Me 109 clashed in combat. The Fighter Command book of tactics was immediately found to be impractical in modern, fast, day-fighter battles and quickly rejected. It then fell to those fighter leaders with a tactical mind to work things out for themselves. Sailor Malan soon had 74 Squadron flying not the recommended, suicidal, vic of three but in a line astern section of four. So it went on, experimenting and sharing the knowledge. During the Battle of Britain he and 74 Squadron were heavily engaged, and then the fighting changed to the offensive operations, with a two-way sea crossing, of 1941. Throughout this time, Sailor Malan, the best shot in the RAF, accumulated his great score – exceeded only by Johnnie Johnson, who, as the Air Vice-Marshal has said that his was a very different and in many ways easier war. Without any disrespect to Johnnie, who I know would agree with me, Sailor Malan, therefore, will always be remembered as the greatest RAF fighter pilot of them all. It is also to his great credit that, recognising the signs of exhaustion and negative, possibly fatal, implications for the team as a whole, he voluntarily rested from operations. He also clearly cared deeply about giving new pilots the best possible advice and training, passing on is hard-earned experience via the famous 'Ten Commandments'.

Jonathan Malan recalls, however, how uncomfortable his father was when lionized by the media as having been the all-conquering Battle of Britain hero:

'It was the only time I saw my Dad intimidated or looking shy. He looked uncomfortable and a little bit embarrassed. He used to tell me, he would say, "Jonathan, just remember, there were nearly three thousand of us, it wasn't just me."'

The only potential blight on Sailor Malan's exceptional service career remains the tragic friendly fire incident dubbed the 'Battle of Barking Creek'. We have explored this incident and while no definitive conclusion can be drawn, my own is that *if* Sailor lied, as accused by defence counsel, it would have been totally contrary to everything we know about him – who set the highest bar for both courage and integrity. Personally, I cannot believe it. Much more likely, I suspect, is that the comparatively primitive radio was to blame. But who knows? And the Court of Inquiry report on the incident remains closed until 2040. Perhaps then the truth will out, at long last, and the matter will be finally resolved.

When the epic *Battle of Britain* film was made in the late 1960s, the characters at operational squadron level were essentially anonymous, although, according to Leonard Mosley in his book *Battle of Britain*, about making the film, 'Audiences could be forgiven if they suspected that a character called Skipper with a very rough manner sounds like the late "Sailor" Malan.' It was originally envisioned, Mosley tells us, that Skipper would be 'a kind of father figure, a sort of flying Mr Chips, who treated the members of the squadron he commanded during the Battle with paternalistic concern. Robert Shaw, one of the principal actors (author's note: and cast in the role of Skipper), at once sent for the files and reminiscences and soon confirmed his suspicion that "Sailor" Malan was not that kind of man at all.' According to Shaw, Sailor was 'ruthless and he was efficient... He had a black hatred for the Germans. He ran his own squadron like an efficient business, and he despised anyone who wasn't up to the job. He wasn't running a public school, he was in the business of killing Germans – and he was out to get results.' While much of what Shaw says, in a sense, is correct, Sailor certainly did not have a 'rough manner'; if anything he was shy and softly spoken – but as a leader he was the consummate professional. During the Battle of Britain, Sailor was 30; in 1969, Shaw was 42, so significantly older. To me, it was never a convincing portrayal of Sailor Malan, Skipper seemed much more like Douglas Bader, but at least Shaw gave Sailor's wartime story currency.

After the war, schoolboys read of the great air ace's exploits in war-themed weekly comics and magazines. Or at least they did outside South Africa. As Yvonne Malan says, 'Most South Africans have no idea who he was.' In South Africa, the Torch Commando story was not just erased from the record – it was never written into the nationalist narrative in the first place. D.F. Malan's government was determined that heroes would not be made of the war veterans involved. Consequently, the name of Group Captain Malan remains obscure in his country of birth, where opinion remains divided over which side South Africa should have supported during the Second World War. Sailor's mother being English exacerbates the situation further, considering the anti-British feeling prevalent in Afrikaner society.

Professor Thula Simpson, however, perfectly sums up the importance of Sailor Malan to his country's post-war story:

'Sailor Malan belongs within the history of white opposition politics to the National Party. He takes his place in the pantheon alongside the Liberal Party and the Progressive Party... in terms of upholding the values of constitutionalism, and in terms of fighting to defend the coloured voting right, and in terms of fighting for the principle of non-racialism in the constitution, Sailor Malan has a position within that trajectory of Apartheid and Anti-apartheid history.

'Sailor Malan is one of the few global South Africans of the 20th century. Not at the same stature I would say of Nelson Mandela and Jan Smuts, but one of the people who has excelled on the international stage.'

Nelson Mandela needs no introduction. A black South African anti-apartheid revolutionary, in 1962 Mandela was imprisoned and in 1964 sentenced to a life behind bars for conspiring to overthrow the nationalist government. By that time, D.F. Malan was dead, but the National Party remained in power – and did so for over forty years. By the 1980s, resistance to apartheid was increasing though, along with violent protest to such an extent that President P.W. Botha entered into talks with Mandela, who, even from a prison cell, remained all-powerful as the resistance's iconic figurehead. In February 1985 Botha offered Mandela freedom, provided that he rejected violence as a means of effecting political change. Mandela refused the offer. Further talks continued over the next three years, Mandela rejecting all offers and insisting that the ANC would only end armed struggle when the government also renounced violence. In 1989, F.W. de Klerk became President and considered apartheid unsustainable. While the ANC's armed resistance was ineffective, economic sanctions imposed upon South Africa by many countries were devastating. While believing that the National Party could survive in power another decade, de Klerk knew that the economy would not; a solution had to be found, and hence the new, forward-thinking, dialogue.

The previous year, Mandela's seventieth birthday had attracted massive global interest, greatly assisted by the famous tribute concert at Wembley Stadium, watched on TV by a staggering 200 million people worldwide. In

November 1989 the infamous Berlin Wall, separating the democratic west from the communist east, came tumbling down as the Soviet bloc collapsed. Times were changing. Recognising this, de Klerk lifted the ban on all prohibited political parties and, on 11 February 1990, Nelson Mandela was released from Victor Verster Prison. It was an incredible moment for democracy and human rights. Over the next few years, apartheid was dismantled, to the extent that on 10 May 1994, Nelson Mandela became South Africa's first black President, with both F.W. de Klerk and Thabo Mbeki sharing the deputy presidency. Now followed the transition from apartheid minority rule to a democracy, with Mandela considering national reconciliation vital for the 'Rainbow Nation' in which diversity was embraced and respected. And therein lies another reason why Sailor Malan's story remains so obscure: the ANC has been the ruling political party since Mandela's presidency (although Mandela died in 2013), and the Torch Commando story is inconvenient to the narrative of the multicultural struggle against apartheid – on account of its having been an exclusively white organization.

Little wonder, then, that my friend the independent film-maker Desmond Naidoo has struggled to achieve funding for our proposed South African-made documentary about Sailor Malan.

Valerie Crankshaw makes a final comment on her father's legacy:

'He should be regarded as one of many special people to have come out of this country.

'He had a morality about him, he knew what was right and what was wrong. That was his moral fibre, he just did not like injustice.'

Certainly, Sailor's was a life lived to the full – and he made a difference. The world was poorer for his premature passing. His loving wife, Lynda, survived Sailor until 1997, having never remarried. His father, Willie, had died shortly after his famous son's return to South Africa; Sailor's mother, Evelyn, outlived three of her sons and died in 1973.

For Sailor Malan, progressive, free-thinker, champion of freedom, democracy and human rights in war and peace, the only possible epitaph is the motto of his beloved 'Tiger' Squadron:

'I Fear No Man.'

Bibliography

Various documents were consulted which are preserved by The National Archive. The following can be downloaded as PDF files. The reader may find these of particular interest:

74 Sqn Operations Record Book   AIR27/640 & 641
74 Sqn Combat Reports   AIR50/32

The National Archive website: nationalarchives.gov.uk

Unpublished Sources

Wylam, EA, *Dunkirk and the BEF, 1940*, unpublished memoir.

Desmond Naidoo's video interviews of:

Mr Jonathan Malan
Mrs Valerie Crankshaw
Mr Jeremy Lawrence
Mr John Kane-Berman
Professor Bill Nasson
Professor Thula Simpson

Published Sources

Balfour, H, *Wings Over Westminster*, Hutchinson, London, 1973
Bialer, U, *The Shadow of the Bomber: The Fear of Air Attack and British Politics 1932-39*, Royal Historical Society, London, 1980
Black, N, *Revisiting the Battle of Barking Creek*, 6 September 1939, unpublished dissertation, University of Suffolk, Ipswich, 2020.

Branson, N, & Heinemann, M, *Britain in the 1930s*, Weidenfeld & Nicolson, London, 1971

Brickhill, P, *Reach for the Sky*, Collins, London, 1954

Calder, A, *The People's War: Britain 1939-45*, Pimlico, London, 2008

Caldwell, D, *The JG26 War Diary, Volume One, 1939-1942*, Grub Street, London, 1996, and *Volume Two, 1943-1945*, 1998

Campion, G, *The Good Fight: Battle of Britain Propaganda and the Few*, Palgrave Macmillan, Basingstoke, 2010

Clapson, M, *The Routledge Companion to Britain in the Twentieth Century*, Routledge, London, 2009

Cornwell, P, *The Battle of France Then & Now: Six Nations Locked in Aerial Combat September 1939 to June 1940*, Battle of Britain International Ltd, Old Harlow, 2007

Dean, Sir Maurice, *The Royal Air Force in Two World Wars*, Cassell, London, 1979

Deere, Air Commodore AC, *Nine Lives*, Hodder Paperbacks Ltd, London, 1959

Dezarrois, A (ed), *The Mouchotte Diaries 1940-43*, Staples, London, 1956

February, V, *The Afrikaners of South Africa*, Keegan Paul International Ltd, London, 1991

Foreman, J, *RAF Fighter Command Victory Claims of World War Two, Part One 1939-1940*, Red Kite, Walton-on-Thames, 2003

Francis, M, *The Flyer: British Culture and the Royal Air Force 1939-45*, OUP, Oxford, 2008

Franks, NLR, *Sky Tiger: The Story of Sailor Malan*, Crécy Publishing Ltd, Manchester, 1980

Franks, NLR, *Royal Air Force Fighter Command Losses of the Second World War. Volume 1 Operational Losses: Aircraft and Crews 1939-41*, Midland Publishing, Hersham, 1997

Franks, NLR, *Air Battle For Dunkirk 26 May – 3 June 1940*, Grub Street, London, 2006

Ishoven, A van *The Luftwaffe in the Battle of Britain*, Ian Allen, Shepperton, 1980

James, J, *The Palladins: A Social History of the RAF up to the Outbreak of World War 2*, Futura Publications, London, 1990.

James, TCG, *The Battle of Britain*, Frank Cass, London, 2000

Jones, Wing Commander I, *Tiger Squadron*, WH Allen & Co, London, 1954

Kaplan, P, *Sailor, Battle of Britain Legend: Adolph Malan*, Pen & Sword Ltd, Barnsley, 2012

BIBLIOGRAPHY

Lodge, T, *Black Politics in South Africa Since 1945*, Longman, London and New York, 1983

MacKenzie, SP, *The Battle of Britain on Screen: The 'Few' in British Film and Television Drama*, Edinburgh University Press, Edinburgh, 2007

Mosley, L, *Battle of Britain: The Making of a Film*, Pan, London, 1969

Mowat, CL, *Britain Between the Wars, 1918-40*, Taylor & Francis, London, 1968

Nasson, B, 'A Flying Springbok of wartime British Skies: AG "Sailor" Malan', *Kronos*, University of Western Cape, No 35 (November 2009), pp. 71-97

Orange, V, *Park: The Biography of Air Chief Marshal Sir Keith Park*, Methuen, London, 1984

Orange, V, *Dowding of Fighter Command: Victor of the Battle of Britain*, Grub Street, London, 2008

Order, C, *Pilots of Fighter Command*, Harrap, London, 1942

Oxspring, Group Captain RW, *Spitfire Command*, William Kimber, London, 1984

Ramsey, W (Ed), *The Battle of Britain Then & Now*, Battle of Britain Prints International, London, 1989

Ramsey, W (Ed), *The Blitz Then & Now, Volume One*, Plaistow Press, London, 1987,

Volume Two, 1988, *Volume Three*, 1990

Romain, G, *Race, Sexuality & Identity in Britain and Jamaica: The Biography of Patrick Nelson, 1916-1963*, Bloomsbury Publishing, London, 2017

Ross, R, 'Oppression, Sexuality and Slavery at the Cape of Good Hope', *Reflections Historique*, 6, 2: 421;33, 1979

Sarkar, D, *The Few: The Battle of Britain in the Words of the Pilots*, Amberley Publishing, Stroud, 2009

Sarkar, D, *How the Spitfire Won the Battle of Britain*, Amberley Publishing, Stroud, 2010

Sarkar, D, *Spitfire! The Story of a Unique Battle of Britain Spitfire Squadron*, Pen & Sword, Barnsley, 2019

Spurdle, B, *The Blue Arena*, William Kimber & Co, London, 1986

Terraine, J, *The Right of the Line: The Role of the RAF in World War Two*, Hodder & Stoughton, London, 1985

Tidy, D, *I Fear No Man: The Story of No 74 (Fighter) Squadron Royal Flying Corps & Royal Air Force (The Tigers)*, MacDonald, London, 1972

Walker, O, *Sailor Malan: A Biography*, Cassell, London, 1953

Wallace, G, *RAF Biggin Hill*, Putnam & Co, London, 1957

Welsh, F, *A History of South Africa*, Harper Collins, London, 2000

Yeoman, C, and Freeborn, J, *Tiger Cub: A 74 Squadron Fighter Pilot in World War II. The Story of John Connell Freeborn DFC**, Pen & Sword, 2009

Ziegler, F, *The Story of 609 Squadron: Under the White Rose*, MacDonald, London, 1971

Films

Desmond Naidoo's trailer for our proposed documentary 'Freedom Flyer':

youtube.com/watch?v=C4jvpZA1GI4&feature=youtu.be&ab_channel=DesmondNaidoo

The Lion Has Wings, Directed by Michael Powell, Brian Desmond Hurst and Adrian Brunel (London Films, 1939). This film can be viewed on YouTube at:

youtube.com/watch?v=41h3ex7GqbQ

Wing Commander Malan's BBC radio broadcast of 28 June 1941:

youtube.com/watch?v=g4I5MpMj84A

'RAF Air Ace's Son Christened Winston', *British Movietone News* item of 10 August 1941:

youtube.com/watch?v=vj6y108rg68

'Malan v Malan: Torch Commandos Against the Government', *British Movietone News*, May 1951:

youtube.com/watch?v=pW8gNsq5_n8

Salzman, H & Fisz, SB, *Battle of Britain* (Spitfire Productions 1969)

Also:

In Britain, sufferers from Parkinson's disease and carers are supported by the charity Parkinson's UK – parkinsons.org.uk

Other Books by Dilip Sarkar

(in order of publication)

Spitfire Squadron: No 19 Squadron at War, 1939-41
The Invisible Thread: A Spitfire's Tale
Through Peril to the Stars: RAF Fighter Pilots Who Failed to Return, 1939-45
Angriff *Westland: Three Battle of Britain Air Raids Through the Looking Glass*
A Few of the Many: Air War 1939-45, A Kaleidoscope of Memories
Bader's Tangmere Spitfires: The Untold Story, 1941
Bader's Duxford Fighters: The Big Wing Controversy
Missing in Action: Resting in Peace?
Guards VC: Blitzkrieg 1940
Battle of Britain: The Photographic Kaleidoscope, Volumes I-IV
Fighter Pilot: The Photographic Kaleidoscope
Group Captain Sir Douglas Bader: An Inspiration in Photographs
Johnnie Johnson: Spitfire Top Gun, Part I
Johnnie Johnson: Spitfire Top Gun, Part II
Battle of Britain: Last Look Back
Spitfire! Courage & Sacrifice
Spitfire Voices: Heroes Remember
The Battle of Powick Bridge: Ambush a Fore-thought
Duxford 1940: A Battle of Britain Base at War
The Few: The Battle of Britain in the Words of the Pilots
Spitfire Manual 1940
The Sinking of HMS Royal Oak In the Words of the Survivors (re-print of Hearts of Oak)
The Last of the Few: Eighteen Battle of Britain Pilots Tell Their Extraordinary Stories
Hearts of Oak: The Human Tragedy of HMS Royal Oak
Spitfire Voices: Life as a Spitfire Pilot in the Words of the Veterans
How the Spitfire Won the Battle of Britain
Spitfire Ace of Aces: The True Wartime Story of Johnnie Johnson

Douglas Bader
Fighter Ace: The Extraordinary Life of Douglas Bader, Battle of Britain Hero (re-print of above)
Spitfire: The Photographic Biography
Hurricane Manual 1940
River Pike
The Final Few: The Last Surviving Pilots of the Battle of Britain Tell Their Stories
Arnhem 1944: The Human Tragedy of the Bridge Too Far
Spitfire! The Full Story of a Unique Battle of Britain Fighter Squadron
Battle of Britain 1940: The Finest Hour's Human Cost
Letters From The Few: Unique Memories of the Battle of Britain
Johnnie Johnson's 1942 Diary: The War Diary of the Spitfire Ace of Aces
Johnnie Johnson's Great Adventure: The Spitfire Ace of Ace's Last Look Back
Spitfire Ace of Aces – The Album: The Photographs of Johnnie Johnson

Index

INDEX

INDEX

INDEX